GIFTED TO

FROM

DATE

DAILY DEVOTIONAL 2025

365 Days Of Reflection And Inspirational Devotions For Walking With God, Building Faith, Strength And Overcoming Fear Through The Year.

Mount Hermon Publications

PREFACE

Life can be complex, filled with joys and challenges, responsibilities and dreams. As you navigate this intricate tapestry, we invite you to take a moment each day to pause, to reflect, and to be inspired. Our hope is that these devotions will be a source of encouragement, wisdom, and inspiration as you strive to live a life aligned with your faith and values.

Whether you are seeking courage to face your fears, clarity to pursue your calling, strength to endure trials, joy in giving, wisdom in your thoughts, or purpose in your reflection, this book is designed to meet you where you are and walk with you in your journey.

Each day, you'll find a short exploration of a specific theme followed by actionable steps to apply these principles to your life. Our desire is for you to not only read but also practice, as faith without action is like a ship without a sail—beautiful but motionless.

We invite you to make this devotional a part of your daily routine—a moment to center yourself, to connect with your faith, and to draw inspiration for the day ahead. May it serve as a faithful companion, a steady guide, and a wellspring of hope throughout the year.

HOW TO USE THIS GUIDE

We've crafted this book with the aim of making it a valuable and practical resource for your spiritual growth and daily life. Here's a simple guide on how to make the most of this devotional:

1. Set a Daily Routine: Choose a specific time each day to engage with this devotional. It could be in the morning to start your day with inspiration or in the evening as a reflective way to end your day. Consistency is key in establishing a routine that works for you.

2. Find a Quiet Space: Select a quiet and comfortable space where you can focus without distractions. It could be your favorite chair, a peaceful corner of your home, or even a spot outdoors where you can connect with nature.

3. Read the Daily Entry: Start by reading the daily devotional entry. Each day presents a specific theme, a scripture reference, and a creative exploration of that theme. Take your time to absorb the message and reflect on its relevance to your life.

4. Meditate on Scripture: After reading the devotional, take a moment to meditate on the scripture reference provided. Consider how it aligns with the theme and how it can guide your thoughts and actions throughout the day.

5. Reflect and Apply: Following the devotional and scripture, spend a few moments reflecting on how the theme relates to your life. What insights or lessons can you draw from it? Then, consider the actionable steps provided and think about how you can apply them in your daily life.

6. Journal Your Thoughts: Consider keeping a journal or notebook alongside this devotional. Use it to jot down your reflections, insights, and personal experiences related to each day's theme. Journaling can be a powerful tool for self-discovery and growth.

7. *Take Action:* Faith without action is incomplete. The action steps provided in each devotional are designed to help you apply the principles discussed. Commit to taking action on at least one of the suggested steps each day, whether it's a practical act of kindness, a moment of prayer, or a change in your thought patterns.

8. *Share and Discuss:* Consider sharing your daily reflections and experiences with a friend, family member, or a small group of like-minded individuals. Engaging in discussions can deepen your understanding of the daily themes and provide additional insights.

9. *Make It Your Own:* Feel free to adapt this devotional to suit your needs. You can revisit previous entries, skip ahead, or use it as a springboard for deeper Bible study and prayer. Make it a personalized experience that aligns with your unique spiritual journey.

10. *Embrace Grace:* Remember that the journey of faith is not about perfection but progress. There may be days when you miss a reading or stumble in your actions. Embrace grace and keep moving forward, knowing that each day is an opportunity for growth and renewal.

As you embark on this daily journey of faith, may you find inspiration, wisdom, and transformation. May your heart be filled with courage, your mind with clarity, and your spirit with purpose. Above all, may you draw closer to the Creator and discover the fullness of your calling as a man of faith in 2025.

Heavenly Father,

As I embark on this journey of spiritual growth and reflection, I come before You with open hearts and humble spirits. Grant me the wisdom to seek Your guidance, the strength to face life's challenges, and the gratitude to appreciate Your countless blessings.

May this time of devotion be a source of inspiration, purpose, and connection with You. Bless my efforts as I meditate on Your word.

In Your holy name, I begin this journey. Amen.

DAY 01

God's Creation

"In the beginning, God created the heavens and the earth." -
Genesis 1:1 (NIV)

Genesis 1:1 is not just an opening line; it is a proclamation of God's sovereign artistry and intentional design. Every sunrise that bathes the world in golden light, every star that twinkles in the night sky, and every leaf that dances in the wind speaks of His handiwork. God's creation is a testament to His glory, a living, breathing canvas painted with love, purpose, and splendor.

Imagine the care with which God crafted the mountains, the oceans, and every living creature. He spoke, and out of nothing, beauty and life sprang forth. But among all His creations, humanity holds a unique place. We are made in His image, designed to reflect His character and to steward His creation.

Yet, as we marvel at the wonders around us, we are also called to recognize our responsibility. God's creation is a gift entrusted to us, not just to admire but to protect and nurture. Each day presents us with opportunities to honor God through our actions toward the environment and each other.

Heavenly Father, thank You for the incredible gift of Your creation. Help us to see Your glory in the world around us and to honor You by taking care of it. Give us wisdom and strength to be faithful stewards of all that You have made. May our actions reflect our gratitude and bring glory to Your name. In Jesus' name, we pray. Amen.

DAY 02

The Love of God

"For I am convinced that neither death nor life, neither angels nor demons, neither the present nor the future, nor any powers, neither height nor depth, nor anything else in all creation, will be able to separate us from the love of God that is in Christ Jesus our Lord."
- Romans 8:38-39 (NIV)

Romans 8:38-39 beautifully encapsulates this divine assurance, reminding us that nothing in all creation can sever us from God's love. This love is not dependent on our actions or worthiness; it is a steadfast promise grounded in the sacrifice of Jesus Christ.

Reflect on the depth of this love. God's love is patient and kind, reaching out to us even when we feel unworthy or lost. It is a love that sent Jesus to the cross, bearing our sins so that we might be reconciled with our Heavenly Father. This sacrificial love is a beacon of hope and a source of unshakeable security.

Understanding and embracing God's love transforms our lives. It calls us to love others as He loves us, with grace, compassion, and forgiveness. It empowers us to face trials with courage and to extend kindness even in difficult situations. God's love is a guiding light, leading us to live with purpose and joy.

Heavenly Father, thank You for Your boundless and unchanging love. May Your love overflow in our hearts, guiding our actions and words. Enable us to love others as You have loved us, spreading Your light in a world in need. In Jesus' name, we pray. Amen.

DAY 03

Faith and Trust in God

"Trust in the Lord with all your heart and lean not on your own understanding; in all your ways submit to him, and he will make your paths straight." - Proverbs 3:5-6 (NIV)

Faith and trust in God are the cornerstones of our spiritual journey. Proverbs 3:5-6 calls us to relinquish our anxieties and lean wholly on God's wisdom and guidance. This scripture is a profound reminder that our human understanding is limited, but God's knowledge and love for us are boundless.

In life's uncertain moments, it's easy to be overwhelmed by fear and doubt. We often try to control every aspect of our lives, forgetting that God, in His infinite wisdom, holds the blueprint of our destiny. Trusting in Him means acknowledging that His plans are greater than our own, even when we can't see the path ahead clearly.

Faith is not just a passive belief but an active reliance on God's promises. It means stepping out in confidence, knowing that He is always with us, guiding and protecting us. It's about finding peace in His presence, even amid life's storms. When we trust God, we find the courage to face challenges, the strength to endure hardships, and the hope that sustains us through every trial.

Heavenly Father, thank You for Your unfailing love and wisdom. Help us to trust You with all our hearts, especially when we don't understand the circumstances we face. Strengthen our faith so that we may lean on You and not on our own understanding. Guide our steps and make our paths straight, according to Your perfect will. In Jesus' name, we pray. Amen.

DAY 04

The Power of Prayer

"Therefore I tell you, whatever you ask in prayer, believe that you have received it, and it will be yours." - Mark 11:24 (NIV)

Prayer is one of the most powerful gifts God has given us. It is our direct line of communication with the Creator of the universe, a sacred conversation where hearts are opened and burdens are shared. This is not a promise of getting everything we want, but rather an invitation to align our hearts with God's will, trusting in His perfect plan for our lives.

Those moments when your heart feels lighter, and your spirit is uplifted. Prayer is more than a list of requests; it is a deeply intimate experience that brings us closer to God. It is where we find comfort in times of sorrow, strength in moments of weakness, and guidance when we are lost.

The power of prayer is also seen in the way it unites believers. When we come together in prayer, our faith is strengthened, and our bond as the body of Christ is deepened. Whether praying alone in the quiet of the morning or joining others in collective prayer, we are reminded that we are never alone. God hears every word, every whisper, and every cry.

Heavenly Father, thank You for the gift of prayer. Help us to approach You with faith and confidence, knowing that You hear us. Strengthen our faith and draw us closer to You through our times of prayer. In Jesus' name, we pray. Amen.

DAY 05

The Holy Trinity

"May the grace of the Lord Jesus Christ, and the love of God, and the fellowship of the Holy Spirit be with you all." - 2 Corinthians 13:14 (NIV)

In 2 Corinthians 13:14, we are greeted by the fullness of God's nature: the grace of Jesus Christ, the love of God the Father, and the fellowship of the Holy Spirit. This verse encapsulates the divine relationship that exists within the Trinity, inviting us into a deeper understanding and experience of God's presence.

Jesus Christ, the Son, our Savior, who poured out His grace upon us through His sacrifice; and the Holy Spirit, our Comforter and Guide, who dwells within us and empowers us to live out our faith. Together, they form a harmonious and dynamic relationship that reveals the fullness of God's nature and His desire for a deep, personal relationship with us.

It calls us to live in unity with one another, to extend grace as Jesus did, to love as the Father loves, and to seek the guidance of the Holy Spirit in our daily lives. The Trinity reminds us that we are never alone; we are always enveloped in the love, grace, and fellowship of our Triune God.

Heavenly Father, thank You for the incredible gift of Your love. Lord Jesus, we are grateful for Your grace and sacrifice. Help us to live in unity and love, reflecting the beautiful relationship of the Trinity in our own lives. May we grow closer to You and to one another each day. In Jesus' name, we pray. Amen.

DAY 06

The Beatitudes

"Blessed are the poor in spirit, for theirs is the kingdom of heaven." - Matthew 5:3 (NIV)

Each Beatitude reveals a facet of the kingdom of God and offers a glimpse into the heart of Christ's teaching. They call us to a life of humility, compassion, righteousness, mercy, purity, peace, and endurance in the face of persecution. These blessings are counter-cultural, challenging our worldly understanding of success and happiness.

Jesus begins with, "Blessed are the poor in spirit," reminding us that true blessing starts with recognizing our need for God. It is in our humility and acknowledgment of spiritual poverty that we open our hearts to the richness of God's kingdom. As we journey through the Beatitudes, we encounter a divine paradox: those who mourn find comfort, the meek inherit the earth, and those who hunger and thirst for righteousness are filled.

These teachings are not mere ideals but practical truths meant to transform our lives. They guide us in living out our faith in a way that reflects Christ's love and grace. The Beatitudes call us to live differently, to embody the values of God's kingdom in our daily interactions and decisions.

Dear Lord, thank You for the wisdom and guidance of the Beatitudes. Help us to embrace these truths and let them transform our hearts and minds. May our lives be a testimony to the hope and joy found in Your kingdom. In Jesus' name, we pray. Amen.

DAY 07

The Ten Commandments

"And God spoke all these words: 'I am the Lord your God, who brought you out of Egypt, out of the land of slavery. You shall have no other gods before me.'" - Exodus 20:1-3 (NIV)

The Ten Commandments are not just ancient rules carved in stone; they are the heartbeat of God's covenant with His people, a divine framework for living a life that honors Him and blesses others. Given to Moses on Mount Sinai, these commandments were spoken directly by God, revealing His character and His desires for how we should relate to Him and to one another.

The first four commandments focus on our relationship with God, urging us to worship Him alone, to avoid idolatry, to honor His name, and to keep the Sabbath holy. These commandments remind us of God's supremacy and our need to prioritize Him in every aspect of our lives.

The remaining six commandments guide us in our relationships with others: honoring our parents, valuing life, keeping our commitments, respecting others' property, speaking truthfully, and nurturing contentment. These directives teach us to live in community with integrity, respect, and compassion.

Heavenly Father, thank You for giving us the Ten Commandments as a guide for our lives. Strengthen us to honor You in all we do and to treat others with the respect and kindness You desire. Draw us closer to You and transform our hearts to reflect Your holiness. In Jesus' name, we pray. Amen.

DAY 08

The Sermon on the Mount

"Blessed are the poor in spirit, for theirs is the kingdom of heaven." - Matthew 5:3 (NIV)

It begins with the Beatitudes, where Jesus turns the world's values upside down, proclaiming blessings on the meek, the merciful, the peacemakers, and those who hunger and thirst for righteousness. This radical sermon calls us to a higher standard of living, one that reflects the heart of God and His kingdom.

Jesus' words challenge us to look beyond mere outward compliance to the law and to embrace a deeper, heart-level righteousness. He calls us to love our enemies, to forgive without limits, to give without seeking recognition, and to seek first His kingdom and righteousness. In doing so, we become salt and light in a world desperately in need of hope and truth.

The Sermon on the Mount is not just a list of rules; it is a roadmap to true joy and fulfillment. It reveals that true blessedness is found not in wealth, power, or comfort, but in a humble, obedient, and surrendered heart. Jesus invites us into a life of authentic discipleship, where our actions flow from a transformed heart that mirrors His love and compassion.

Lord Jesus, thank You for the Sermon on the Mount and the powerful truths it holds. Help us to internalize Your teachings and to live them out in our daily lives. Transform our hearts so that we may reflect Your love, mercy, and righteousness to the world. Guide us to be faithful disciples who bring glory to Your name. Amen.

DAY 09

The Lord's Prayer

"Pray then like this: 'Our Father in heaven, hallowed be your name.'" - Matthew 6:9 (ESV)

In Matthew 6:9, Jesus imparts to His disciples a profound and transformative gift: the Lord's Prayer. This divine template for prayer is not merely a string of words to recite, but a pathway to intimacy with our Heavenly Father. Each word, each phrase, holds the power to elevate our hearts and align our desires with God's will.

When we utter the words, "Our Father," we acknowledge our relationship with God as His beloved children. We recognize His sovereignty and our dependence on His love and provision. Through this prayer, we are invited into the sacred space of communion with the One who knows us intimately and cares for us deeply.

As we declare, "hallowed be your name," we exalt the holiness and majesty of God. His name is not to be taken lightly but revered above all else. In a world filled with distractions and noise, the Lord's Prayer reminds us to center our hearts on the One who is worthy of all praise and adoration.

Gracious Father, thank You for the gift of the Lord's Prayer, a sacred invitation into Your presence. Help us to approach You with reverence and awe, acknowledging You as our loving Father in heaven. May Your name be hallowed in our hearts and lives as we seek to align our will with Yours. Guide us in the practice of prayer, that we may grow closer to You each day. In Jesus' name, we pray. Amen.

DAY 10

The Great Commission

"Go therefore and make disciples of all nations, baptizing them in the name of the Father and of the Son and of the Holy Spirit, teaching them to observe all that I have commanded you. And behold, I am with you always, to the end of the age." - Matthew 28:19-20 (ESV)

It's not merely a suggestion or a request; it's a divine mandate, a charge given to every believer to go forth and spread the good news of salvation to all corners of the earth. This commission embodies the heartbeat of God, His relentless pursuit of reconciliation with humanity.

The Great Commission isn't just about evangelism; it's about discipleship. Jesus doesn't just instruct us to make converts but to make disciples – individuals who are transformed by the power of His love and committed to following Him wholeheartedly.

Imagine the ripple effect of obediently carrying out the Great Commission. Lives are transformed, communities are revitalized, and nations are impacted. Each soul won for Christ is a testament to His redeeming love and the fulfillment of His promise to be with us always.

Lord Jesus, thank You for entrusting us with the privilege and responsibility of sharing Your gospel with the world. May Your Holy Spirit empower and guide us every step of the way. Use us to bring glory to Your name and to see Your kingdom advance on earth. In Your mighty name, we pray. Amen.

DAY 11

The Fruit of the Spirit

"But the fruit of the Spirit is love, joy, peace, forbearance, kindness, goodness, faithfulness, gentleness and self-control. Against such things there is no law." - Galatians 5:22-23 (NIV)

Like a tender gardener nurturing a precious orchard, the Holy Spirit works within us, producing a rich abundance of virtues that reflect the character of Christ. Galatians 5:22-23 paints a vivid picture of this spiritual fruit basket, each attribute ripe with significance and purpose.

Love, the first and foremost fruit, serves as the foundation upon which the others flourish. It is a selfless, unconditional love that mirrors the love of our Heavenly Father. Joy follows, not as fleeting happiness dependent on circumstances, but a deep-rooted gladness that springs from knowing Christ. Peace, like a gentle stream, flows through our souls, calming the storms of life and bringing tranquility in every season.

As we walk in the Spirit, we also bear the fruit of forbearance, showing patience and understanding toward others. Kindness and goodness overflow from hearts transformed by grace, reaching out to touch lives with compassion and generosity.

Heavenly Father, thank You for the precious gift of Your Spirit and the fruit He produces within us. Help us to daily surrender to Your work in our lives, bearing fruit that honors and glorifies You. Give us the strength and courage to live out these virtues, becoming more like Christ each day. May our lives be a testimony to Your grace and love. In Jesus' name, we pray. Amen.

DAY 12

The Armor of God

"Put on the full armor of God, so that you can take your stand against the devil's schemes." - Ephesians 6:11 (NIV)

Just as a soldier equips themselves with armor before going into battle, so too are we called to put on the full armor of God to stand against the enemy's schemes.

The imagery of armor is rich with symbolism, representing the strength, protection, and readiness that God offers us. Each piece holds significance, from the belt of truth that girds our loins to the helmet of salvation that guards our minds. As we clothe ourselves with this spiritual armor, we are not merely preparing for a physical confrontation but for the unseen battles waged in the spiritual realm.

The enemy seeks to deceive, discourage, and destroy, but with the armor of God, we are equipped to withstand his attacks. We are fortified by the truth of God's Word, emboldened by the righteousness of Christ, and empowered by the gospel of peace. Our faith serves as a shield against doubt and fear, and the Word of God is our sword, a weapon of offense against the enemy's lies.

Heavenly Father, thank You for providing us with the armor we need to stand firm against the enemy's attacks. Help us to be diligent in putting on each piece, that we may be equipped to face the challenges of each day with courage and strength. May Your truth guide us, your righteousness protect us, and Your peace sustain us. In Jesus' name, we pray. Amen.

DAY 13

The Grace of God

"For it is by grace you have been saved, through faith—and this is not from yourselves, it is the gift of God— not by works, so that no one can boast." - Ephesians 2:8-9 (NIV)

Grace – it's a word that carries the weight of eternity within its syllables. In Ephesians 2:8-9, we're reminded of the profound truth that our salvation is not earned through our own efforts but is a lavish gift from God. It is by grace that we are redeemed, by grace that we are forgiven, and by grace that we are made new.

The grace of God is a concept so vast and profound that it's almost impossible to fully grasp. It's a love that knows no bounds, a mercy that reaches beyond our understanding. When we were lost in our sin, God's grace pursued us relentlessly, drawing us into His embrace with arms outstretched on the cross.

This grace is not something we can buy or achieve; it's freely given to all who believe. It's the great equalizer, leveling the playing field and reminding us that we are all sinners in need of a Savior. In the face of our inadequacies and failures, God's grace shines like a beacon of hope, offering forgiveness and restoration.

Gracious Father, thank You for Your unending grace poured out upon us. Help us to fully grasp the depth of Your love and mercy, and to live our lives in response to Your grace. Empower us to extend that same grace to those around us, showing them the same love and forgiveness You have shown us. In Jesus' name, we pray. Amen.

DAY 14

The Mercy of God

"But you, O Lord, are a God merciful and gracious, slow to anger and abounding in steadfast love and faithfulness." - Psalm 86:15 (ESV)

His mercy is not just a characteristic; it is His very nature. As human beings, we often fall short, stumbling along the journey of life, but in the midst of our failures, we find solace in the boundless mercy of our Heavenly Father.

The mercy of God is a beacon of hope in a world filled with brokenness and pain. It is a lifeline extended to us when we least deserve it, a gentle whisper of forgiveness that echoes through the depths of our souls. No matter how far we may stray, His mercy reaches out to embrace us, drawing us back into His loving arms.

Through the sacrifice of Jesus Christ on the cross, we see the ultimate demonstration of God's mercy. Despite our sinfulness, God sent His Son to die for us, offering redemption and reconciliation to all who believe. It is through this act of divine mercy that we find forgiveness for our sins and restoration to a right relationship with God.

Gracious Father, thank You for Your boundless mercy that knows no bounds. Help us to truly grasp the depth of Your love and forgiveness, and may it transform our hearts and minds. Empower us to extend mercy to others as You have shown mercy to us. May our lives be a testament to Your grace and compassion. In Jesus' name, we pray. Amen.

DAY 15

Forgiveness

"Be kind to one another, tenderhearted, forgiving one another, as God in Christ forgave you." - Ephesians 4:32 (ESV)

Forgiveness is a cornerstone of the Christian faith, rooted deeply in the grace and mercy of God. Ephesians 4:32 beautifully encapsulates this truth, reminding us of the immense love demonstrated by Christ's sacrifice on the cross. In His ultimate act of forgiveness, Jesus showed us the way to reconciliation and restoration.

To forgive is to release the hold of bitterness and resentment, allowing the healing balm of grace to soothe the wounds of our hearts. It is a choice, often challenging and yet profoundly liberating. When we extend forgiveness, we mirror the boundless compassion of our Heavenly Father, who forgives us time and time again, despite our failings.

Forgiveness is not excusing or minimizing the offense; rather, it is acknowledging the pain while choosing to let go of the desire for vengeance. It is a journey of healing, both for the one who forgives and for the one who is forgiven. As we extend grace to others, we experience the transformative power of God's love working within us.

Gracious God, thank You for the immeasurable gift of forgiveness through Your Son, Jesus Christ. Help us to embody His spirit of compassion and grace in our interactions with others. May Your healing power flow through our hearts, bringing reconciliation and peace. In Jesus' name, we pray. Amen.

DAY 16

Redemption

"For you know that it was not with perishable things such as silver or gold that you were redeemed from the empty way of life handed down to you from your ancestors, but with the precious blood of Christ, a lamb without blemish or defect." - 1 Peter 1:18-19 (NIV)

The concept of redemption is woven deeply into the fabric of Christian faith. It is a theme that runs throughout Scripture, culminating in the ultimate act of redemption through the sacrifice of Jesus Christ on the cross. 1 Peter 1:18-19 reminds us that our redemption is not bought with material wealth but with something far more precious—the blood of Christ.

It signifies a new beginning, a second chance, and the promise of transformation. Before Christ, we were enslaved by sin, trapped in a cycle of brokenness and despair. But through His sacrificial love, we have been set free from the power of sin and death. We have been redeemed.

This redemption is not merely a transaction; it is a profound expression of God's relentless love for us. He saw our brokenness and reached out with arms of mercy to redeem us.

Gracious God, we thank You for the incomparable gift of redemption through Your Son, Jesus Christ. Thank You for loving us enough to rescue us from sin and restore us to relationship with You. Give us eyes to see the brokenness around us and hearts willing to offer hope and healing in Your name. In Jesus' name, we pray. Amen.

DAY 17

Salvation

"For God so loved the world that he gave his one and only Son, that whoever believes in him shall not perish but have eternal life."
- John 3:16 (NIV)

Salvation is not just a theological concept; it is a divine rescue mission born out of God's immeasurable love for humanity. It is the ultimate demonstration of His grace and mercy, offering redemption and eternal life to all who believe.

At the heart of salvation is the recognition of our need for a Savior. Sin has separated us from God, tarnishing our souls and leaving us spiritually destitute. But in His boundless compassion, God sent His Son, Jesus Christ, to bridge the gap between heaven and earth. Through His sacrificial death on the cross, Jesus paid the price for our sins, offering us forgiveness and reconciliation with God.

Salvation is not something we can earn through our own efforts or merits. It is a gift freely given by God, available to anyone who accepts it with faith and humility. This truth should stir our hearts with gratitude and awe.

Heavenly Father, thank You for the gift of salvation through Your Son, Jesus Christ. Help us to grasp the depth of Your love and the magnitude of Your sacrifice. Empower us to live as grateful recipients of Your grace and to share the hope of salvation with others. May Your love shine through us, drawing hearts to You. In Jesus' name, we pray. Amen.

DAY 18

Eternal Life

"For God so loved the world that he gave his one and only Son,
that whoever believes in him shall not perish but have eternal life."
- John 3:16 (NIV)

It is a longing for eternity, a whisper of the divine woven into the fabric of our being. John 3:16 encapsulates the essence of this longing and the promise of fulfillment found in Christ: eternal life.

Eternal life is not merely an extension of our earthly existence but a transformation into a state of everlasting communion with God. It is the culmination of His redemptive plan, offered freely to all who believe in His Son.

Imagine the sheer magnitude of this promise – to live in unbroken fellowship with the Creator of the universe, to bask in His love and glory for all eternity. It is a hope that transcends the trials and tribulations of this world, a beacon of light in the midst of darkness.

Yet, while the gift of eternal life is freely given, it calls for a response from us. We are called to embrace this gift with faith and surrender, to live each day in the light of eternity.

Gracious Lord, thank You for the incomprehensible gift of eternal life through Your Son, Jesus Christ. Help us to grasp the depth of Your love and the reality of eternity. Guide us in living each day with an eternal perspective, that our lives may reflect Your glory and draw others into Your kingdom. In Jesus' name, we pray.
Amen.

DAY 19

God's Promises

"For no matter how many promises God has made, they are 'Yes' in Christ. And so through him the 'Amen' is spoken by us to the glory of God." - 2 Corinthians 1:20 (NIV)

The Bible is a treasure trove of divine pledges, each one a testament to God's faithfulness and love for His people. 2 Corinthians 1:20 reminds us that every promise God has made finds its fulfillment in Christ. Through Him, we can confidently declare "Amen," affirming our trust in God's word and bringing glory to His name.

God's promises are not empty words; they are declarations of His character and intentions toward us. From the promise of salvation and eternal life to the assurance of His presence and provision in our daily lives, His promises are a source of strength, comfort, and guidance. They remind us that we are never alone, that our future is secure in His hands, and that His plans for us are good.

But knowing God's promises is only the beginning. We are called to believe them, to hold onto them in times of trial and to live in the confidence that they will come to pass.

Gracious God, thank You for Your precious promises that sustain us in every season of life. Help us to cling to Your word with unwavering faith, knowing that You are faithful to fulfill all that You have spoken. Strengthen us to trust in Your promises, even when circumstances seem bleak. May our lives be a testimony to Your faithfulness, as we live in the assurance of Your love and provision. In Jesus' name, we pray. Amen.

DAY 20

The Bible as God's Word

*"For no matter how many promises God has made, they are 'Yes'
in Christ. And so through him the 'Amen' is spoken by us to the
glory of God." - 2 Corinthians 1:20 (NIV)*

The Bible is a treasure trove of divine pledges, each one a testament to God's faithfulness and love for His people. 2 Corinthians 1:20 reminds us that every promise God has made finds its fulfillment in Christ. Through Him, we can confidently declare "Amen," affirming our trust in God's word and bringing glory to His name.

God's promises are not empty words; they are declarations of His character and intentions toward us. From the promise of salvation and eternal life to the assurance of His presence and provision in our daily lives, His promises are a source of strength, comfort, and guidance. They remind us that we are never alone, that our future is secure in His hands, and that His plans for us are good.

But knowing God's promises is only the beginning. We are called to believe them, to hold onto them in times of trial and to live in the confidence that they will come to pass.

*Gracious God, thank You for Your precious promises that sustain
us in every season of life. Help us to cling to Your word with
unwavering faith, knowing that You are faithful to fulfill all that
You have spoken. Strengthen us to trust in Your promises, even
when circumstances seem bleak. May our lives be a testimony to
Your faithfulness, as we live in the assurance of Your love and
provision. In Jesus' name, we pray. Amen.*

DAY 21

The Role of the Church

"And let us consider how we may spur one another on toward love and good deeds, not giving up meeting together, as some are in the habit of doing, but encouraging one another—and all the more as you see the Day approaching." - Hebrews 10:24-25 (NIV)

Hebrews 10:24-25 reminds us of the essential role of the church in our lives. It calls us to gather together, to uplift and support one another in our journey of faith. In a world marked by division and isolation, the church stands as a beacon of hope, love, and unity.

The role of the church extends far beyond Sunday services. It is a place where broken hearts find healing, where the lost find direction, and where the weary find rest. Through worship, fellowship, and the preaching of God's Word, the church nurtures and strengthens our faith, equipping us to face life's challenges with courage and resilience.

As members of the body of Christ, we are called to actively participate in the life of the church. This means not only attending services but also investing in relationships, serving others, and sharing the love of Christ with those around us.

Heavenly Father, thank You for the gift of the church, a place where we can gather together to worship You and support one another. Help us to recognize the importance of active participation in our church community and to contribute to its growth and vitality. May Your love shine through us as we serve and encourage one another. In Jesus' name, we pray. Amen.

DAY 22

Fellowship with Believers

"And let us consider how we may spur one another on toward love and good deeds, not giving up meeting together, as some are in the habit of doing, but encouraging one another—and all the more as you see the Day approaching." - Hebrews 10:24-25 (NIV)

Fellowship with fellow Christians is not merely a social activity; it is a vital aspect of our spiritual journey. It is in the company of believers that we find encouragement, accountability, and strength to navigate life's challenges and grow in our faith.

When we come together in fellowship, we create a space for mutual edification and support. We share our joys and sorrows, our triumphs and struggles, knowing that we are not alone. In the bond of Christian fellowship, we find acceptance, love, and understanding. It is a place where we can be vulnerable, knowing that we will be met with compassion and empathy.

As believers, we are called to actively participate in fellowship, not only for our own benefit but also for the benefit of others. Our presence, encouragement, and prayers can make a significant difference in the lives of our brothers and sisters in Christ.

Heavenly Father, thank You for the gift of Christian fellowship. Help us to cherish and nurture the bonds we share with our brothers and sisters in Christ. May our fellowship be a reflection of Your love and grace, drawing others into relationship with You. In Jesus' name, we pray. Amen.

DAY 23

Worship

"And let us consider how we may spur one another on toward love and good deeds, not giving up meeting together, as some are in the habit of doing, but encouraging one another—and all the more as you see the Day approaching." - Hebrews 10:24-25 (NIV)

Fellowship with fellow Christians is not merely a social activity; it is a vital aspect of our spiritual journey. It is in the company of believers that we find encouragement, accountability, and strength to navigate life's challenges and grow in our faith.

When we come together in fellowship, we create a space for mutual edification and support. We share our joys and sorrows, our triumphs and struggles, knowing that we are not alone. In the bond of Christian fellowship, we find acceptance, love, and understanding. It is a place where we can be vulnerable, knowing that we will be met with compassion and empathy.

As believers, we are called to actively participate in fellowship, not only for our own benefit but also for the benefit of others. Our presence, encouragement, and prayers can make a significant difference in the lives of our brothers and sisters in Christ.

Heavenly Father, thank You for the gift of Christian fellowship. Help us to cherish and nurture the bonds we share with our brothers and sisters in Christ. May our fellowship be a reflection of Your love and grace, drawing others into relationship with You. In Jesus' name, we pray. Amen.

DAY 24

Tithing and Giving

"Each of you should give what you have decided in your heart to give, not reluctantly or under compulsion, for God loves a cheerful giver." - 2 Corinthians 9:7 (NIV)

Tithing and giving are not merely acts of duty; they are expressions of our love and gratitude towards God. When we give freely and willingly, we participate in God's work of blessing others and advancing His kingdom here on earth.

Tithing, traditionally understood as giving ten percent of one's income, is a practice rooted in biblical principles. It symbolizes our acknowledgment that all we have ultimately belongs to God, and our willingness to trust Him with our finances. However, beyond the prescribed percentage, giving is a matter of the heart.

When we give cheerfully, we align our hearts with God's generous nature. We become conduits of His grace, spreading love and hope to those around us. Our giving becomes a testimony of God's faithfulness and provision, both to us and to those who benefit from our generosity.

Dear Lord, thank You for the countless blessings You have bestowed upon us. Help us to give generously and cheerfully, knowing that everything we have comes from You. Show us how to be good stewards of the resources You've entrusted to us, and guide us in using them to bless others and advance Your kingdom. May our giving be a reflection of Your love and grace in our lives. In Jesus' name, we pray. Amen.

DAY 25

Serving Others

"For even the Son of Man did not come to be served, but to serve, and to give his life as a ransom for many." - Mark 10:45 (NIV)

Mark 10:45 beautifully encapsulates the heart of Christian service. Jesus, the perfect example of humility and love, came not to be served, but to serve. His life was a living demonstration of selflessness, compassion, and sacrifice. As followers of Christ, we are called to emulate His example by serving others with the same love and grace.

Serving others is more than just a good deed; it's a reflection of our faith in action. It's about putting the needs of others before our own, extending a helping hand to those who are hurting, and being a source of hope and encouragement in a world filled with darkness. When we serve others, we become vessels of God's love, shining His light into the lives of those around us.

True service is not always glamorous or easy. It often requires humility, patience, and a willingness to step out of our comfort zones. Yet, in serving others, we experience the profound joy and fulfillment that comes from making a difference in someone else's life.

Heavenly Father, thank You for the example of Jesus, who came to serve and to give His life for us. Teach us to follow His example by serving others with humility and love. May our lives be a reflection of Your love and grace in the world. In Jesus' name, we pray.
Amen.

DAY 26

Loving Your Neighbor

"Love your neighbor as yourself." - Mark 12:31b (NIV)

"Love your neighbor as yourself." This commandment cuts to the core of our relationships, challenging us to extend the same love, compassion, and kindness to others that we desire for ourselves. Loving our neighbor isn't just a suggestion; it's a fundamental aspect of our faith that reflects the very heart of God.

But who is our neighbor? Our neighbor is anyone whom we encounter in our daily lives - family, friends, colleagues, strangers, even those who may be different from us or whom we find challenging to love. Jesus calls us to see beyond differences and to recognize the inherent worth and dignity of every individual. When we love our neighbor, we mirror God's unconditional love for us and fulfill the greatest commandment to love Him with all our heart, soul, mind, and strength.

Loving our neighbor isn't always easy. It requires selflessness, forgiveness, and empathy. It means stepping out of our comfort zones, reaching out to those in need, and actively seeking ways to serve and support others. Yet, in doing so, we experience the transformative power of love, both in our own lives and in the lives of those around us.

Heavenly Father, thank You for the commandment to love our neighbor as ourselves. Help us to see others through Your eyes, with compassion, grace, and understanding. May our actions reflect Your love and bring glory to Your name. In Jesus' name, we pray. Amen.

DAY 27

Compassion

"Be kind and compassionate to one another, forgiving each other, just as in Christ God forgave you." - Ephesians 4:32 (NIV)

Ephesians 4:32 encapsulates the essence of compassion as a central theme in the life of a Christian. Compassion is more than just feeling sorry for someone; it's about entering into the suffering of others with empathy and actively seeking to alleviate it. Just as Christ demonstrated boundless compassion in His ministry, we are called to reflect His love and mercy in our interactions with others.

Compassion is a reflection of God's character and His deep love for humanity. It moves us to extend a helping hand to the hurting, to listen with empathy, and to offer support and encouragement to those in need. It's a powerful force that breaks down barriers, bridges divides, and brings healing to broken hearts and wounded souls.

It should guide our words, our actions, and our attitudes towards others. Whether it's showing kindness to a stranger, extending forgiveness to someone who has wronged us, or lending a listening ear to a friend in distress, every act of compassion has the potential to make a profound difference in someone's life.

Heavenly Father, thank You for the example of compassion You have set for us through Your Son, Jesus Christ. Help us to embody His love and mercy in our interactions with others. Open our eyes to the needs of those around us and give us the courage and compassion to reach out and make a difference. May our lives be a testimony to Your boundless love and grace. In Jesus' name, we pray. Amen.

DAY 28

Humility

"Do nothing out of selfish ambition or vain conceit. Rather, in humility value others above yourselves." - Philippians 2:3 (NIV)

Humility is not merely a posture of self-effacement; it is a radical shift in perspective that places the needs and well-being of others above our own. It's about recognizing our inherent worth as children of God while also acknowledging the value and dignity of every person we encounter.

Jesus, the ultimate example of humility, willingly laid aside His divine glory to serve humanity, even to the point of death on the cross. His humility was not weakness but strength, not submission to oppression but a revolutionary act of love that ushered in redemption for all mankind.

To cultivate humility in our lives, we must first surrender our pride and ego at the feet of Jesus. We must acknowledge that true greatness lies not in status or achievement but in service and sacrifice. Humility opens the door to deeper relationships, greater empathy, and a heightened awareness of the needs of others.

Heavenly Father, teach us to walk in the way of humility as Jesus did. Help us to value others above ourselves and to serve with love and compassion. Remove from us any pride or selfish ambition that hinders our ability to reflect Your character to the world. May humility be the hallmark of our lives, drawing others closer to You. In Jesus' name, we pray. Amen.

DAY 29

Patience

"But if we hope for what we do not yet have, we wait for it patiently." - Romans 8:25 (NIV)

Romans 8:25 reminds us that patience is not merely the ability to wait but the willingness to trust in God's perfect timing. It is an active expression of our faith, demonstrating our confidence in God's promises even when they seem delayed.

In a world that values instant gratification and quick results, practicing patience can be challenging. We live in a culture of immediacy, where waiting is often seen as a burden rather than an opportunity for growth. However, as followers of Christ, we are called to a different standard. We are called to wait patiently, knowing that God's timing is always perfect.

Patience is not passive resignation but active endurance. It requires us to hold onto hope and faith even in the midst of uncertainty. It's about trusting that God is at work behind the scenes, orchestrating every detail for our good and His glory. As we wait patiently, we are invited to lean into God's presence, seeking His wisdom and guidance in every season of waiting.

Heavenly Father, teach us to wait patiently for Your perfect timing. Help us to trust in Your plans and promises, even when we cannot see the way forward. Give us strength to endure the waiting seasons with grace and faith, knowing that You are always working for our good. May our hearts be filled with gratitude and hope as we wait expectantly for Your promises to be fulfilled. In Jesus' name, we pray. Amen.

DAY 30

Kindness

"And be kind and compassionate to one another, forgiving one another, just as God also forgave you in Christ." - Ephesians 4:32 (CSB)

In Ephesians 4:32, we find a profound call to kindness and compassion, rooted in the very nature of God Himself. As followers of Christ, we are called to embody His love and extend it to others through acts of kindness. Kindness is more than just a polite gesture; it is a reflection of the transformative power of God's love working within us.

To be kind is to extend grace and mercy to those around us, regardless of their circumstances or actions. It is to see others through the eyes of Christ, recognizing their inherent dignity and worth as fellow creations of God. Kindness has the power to heal wounds, mend broken relationships, and bring hope to the weary soul.

As we cultivate a spirit of kindness in our lives, we become vessels of God's love in a world desperate for compassion. Our words and actions have the potential to make a profound impact on those we encounter, revealing the light of Christ in the midst of darkness.

Heavenly Father, thank You for Your boundless love and grace towards us. Help us to walk in the footsteps of Your Son, Jesus Christ, by extending kindness and compassion to those around us. May our lives be a testament to Your goodness and mercy, as we seek to reflect Your kindness to others. In Jesus' name, we pray. Amen.

DAY 31

Goodness

"The Lord is good to all; he has compassion on all he has made." - Psalm 145:9 (NIV)

His goodness extends far beyond our comprehension, reaching every corner of creation and embracing every individual with boundless love and compassion. In a world often marred by darkness and despair, the goodness of God shines as a beacon of hope, illuminating our lives with His grace and mercy.

God's goodness is not contingent upon our circumstances or our actions; it is an intrinsic aspect of His character. Even in the midst of trials and tribulations, we can trust in His unwavering goodness. It is a source of comfort and strength, reminding us that we are never alone, and that His plans for us are filled with hope and purpose.

As recipients of God's goodness, we are called to reflect His character in our own lives. This means striving to embody goodness in our thoughts, words, and actions. It means extending kindness and compassion to those around us, even when it may seem difficult.

Heavenly Father, we thank You for Your boundless goodness and compassion towards us. Help us to be mindful of Your goodness in every aspect of our lives, and empower us to reflect Your character to those around us. Fill us with Your love and grace, that we may be instruments of Your goodness in the world. In Jesus' name, we pray. Amen.

DAY 32

Self-Control

"For the Spirit God gave us does not make us timid, but gives us power, love and self-discipline." - 2 Timothy 1:7 (NIV)

Self-control is not merely an exercise of willpower; it is a manifestation of the power and love of God working within us. As Christians, we are called to live lives that reflect the character of Christ, and self-control plays a crucial role in this pursuit.

Self-control is the ability to govern our thoughts, desires, and actions in alignment with God's will. It empowers us to resist temptations and impulses that lead us away from His plan for our lives. While it may not always be easy, self-control is essential for spiritual growth and maturity. It enables us to live with integrity, honoring God in all that we do.

When we exercise self-control, we demonstrate our trust in God's guidance and sovereignty over our lives. We acknowledge that His ways are higher than our ways, and His plans are always for our good. Through self-discipline, we surrender our own desires to His will, allowing His Spirit to work within us to transform us into the image of Christ.

Heavenly Father, thank You for the gift of Your Spirit, which empowers us to live lives of self-discipline and godliness. Help us to rely on Your strength and guidance as we strive to exercise self-control in all areas of our lives. May our actions bring glory to Your name and reflect Your love to the world. In Jesus' name, we pray. Amen.

DAY 33

Peace

"Peace I leave with you; my peace I give you. I do not give to you as the world gives. Do not let your hearts be troubled and do not be afraid." - John 14:27 (NIV)

In the midst of life's chaos and uncertainty, the promise of peace stands as a beacon of hope for every believer. John 14:27 reminds us that the peace Jesus offers is unlike anything the world can give. It is a deep, abiding peace that transcends circumstances and surpasses understanding. It is the peace that comes from knowing and trusting in our Savior.

Peace, in the biblical sense, is not merely the absence of conflict or turmoil; it is a state of wholeness, harmony, and well-being. It is the assurance that God is in control, working all things together for our good. This peace doesn't depend on external factors but resides within us as a fruit of the Holy Spirit.

In a world filled with strife and discord, experiencing God's peace is a powerful testimony to His presence in our lives. It is a peace that calms our anxious hearts, soothes our troubled minds, and sustains us through the storms of life. When we abide in His peace, we become beacons of light, drawing others to the source of true peace.

Heavenly Father, thank You for the gift of Your peace that surpasses all understanding. In the midst of life's storms, help us to anchor our hearts in Your unshakable peace. May Your peace guard our hearts and minds in Christ Jesus, and may it overflow to those around us, bringing healing and hope to a broken world. In Jesus' name, we pray. Amen.

DAY 34

Hope

"Now faith is confidence in what we hope for and assurance about what we do not see." - Hebrews 11:1 (NIV)

Hope is not merely wishful thinking; it is a deep-seated confidence in the promises of God, even when circumstances seem bleak. It is the assurance that God is faithful and that His plans for us are good, regardless of our present struggles.

In a world often marked by uncertainty and despair, hope shines as a beacon of light, guiding us through the darkest of nights. It is the antidote to fear and despair, reminding us that our story does not end with our current challenges. Hope whispers to our hearts that there is more to come, that God is working all things together for our good.

Our faith in God fuels our hope. As we trust in His character and His promises, our hope grows stronger. We can look beyond our present circumstances and fix our eyes on the eternal glory that awaits us. This hope is not fleeting or fragile; it is an anchor that holds firm amidst life's storms.

Heavenly Father, thank You for the gift of hope that sustains us through every trial and tribulation. Help us to anchor our souls in Your promises and to trust in Your unfailing love. Strengthen our faith and fill us with confident hope, knowing that You are always with us and that Your plans for us are good. In Jesus' name, we pray. Amen.

DAY 35

The Second Coming of Christ

"For as lightning that comes from the east is visible even in the west, so will be the coming of the Son of Man." - Matthew 24:27 (NIV)

For Christians, the anticipation of Christ's return is both a source of comfort and urgency. It reminds us of the promise of eternal life with our Savior and the fulfillment of God's kingdom on earth.

The Second Coming is not just a future event; it is a foundational truth that shapes our present lives. It calls us to live with a sense of readiness and expectation, knowing that at any moment, Christ could return to establish His reign of righteousness and peace. In a world marked by uncertainty and turmoil, the hope of His return sustains us, reminding us that God's ultimate victory is assured.

As we wait for Christ's return, we are called to action. Our lives should reflect the values of His kingdom, characterized by love, justice, and compassion. We are to be faithful stewards of the gifts and resources entrusted to us, using them to glorify God and further His purposes on earth. Our words and deeds should bear witness to the transforming power of Christ in our lives, drawing others to Him and preparing the way for His return.

Heavenly Father, we thank You for the promise of Christ's Second Coming, a hope that sustains us in times of trial and uncertainty. Help us to live with eager anticipation of His return, ready to greet Him with joy and longing. May our lives be a reflection of Your glory, as we eagerly await the coming of our Savior. In Jesus' name, we pray. Amen.

DAY 36

Spiritual Warfare

"For our struggle is not against flesh and blood, but against the rulers, against the authorities, against the powers of this dark world and against the spiritual forces of evil in the heavenly realms." - Ephesians 6:12 (NIV)

As believers, we are engaged in a battle that transcends the physical realm. Our struggle is not against mere mortal adversaries, but against the spiritual forces of darkness that seek to undermine God's purposes and lead us astray.

Spiritual warfare encompasses the ongoing conflict between good and evil, light and darkness. It manifests in various forms, including temptations, doubts, fears, and spiritual attacks. The enemy, Satan, prowls like a roaring lion, seeking whom he may devour (1 Peter 5:8). But we are not defenseless in this battle. God equips us with spiritual armor, described in Ephesians 6:13-18, to stand firm against the schemes of the devil.

While the concept of spiritual warfare may evoke fear or apprehension, it is also a reminder of the power and victory we have in Christ. Through His death and resurrection, Jesus triumphed over sin and death, disarming the powers and authorities, and making a public spectacle of them (Colossians 2:15).

Heavenly Father, we thank You for the victory we have in Christ Jesus. Help us to be vigilant and discerning in recognizing the spiritual battles we face. Fill us afresh with Your Holy Spirit, empowering us to overcome evil with good and to advance Your kingdom in the world. In Jesus' name, we pray. Amen.

DAY 37

Temptation

"No temptation has overtaken you except what is common to mankind. And God is faithful; he will not let you be tempted beyond what you can bear. But when you are tempted, he will also provide a way out so that you can endure it." - 1 Corinthians 10:13 (NIV)

Temptation is a universal experience, one that every person encounters in various forms throughout life. It seeks to lure us away from God's will and into paths of disobedience and destruction. Yet, even in the midst of temptation, we find assurance in God's promise: He will not allow us to be tempted beyond what we can bear, and He always provides a way out.

Temptation often comes unexpectedly, catching us off guard in moments of weakness or vulnerability. It may present itself as a subtle whisper, enticing us with promises of pleasure or fulfillment. Other times, it may confront us boldly, challenging our convictions and testing our faith. But regardless of its form, temptation is not insurmountable. With God's strength and guidance, we can overcome its grip and emerge victorious.

Heavenly Father, thank You for Your faithfulness in the midst of temptation. Give us strength to resist the schemes of the enemy and wisdom to discern Your way out. Help us to rely on Your power and provision, knowing that You are greater than any temptation we may face. Guide us in walking uprightly and honoring You in all we do. In Jesus' name, we pray. Amen.

DAY 38

Overcoming Sin

"For sin shall no longer be your master, because you are not under the law, but under grace." - Romans 6:14 (NIV)

Through the grace of God, we are empowered to overcome sin and live victoriously in His righteousness. However, the journey of overcoming sin is not always easy. It requires intentionality, perseverance, and a deep reliance on God's strength.

Sin separates us from God and hinders our spiritual growth. It enslaves us in patterns of behavior that lead to guilt, shame, and spiritual stagnation. Yet, as believers, we are called to a life of freedom and transformation. Through the power of the Holy Spirit, we have the ability to break free from the chains of sin and walk in the fullness of God's grace.

Overcoming sin begins with acknowledging our need for God's help. We cannot overcome sin through our own efforts alone; it is only by surrendering to God and allowing His Spirit to work within us that true victory is possible. We must also be vigilant and proactive in guarding our hearts and minds against temptation. This may involve prayer, scripture meditation, accountability, and practical steps to avoid situations that lead to sin.

Heavenly Father, thank You for the gift of Your grace that empowers us to overcome sin. Give us the strength and wisdom to walk in obedience to Your will, and to resist the temptations that seek to ensnare us. Help us to rely on Your Spirit to guide us in the paths of righteousness, and to lead us into freedom and abundant life. In Jesus' name, we pray. Amen.

DAY 39

The Authority of Scripture

"All Scripture is God-breathed and is useful for teaching, rebuking, correcting and training in righteousness, so that the servant of God may be thoroughly equipped for every good work."
- 2 Timothy 3:16-17 (NIV)

The Bible is not merely a collection of ancient writings; it is the inspired word of God, given to us for our instruction, correction, and spiritual growth. As Christians, understanding and affirming the authority of Scripture is essential for our faith journey.

The authority of Scripture means that it serves as the ultimate standard by which we measure truth and discern God's will for our lives. In a world filled with competing voices and conflicting ideologies, the Bible stands as a steadfast anchor, offering wisdom and guidance in every situation. Its timeless truths provide a solid foundation upon which we can build our lives, shaping our beliefs, values, and actions according to God's word.

Embracing the authority of Scripture also requires humility and obedience. It means surrendering our own preferences and opinions to the truth revealed in God's word, even when it challenges or convicts us.

Heavenly Father, thank You for the gift of Your word. Help us to recognize and affirm its authority in our lives. Give us a hunger for Your truth and a willingness to submit ourselves to Your word. May Your word dwell richly in our hearts, leading us into a deeper relationship with You. In Jesus' name, we pray. Amen.

DAY 40

The Importance of Community

*"And let us consider how we may spur one another on toward love
and good deeds, not giving up meeting together, as some are in the
habit of doing, but encouraging one another—and all the more as
you see the Day approaching." - Hebrews 10:24-25 (NIV)*

God designed us to thrive in relationships, to uplift and support one
another as we journey through life. In a world often marked by
isolation and self-sufficiency, the value of community cannot be
overstated. It is within the context of loving, supportive
relationships that we experience God's presence in profound ways.

Community provides us with a sense of belonging and identity. It
is where we find acceptance, encouragement, and accountability.
When we gather with fellow believers, we are reminded that we
are not alone in our faith journey.

Community is essential for spiritual growth. Through fellowship,
we sharpen one another, spurring each other on toward love and
good deeds. We learn from one another's experiences,
perspectives, and gifts, enriching our understanding of God's Word
and deepening our relationship with Him.

*Heavenly Father, thank You for the gift of community. Help us to
appreciate the beauty of fellowship and the strength found in unity.
May we be faithful in encouraging and uplifting one another,
bearing witness to Your love and grace through our interactions.
In Jesus' name, we pray. Amen.*

DAY 41

Christian Leadership

"But among you it will be different. Whoever wants to be a leader among you must be your servant." - Mark 10:43 (NLT)

He teaches us that true leadership in the kingdom of God is not about power, status, or authority over others. Instead, it is about service, humility, and sacrificial love. Christian leadership is exemplified by the heart of a servant, following the example set by Jesus Himself.

As Christians, we are called to lead by serving others. This means putting the needs of others before our own, leading with compassion, and guiding with wisdom and grace. It is a leadership style that seeks to empower, uplift, and encourage those around us, rather than seeking recognition or self-promotion.

Christian leadership is about influencing others to grow in their faith, to discover their God-given talents, and to fulfill their potential. It is about leading by example, living a life that reflects the love and character of Christ in all that we do.

Heavenly Father, thank You for showing us the true meaning of leadership through the example of Your Son, Jesus Christ. Help us to embrace the call to serve others with humility and love, following in His footsteps. Grant us wisdom and strength to lead by example, and to influence others for Your kingdom. May our leadership be a reflection of Your grace and glory in the world. In Jesus' name, we pray. Amen.

DAY 42

Discipleship

"Then Jesus said to his disciples, 'Whoever wants to be my disciple must deny themselves and take up their cross and follow me.'" - Matthew 16:24 (NIV)

To be a disciple of Christ is not merely to believe in Him, but to follow Him wholeheartedly, embracing His teachings and embodying His love in our lives.

Discipleship is a journey of transformation, a process of becoming more like Jesus in every aspect of our being. It's about surrendering our will and desires to His, allowing His Spirit to work in us and through us to bring about His purposes in the world. This journey requires sacrifice, as we let go of our own ambitions and comforts to pursue the will of God.

But discipleship is also a journey of incredible joy and fulfillment. It's an invitation to experience the abundant life that Jesus promised to those who follow Him faithfully. As we walk in obedience to His commands, we find peace, purpose, and a deep sense of belonging in His kingdom.

Heavenly Father, thank You for calling us to be Your disciples. Give us the strength and courage to follow You wholeheartedly, even when it requires sacrifice. Help us to surrender our will to Yours and to walk in obedience to Your commands. May our lives be a reflection of Your love and grace to the world. In Jesus' name, we pray. Amen.

DAY 43

The Sabbath

"Remember the Sabbath day by keeping it holy." - Exodus 20:8
(NIV)

The Sabbath is a sacred time set apart for rest, reflection, and worship. It is a gift from God, designed not as a burden, but as a source of spiritual renewal and rejuvenation for His people.

In our fast-paced world, the concept of rest often seems foreign. We fill our schedules with endless tasks and commitments, leaving little time for rest and reflection. Yet, God, in His wisdom, knew the importance of rest for our well-being, both physically and spiritually. The Sabbath serves as a reminder that our worth is not determined by our productivity, but by our identity as beloved children of God.

On the Sabbath, we are invited to cease our striving and enter into God's rest. It is a time to pause, to reflect on His goodness, and to cultivate deeper intimacy with Him. In the stillness of the Sabbath, we find refuge from the chaos of the world, and our souls are refreshed by the presence of our Heavenly Father.

Heavenly Father, thank You for the gift of the Sabbath, a sacred time of rest and renewal. Help us to honor this day by keeping it holy, and by drawing near to You with grateful hearts. May we find true rest in Your presence, and may our souls be nourished by Your love and grace. In Jesus' name, we pray. Amen.

DAY 44

The Fear of the Lord

"The fear of the Lord is the beginning of wisdom, and knowledge of the Holy One is understanding." - Proverbs 9:10 (NIV)

Proverbs 9:10 teaches us that the fear of the Lord is the foundation of wisdom. But what does it mean to fear the Lord? It's not a trembling, cowering fear, but rather a deep reverence, awe, and respect for the Almighty God. It's an acknowledgment of His holiness, His power, and His sovereignty over all creation.

When we fear the Lord, we recognize our dependence on Him and our need for His guidance and direction in our lives. It's a posture of humility, understanding that we are finite beings in the presence of the infinite God. This fear leads us to seek His will above our own, to align our hearts with His purposes, and to live in obedience to His commands.

The fear of the Lord also brings wisdom and understanding. It opens our hearts and minds to receive God's truth and to discern right from wrong. It shapes our character, guiding us to live lives that honor and please Him. In essence, the fear of the Lord is the key that unlocks the treasures of wisdom and knowledge found in God Himself.

Heavenly Father, we come before You in awe of Your majesty and holiness. Teach us to fear You rightly, to recognize Your sovereignty over our lives, and to live in obedience to Your commands. Grant us wisdom and understanding as we seek to honor You in all that we do. May our lives be a testament to Your glory and grace. In Jesus' name, we pray. Amen.

DAY 45

God's Righteousness

"For I tell you that unless your righteousness surpasses that of the Pharisees and the teachers of the law, you will certainly not enter the kingdom of heaven." - Matthew 5:20 (NIV)

God's righteousness is not simply about following rules or appearing holy; it's about aligning our hearts with His perfect and unwavering standard of goodness and justice. It's about living in a way that reflects His character and brings glory to His name.

God's righteousness is rooted in His character. He is holy, just, and true in all His ways. His righteousness is not based on human standards or merit but is a gift freely given to us through Christ Jesus. When we accept Jesus as our Savior, His righteousness covers us, and we are made righteous in God's sight.

However, our journey of faith doesn't end with salvation. God calls us to walk in His righteousness daily, allowing His Spirit to transform us from the inside out. This means seeking justice, loving mercy, and walking humbly with our God (Micah 6:8). It means treating others with kindness, forgiveness, and compassion, just as God has shown us.

Heavenly Father, thank You for Your perfect righteousness that covers us through Christ Jesus. Help us to walk in Your ways and live according to Your standard of goodness and justice. Give us the strength and wisdom to be instruments of Your righteousness in the world, shining Your light and bringing glory to Your name. In Jesus' name, we pray. Amen.

DAY 46

Holiness

"But just as he who called you is holy, so be holy in all you do; for it is written: 'Be holy, because I am holy.'" - 1 Peter 1:15-16 (NIV)

Holiness is not merely about following a set of rules or avoiding certain behaviors; it's about living a life set apart for God's purposes. It's about reflecting His character of purity, righteousness, and love in every aspect of our lives.

As followers of Christ, we are called to pursue holiness wholeheartedly. This pursuit requires surrendering our desires, ambitions, and selfish tendencies to the will of God. It means allowing His Spirit to transform us from the inside out, shaping our thoughts, words, and actions to align with His perfect will.

Living a holy life is a journey, not a destination. It's a daily commitment to walk in obedience and righteousness, even when it's challenging or unpopular. It's about striving for excellence in our relationships, our work, and our service to others, all for the glory of God.

Heavenly Father, thank You for calling us to a life of holiness. Help us to understand what it truly means to be set apart for Your purposes. Give us the strength and courage to pursue holiness in every area of our lives, trusting in Your grace to transform us into the image of Your Son, Jesus Christ. May our lives be a testimony of Your goodness and glory. In Jesus' name, we pray. Amen.

DAY 47

Sanctification

"And the very God of peace sanctify you wholly; and I pray God your whole spirit and soul and body be preserved blameless unto the coming of our Lord Jesus Christ." - 1 Thessalonians 5:23 (KJV)

Sanctification is not a one-time event but a lifelong journey of growth and purification in our relationship with God. It involves the renewal of our minds, the purification of our hearts, and the surrender of our wills to God's perfect plan.

As Christians, we are called to be holy as God is holy (1 Peter 1:16). Sanctification is the means by which we increasingly reflect the character of Christ in our thoughts, words, and actions. It is a beautiful work of God's grace, accomplished through the power of His Spirit working within us.

Sanctification requires our active participation. It involves seeking God daily through prayer, studying His Word, and cultivating intimacy with Him. It means surrendering our selfish desires and submitting to His will, even when it goes against our own. It requires humility, perseverance, and faithfulness as we allow God to shape us into vessels fit for His use.

Heavenly Father, thank You for the gift of sanctification. Help us to understand the depth of Your love and the power of Your grace at work within us. May our hearts be continually renewed, our minds transformed, and our wills aligned with Yours. In Jesus' name, we pray. Amen.

DAY 48

Consecration

"Present your bodies as a living sacrifice, holy and acceptable to God, which is your spiritual worship." - Romans 12:1 (ESV)

Consecration is the deliberate act of setting ourselves apart for God's purposes, surrendering our will, desires, and ambitions to His perfect plan.

Consecration goes beyond mere religious rituals; it's a heart posture of devotion and commitment. It's saying to God, "Here I am, wholly Yours, ready to be used by You in whatever way You see fit." It involves laying down our own agendas and allowing God to direct our steps, trusting that His plans for us are good and perfect.

When we consecrate ourselves to God, we invite His presence to dwell within us and work through us. We become vessels of His love, grace, and power, impacting the world around us for His kingdom. Consecration is not a one-time event but a daily choice—a continual surrender of our lives to the One who gave His life for us.

Lord, we come before You with hearts open and willing to be consecrated for Your purposes. Help us to lay aside our own agendas and desires, and to fully surrender ourselves to Your will. Fill us with Your Holy Spirit, that we may be empowered to live as living sacrifices, holy and pleasing to You. May our lives bring glory to Your name and advance Your kingdom here on earth. In Jesus' name, we pray. Amen.

DAY 49

God's Provision

"And my God will meet all your needs according to the riches of his glory in Christ Jesus." - Philippians 4:19 (NIV)

The promise of God's provision extends beyond mere material needs; it encompasses every aspect of our lives. Just as a loving parent cares for the needs of their child, our Heavenly Father tenderly provides for His beloved.

God's provision is not limited by our circumstances or resources. It flows from the inexhaustible riches of His glory, lavished upon us through His Son, Jesus Christ. Whether we find ourselves in times of abundance or scarcity, God remains faithful to meet our needs according to His perfect plan and timing.

As recipients of God's provision, we are called to trust in His faithfulness and to cultivate an attitude of gratitude. We can rest assured that He knows our needs even before we ask and that He delights in providing for His children. In times of uncertainty or hardship, we can find comfort and strength in knowing that our Heavenly Father is always with us, guiding, protecting, and providing for us.

Gracious Father, thank You for Your abundant provision in our lives. Help us to trust in Your unfailing love and faithfulness, knowing that You will always provide for us according to Your perfect plan. Give us grateful hearts that recognize Your hand at work in every aspect of our lives. May Your provision fill us with peace and confidence as we journey through life with You. In Jesus' name, we pray. Amen.

DAY 50

Trusting God's Timing

"But do not forget this one thing, dear friends: With the Lord a day is like a thousand years, and a thousand years are like a day." - 2 Peter 3:8 (NIV)

As humans, we often struggle with impatience and the desire for immediate answers to our prayers and desires. Trusting God's timing requires faith and surrender, but it also brings peace and assurance.

God's timing is always perfect. He knows the beginning from the end, and His plans for us are always for our good, even when they don't align with our expectations or timelines. When we trust in His timing, we acknowledge His sovereignty and wisdom, recognizing that He sees the bigger picture and knows what is best for us.

Trusting God's timing doesn't mean we passively sit back and wait for things to happen. It means actively seeking His will and surrendering our plans and desires to Him. It means praying with faith and perseverance, knowing that God hears our prayers and will answer them in His perfect time. It means living each day with hope and expectation, knowing that God is always working behind the scenes, orchestrating every detail of our lives for His glory.

Dear Heavenly Father, thank You for Your perfect timing and Your unwavering faithfulness. Give us patience and peace as we wait for Your plans to unfold in our lives. Strengthen our faith and help us to surrender our desires to Your will. In Jesus' name, we pray.
Amen.

DAY 51

The Wisdom of God

"Oh, the depth of the riches of the wisdom and knowledge of God!
How unsearchable his judgments, and his paths beyond tracing
out!" - Romans 11:33 (NIV)

His wisdom surpasses human understanding, transcending our limited perception and comprehension. It's a wisdom that permeates every aspect of creation, from the intricate design of the cosmos to the intricate details of our lives.

The wisdom of God is not merely intellectual knowledge; it's practical and transformative. It guides us in making decisions, navigating challenges, and discerning His will for our lives. When we seek God's wisdom, we tap into a wellspring of divine insight and understanding that empowers us to live according to His purposes.

In a world filled with uncertainty and complexity, God's wisdom offers clarity and direction. It illuminates the path before us, showing us the way to walk in righteousness and truth. It teaches us to prioritize what truly matters and to trust in God's sovereignty, even when circumstances seem daunting.

Heavenly Father, we thank You for the richness of Your wisdom that surpasses all understanding. Help us to seek Your wisdom in every aspect of our lives, trusting in Your guidance and direction. May Your wisdom lead us to a life of greater intimacy with You and fulfillment of Your purposes. In Jesus' name, we pray. Amen.

DAY 52

Hearing God's Voice

"My sheep listen to my voice; I know them, and they follow me." - John 10:27 (NIV)

Hearing God's voice is not just a privilege reserved for prophets or spiritual giants; it's a promise for every believer who seeks to know and follow Him.

But in a world filled with competing voices and conflicting messages, how do we discern the voice of God? The key lies in cultivating a heart that is attuned to His presence and a spirit that is sensitive to His leading. It requires spending time in prayer, in the study of His Word, and in quiet reflection, tuning out the clamor of the world to listen for the gentle whisper of His Spirit.

Hearing God's voice is not always dramatic or earth-shattering; often, it comes as a still, small voice speaking peace, wisdom, and direction into our hearts. It may come through Scripture, through the counsel of wise mentors, or through moments of divine revelation. But however God chooses to speak to us, His voice always brings clarity, conviction, and comfort.

Gracious Lord, thank You for the gift of Your presence and the privilege of hearing Your voice. Give us the wisdom to discern Your voice from the noise of the world, and the courage to follow wherever You may lead. May we be faithful listeners and obedient followers of Your Word. In Jesus' name, we pray. Amen.

DAY 53

Spiritual Discernment

"Dear friends, do not believe every spirit, but test the spirits to see whether they are from God, because many false prophets have gone out into the world." - 1 John 4:1 (NIV)

1 John 4:1 reminds us of the importance of testing the spirits to distinguish between what is of God and what is not. Spiritual discernment is the ability to recognize the voice of God amidst the clamor of competing voices, whether they be from within ourselves, from others, or from the enemy.

As followers of Christ, we are called to be vigilant and discerning, not swayed by every wind of doctrine or passing trend. Discernment requires a deep intimacy with God, cultivated through prayer, meditation on His Word, and a surrendered heart. It involves tuning our spiritual ears to hear His voice above all others and aligning our hearts with His truth and wisdom.

But spiritual discernment is not just about avoiding deception; it's also about embracing God's will and direction for our lives. It empowers us to make wise choices, to discern between good and evil, and to walk in the light of His presence.

Heavenly Father, thank You for the gift of spiritual discernment. Help us to test the spirits and to discern Your voice amidst the noise of the world. May Your Spirit guide us into all truth and righteousness, that we may walk in Your ways and bring glory to Your name. In Jesus' name, we pray. Amen.

DAY 54

Courage in Christ

"Be strong and courageous. Do not be afraid; do not be discouraged, for the Lord your God will be with you wherever you go." - Joshua 1:9 (NIV)

Courage in Christ is not the absence of fear, but the presence of faith that empowers us to overcome our fears. It's the assurance that no matter what challenges we face, we are never alone, for God Himself goes before us and walks beside us.

Courage in Christ is rooted in our trust in God's promises and His faithfulness. Just as He promised Joshua as he prepared to lead the Israelites into the Promised Land, God assures us that He will never leave us nor forsake us. In times of uncertainty, doubt, or adversity, we can draw strength from knowing that our Heavenly Father is with us, guiding us, and empowering us to press on with courage and confidence.

When we face trials or obstacles that seem insurmountable, it's easy to give in to fear and doubt. But as followers of Christ, we are called to stand firm in our faith, trusting in His power to see us through. Our courage is not based on our own abilities or circumstances but on the unchanging character of God and His promises to His people.

Heavenly Father, thank You for Your promise to be with us always. Give us the courage to face whatever challenges may come our way, knowing that You are with us and for us. May we live boldly for You, bringing glory to Your name in all that we do. In Jesus' name, we pray. Amen.

DAY 55

Strength in Weakness

"But he said to me, 'My grace is sufficient for you, for my power is made perfect in weakness.' Therefore I will boast all the more gladly about my weaknesses, so that Christ's power may rest on me." - 2 Corinthians 12:9 (NIV)

world often tells us to hide our weaknesses, to cover them up with a facade of strength and self-sufficiency. But God's perspective is radically different. He tells us that His power is most fully displayed in our moments of weakness.

Strength in weakness is not about pretending to be strong when we feel weak; it's about embracing our vulnerability and relying completely on God's strength. It's about recognizing that our limitations are an opportunity for God to demonstrate His power and grace in our lives.

When we acknowledge our weaknesses and lean on God for strength, we experience His sufficiency in a profound way. His grace becomes our sustaining force, carrying us through life's challenges and empowering us to persevere in faith. Our weaknesses become the canvas on which God paints His masterpiece of redemption and transformation.

Heavenly Father, thank You for Your promise that Your power is made perfect in our weakness. Teach us to boast in our weaknesses, knowing that they are opportunities for Your power to be revealed in our lives. May Your grace sustain us and Your strength empower us to walk in faith each day. In Jesus' name, we pray. Amen.

DAY 56

Reconciliation

"So if you are offering your gift at the altar and there remember that your brother or sister has something against you, leave your gift there before the altar and go. First be reconciled to your brother or sister, and then come and offer your gift." - Matthew 5:23-24 (NIV)

Reconciliation is at the heart of the Gospel message. It's about restoring broken connections, healing wounds, and making amends. As followers of Christ, we are called to be agents of reconciliation, both in our relationship with God and with one another.

Reconciliation begins with humility and repentance. It requires us to acknowledge our faults and seek forgiveness from those we have wronged. It also involves extending forgiveness to those who have hurt us, releasing bitterness and resentment to embrace healing and restoration.

True reconciliation goes beyond superficial apologies; it seeks to rebuild trust and foster genuine harmony. It's a process that requires time, patience, and commitment. But the rewards are immeasurable—a restored sense of peace, unity, and the opportunity to reflect God's love and grace to the world.

Lord, You are the ultimate reconciler, bringing us back into right relationship with You through the sacrifice of Your Son, Jesus Christ. May our lives be a testament to Your transformative power and boundless mercy. In Jesus' name, we pray. Amen.

DAY 57

Repentance

"Repent, then, and turn to God, so that your sins may be wiped out, that times of refreshing may come from the Lord." - Acts 3:19 (NIV)

Repentance is not merely feeling sorry for our sins; it is a deep, heartfelt turning away from sin and toward God. It is a recognition of our need for His forgiveness and a willingness to change our thoughts, attitudes, and actions.

Repentance is a journey of humility and surrender. It requires us to confront our own brokenness and to acknowledge the ways in which we have fallen short of God's standards. Yet, in the midst of our failings, there is hope. God's promise is one of restoration and renewal. When we repent and turn to Him, He graciously forgives our sins and offers us the gift of new life in Christ.

Repentance is not a one-time event but a continual process of growth and transformation. It is a daily decision to align our lives with God's will and to walk in obedience to His Word. As we humble ourselves before Him, He pours out His grace upon us, cleansing us from all unrighteousness and leading us into a deeper relationship with Him.

Heavenly Father, thank You for Your incredible love and mercy toward us. We confess that we have sinned against You in thought, word, and deed. Help us to turn away from our sins and to walk in obedience to Your Word. May Your Holy Spirit empower us to live lives that bring honor and glory to Your name. In Jesus' name, we pray. Amen.

DAY 58

The Vine and the Branches

"I am the vine; you are the branches. If you remain in me and I in you, you will bear much fruit; apart from me you can do nothing."
- John 15:5 (NIV)

He is the vine, the source of our life and sustenance, and we are the branches, intimately connected to Him. This metaphor reveals profound truths about our dependence on Christ and the abundant life that flows from abiding in Him.

Just as a branch draws its nourishment and vitality from the vine, so too do we find our strength, purpose, and identity in Jesus. When we remain connected to Him through prayer, worship, and obedience to His Word, His life-giving power flows through us, enabling us to bear fruit that glorifies God.

But apart from Christ, we wither and fade, unable to fulfill our true purpose. It's only by staying firmly rooted in Him that we can experience the fullness of life He promises. This requires an ongoing, intentional relationship with Jesus, one characterized by surrender, trust, and a deepening love for Him.

Heavenly Father, thank You for the privilege of being connected to Jesus, the true vine. Help us to remain steadfast in our relationship with Him, drawing strength and sustenance from His abundant grace. Teach us to abide in Him more fully, that we may bear fruit that brings glory to Your name. May our lives be a reflection of His love and power at work within us. In Jesus' name, we pray.
Amen.

DAY 59

Salt Of The Earth

"You are the salt of the earth. But if the salt loses its saltiness, how can it be made salty again? It is no longer good for anything, except to be thrown out and trampled underfoot." - Matthew 5:13 (NIV)

Salt is not only a seasoning; it is also a preservative and a symbol of purity. As Christians, we are called to be like salt, bringing flavor, preservation, and moral influence to the world around us.

Just as salt enhances the taste of food, we are called to bring flavor to the lives of those we encounter. Our words, actions, and attitudes should reflect the love, grace, and truth of Christ, making the world a more vibrant and fulfilling place. We are called to bring hope to the hopeless, joy to the downtrodden, and healing to the brokenhearted.

Moreover, salt acts as a preservative, preventing decay and corruption. In a world marked by sin and darkness, we are called to stand firm in our faith, preserving moral values and upholding God's standards of righteousness. We are called to be a light in the darkness, shining the truth of God's Word and leading others to Him.

Heavenly Father, thank You for calling us to be the salt of the earth. Help us to embrace this role with humility and courage, knowing that You have empowered us to make a difference in the world. Give us wisdom and discernment to know how best to bring flavor, preservation, and moral influence to those around us. May our lives reflect Your light and love, drawing others to You. In Jesus' name, we pray. Amen.

DAY 60

The Light of the World

"Again Jesus spoke to them, saying, 'I am the light of the world. Whoever follows me will not walk in darkness, but will have the light of life.'" - John 8:12 (ESV)

Light illuminates' darkness, brings clarity to confusion, and guides us on the path of righteousness. Jesus, as the Light of the World, offers hope, truth, and salvation to all who believe in Him.

In a world often shrouded in darkness—darkness of sin, despair, and uncertainty—Jesus shines brightly as the beacon of hope and life. He dispels the shadows of fear and doubt, leading us into the glorious light of His presence. Through His teachings, His sacrificial love, and His resurrection, Jesus offers us the light of eternal life, a life filled with purpose, joy, and peace.

As followers of Christ, we are called to reflect His light to the world around us. Just as a city on a hill cannot be hidden, neither should our faith be concealed.

Lord Jesus, thank You for being the Light of the World. In a world filled with darkness, You shine brightly as our source of hope and salvation. Help us to follow You faithfully, so that we may walk in Your light and share it with others. Guide us by Your Spirit as we seek to be beacons of Your love and truth in the world. May Your light shine through us, drawing others into Your marvelous light. In Your name, we pray. Amen.

DAY 61

The Bread of Life

"Then Jesus declared, 'I am the bread of life. Whoever comes to me will never go hungry, and whoever believes in me will never be thirsty.'" - John 6:35 (NIV)

This powerful metaphor speaks to the deepest hunger and thirst of our souls. Just as bread sustains our physical bodies, Jesus sustains our spiritual lives, providing nourishment, satisfaction, and sustenance that can be found nowhere else.

As the Bread of Life, Jesus satisfies the longings of our hearts in ways that earthly pleasures and possessions never can. He offers us true fulfillment, purpose, and meaning. When we partake of His presence through prayer, worship, and studying His Word, we find our souls nourished and our spirits refreshed.

Moreover, Jesus promises that whoever comes to Him will never hunger or thirst again. This is a profound invitation to experience the abundance of His grace and the richness of His love. No matter how empty or broken we may feel, Jesus offers us hope and wholeness in Himself.

Dear Lord, thank You for being the Bread of Life that satisfies the deepest hunger and thirst of our souls. Help us to come to You daily, seeking nourishment and sustenance for our spirits. May we find true fulfillment and joy in Your presence. Guide us as we seek to grow closer to You and to live lives that honor and glorify Your name. In Jesus' name, we pray. Amen.

DAY 62

The Living Water

"Jesus answered, 'Everyone who drinks this water will be thirsty again, but whoever drinks the water I give them will never thirst. Indeed, the water I give them will become in them a spring of water welling up to eternal life.'" - John 4:13-14 (NIV)

This Living Water quenches the deepest thirst of our souls, providing sustenance not just for this life, but for eternity. But what is this Living Water, and how can we partake of it?

The Living Water that Jesus offers is not physical, but spiritual. It is the Holy Spirit, the source of life and renewal. Just as water is essential for our physical survival, the Living Water is essential for our spiritual well-being. It satisfies our deepest longings and fills us with the abundant life that Jesus promised.

But how do we access this Living Water? Jesus invites us to come to Him, to drink deeply of His grace and love. When we surrender our lives to Him and open our hearts to His Spirit, we are filled with His life-giving presence. The Living Water flows within us, cleansing us from sin, refreshing our souls, and empowering us to live victoriously.

Lord Jesus, thank You for being the source of Living Water that satisfies our deepest thirst. Help us to come to You daily, to drink deeply of Your grace and love. Fill us with Your Spirit, that we may experience the abundant life You promised. May Your Living Water flow through us, bringing hope, healing, and transformation to all we encounter. In Your name, we pray. Amen.

DAY 63

The Lamb of God

"The next day John saw Jesus coming toward him and said, 'Look, the Lamb of God, who takes away the sin of the world!'" - John 1:29 (NIV)

This title encapsulates the sacrificial nature of Jesus' mission on earth—to serve as the ultimate atonement for humanity's sin. Just as the sacrificial lambs of the Old Testament were offered to cleanse people of their sins, Jesus, the perfect Lamb of God, offered Himself as the ultimate sacrifice to reconcile us to God.

Contemplate the depth of love and mercy demonstrated through Jesus' sacrificial act. Despite our waywardness and sinfulness, God sent His Son to bear the weight of our transgressions, to suffer and die in our place so that we might have forgiveness and eternal life. Jesus willingly embraced the cross, enduring unimaginable pain and separation from the Father, all out of love for us.

Reflect on the Lamb of God's purity and innocence. Jesus, sinless and blameless, willingly bore the sins of the world upon His shoulders. His sacrifice provides the pathway to redemption and restoration for all who believe in Him. Through His death and resurrection, we are offered forgiveness, healing, and new life.

Gracious Father, we thank You for sending Your Son, Jesus Christ, as the Lamb of God who takes away the sins of the world. Help us to fully grasp the depth of His sacrifice and to respond with hearts overflowing with gratitude and love. May our lives bear witness to the transformative power of the Lamb who was slain for our salvation. In Jesus' name, we pray. Amen.

DAY 64

The Lion of Judah

"Behold, the Lion of the tribe of Judah, the Root of David, has triumphed." - Revelation 5:5a (NIV)

This imagery of the Lion of Judah carries profound significance for Christians, symbolizing Jesus Christ's sovereignty, strength, and triumph over sin and death.

The tribe of Judah was one of the twelve tribes of Israel, and from it came the lineage of David, the great king of Israel. Jesus, as the descendant of David, fulfills the messianic prophecies of the Old Testament. He is the long-awaited Messiah, the promised Savior who would establish God's kingdom on earth.

As the Lion of Judah, Jesus embodies qualities of courage, leadership, and authority. He is not a timid or passive figure but a fierce and mighty warrior who fights on behalf of His people. His roar resounds through the ages, inspiring awe and reverence in all who hear it.

But the Lion of Judah is not just a symbol of power; He is also a symbol of protection and provision. Like a lion watches over its pride, Jesus watches over His followers with unwavering love and care.

Lord Jesus, thank You for being the Lion of Judah, our mighty Savior and King. May Your roar echo in our hearts, driving out fear and filling us with boldness and faith. Guide us as we follow You, our triumphant Lion, into victory. In Your name, we pray. Amen.

DAY 65

The Alpha and Omega

"I am the Alpha and the Omega, the First and the Last, the Beginning and the End." - Revelation 22:13 (NIV)

This profound declaration encapsulates the eternal nature and sovereignty of our Lord. He is not bound by time or limited by space; He is the timeless Creator of all things, and He holds the entirety of existence in His hands.

As the Alpha, Jesus is the origin and source of all life. He spoke the universe into being and fashioned humanity from the dust of the earth. Every breath we take, every beat of our hearts, is sustained by His power and grace. He is the foundation upon which all things are built, the Author of our faith and the Architect of our salvation.

Yet, Jesus is not just the Beginning; He is also the End. He holds the ultimate authority over the course of history and the destiny of every soul. He is the fulfillment of all prophecy, the culmination of God's redemptive plan for humanity. In Him, all things find their purpose and their meaning, and through Him, all things will be brought to their glorious conclusion.

Lord Jesus, You are the Alpha and the Omega, the Beginning and the End. Help us to trust in Your eternal wisdom and sovereignty, knowing that You hold all things in Your hands. Give us the faith to surrender our lives to Your will and to follow You with courage and obedience. May Your name be glorified in all that we do. In Your holy name, we pray. Amen.

DAY 66

The Great High Priest

"Therefore, since we have a great high priest who has ascended into heaven, Jesus the Son of God, let us hold firmly to the faith we profess." - Hebrews 4:14 (NIV)

In ancient Jewish tradition, the high priest served as the intermediary between God and His people, offering sacrifices for their sins and interceding on their behalf. But Jesus transcends the role of any earthly high priest. He is the perfect and eternal High Priest who not only offers the ultimate sacrifice for our sins but also continually intercedes for us before the Father's throne.

As our Great High Priest, Jesus understands our weaknesses and struggles because He experienced them Himself during His time on earth. He faced temptations, endured suffering, and ultimately conquered sin and death through His sacrificial death on the cross. Because of His victory, we can approach the throne of grace with confidence, knowing that we will find mercy and grace to help us in our time of need (Hebrews 4:16).

Jesus' role as our Great High Priest should fill us with gratitude and assurance. We are not alone in our journey of faith; we have a compassionate advocate who stands before God on our behalf.

Dear Jesus, thank You for being our Great High Priest. Thank You for your sacrifice on the cross and for continually interceding for us before the Father. Help us to hold firmly to the faith we profess, knowing that You are with us always. Strengthen us by Your Spirit to live lives that bring glory to Your name. In Your precious name, we pray. Amen.

DAY 67

The Prince of Peace

"For to us a child is born, to us a son is given, and the government will be on his shoulders. And he will be called Wonderful Counselor, Mighty God, Everlasting Father, Prince of Peace." - Isaiah 9:6 (NIV)

In a world marked by chaos, conflict, and unrest, Jesus came to bring a different kind of peace—a peace that surpasses understanding, transcends circumstances, and transforms lives.

The peace that Jesus offers is not merely the absence of conflict, but a deep, abiding sense of wholeness, harmony, and reconciliation with God. It is a peace that calms the storms of our souls, soothes our fears, and gives us hope in the midst of trials. Through His life, death, and resurrection, Jesus made it possible for us to experience true peace—peace with God and peace with one another.

As followers of Christ, we are called to be ambassadors of His peace in a world desperately in need of it. We are called to embody His love, grace, and forgiveness, extending a hand of reconciliation to those who are broken and hurting. Our words and actions should reflect the peace that Jesus offers, bringing healing and restoration wherever we go.

Dear Jesus, Prince of Peace, thank You for the peace that surpasses all understanding. May Your peace reign in our hearts and in the hearts of all who call upon Your name. In Your precious name, we pray. Amen.

DAY 68

The Mighty God

"For to us a child is born, to us a son is given, and the government will be on his shoulders. And he will be called Wonderful Counselor, Mighty God, Everlasting Father, Prince of Peace." - Isaiah 9:6 (NIV)

He is not just a God who is distant or indifferent to our struggles; He is the Mighty God who reigns supreme over all creation. This title speaks of His power, His strength, and His ability to overcome any challenge we may face. He is the One who spoke the universe into existence, who calms the storms with a word, and who conquered sin and death through the sacrifice of His Son, Jesus Christ.

The Mighty God is not just a concept to be pondered; He is a reality to be experienced. In times of weakness, He gives us strength. In times of fear, He offers us courage. In times of despair, He provides us with hope. There is no problem too big, no mountain too high, and no situation too difficult for our Mighty God to handle. He is our refuge and our fortress, our ever-present help in times of trouble.

Heavenly Father, thank You for revealing Yourself to us as the Mighty God. Help us to trust in Your strength and power, especially in the midst of our weaknesses and struggles. Give us the courage to surrender every aspect of our lives to You, knowing that You are able to do immeasurably more than we could ever ask or imagine. May Your mightiness be glorified in our lives today and always. In Jesus' name, we pray. Amen.

DAY 69

The Everlasting Father

"For to us a child is born, to us a son is given, and the government will be on his shoulders. And he will be called Wonderful Counselor, Mighty God, Everlasting Father, Prince of Peace." - Isaiah 9:6 (NIV)

As our Everlasting Father, Jesus embodies the qualities of a perfect parent: unconditional love, boundless compassion, and unwavering protection. He cares for us with a depth of love that surpasses human understanding, nurturing us with grace and mercy even in our weakest moments. His fatherly love is constant and unchanging, extending throughout eternity.

No matter what trials or challenges we face, we can find comfort and security in the arms of our Everlasting Father. He is our refuge in times of trouble, our source of strength when we are weary, and our guiding light in the darkness. His love never fails, and His promises are forever true.

Dear Jesus, thank You for being our Everlasting Father, a source of unconditional love and unwavering protection. Help us to trust in Your faithfulness and to find refuge in Your arms in times of trouble. May Your love fill us with peace and assurance, knowing that You are always with us, now and forever. In Your precious name, we pray. Amen.

DAY 70

Jesus as Friend

"Greater love has no one than this: to lay down one's life for one's friends." - John 15:13 (NIV)

This profound statement offers us a glimpse into the intimate relationship He desires to have with each of us. Jesus, the Son of God, the Savior of the world, desires to be not only our Lord and Master but also our Friend.

As our Friend, Jesus walks alongside us through every season of life. He rejoices with us in moments of joy and celebration, and He comforts us in times of sorrow and despair. He understands our struggles, our doubts, and our fears, and He offers us His hand in friendship, inviting us to share our burdens with Him.

Jesus as our Friend is not a distant or aloof figure, but a compassionate and caring companion. He knows us intimately, yet He loves us unconditionally. He is always there to listen to our prayers, to offer guidance and wisdom, and to extend His grace and forgiveness.

Lord Jesus, thank You for calling us Your friends and for the deep love and friendship You offer us. Help us to truly grasp the depth of Your love and to cultivate a closer relationship with You each day. May we lean on You as our Friend, finding comfort, strength, and joy in Your presence. In Your precious name, we pray. Amen.

DAY 71

Jesus as Savior

*"For the Son of Man came to seek and to save the lost." - Luke
19:10 (NIV)*

He came not for the righteous, but for the lost, the broken, and the
hurting. Jesus' sacrificial love knows no bounds, reaching out to
each of us with open arms, offering forgiveness, redemption, and
eternal life.

As our Savior, Jesus offers us the greatest gift imaginable:
salvation. Through His death on the cross and resurrection from
the grave, He conquered sin and death, paving the way for us to be
reconciled to God. No matter how far we may have wandered or
how deep we may have fallen, Jesus is always ready to welcome us
back into the loving embrace of our Heavenly Father.

The truth of Jesus as Savior should fill us with awe and gratitude.
It's a reminder that we are not alone in our struggles, but that we
have a Savior who understands our pain and walks beside us every
step of the way. His love is unchanging and unconditional, offering
hope and healing to all who call upon His name.

*Heavenly Father, thank You for sending Your Son, Jesus, to be our
Savior. Thank You for His sacrificial love and the gift of salvation
that He offers to each of us. Give us the courage to live as children
of the light, sharing His love and truth with a world in need. In
Jesus' name, we pray. Amen.*

DAY 72

Jesus as Healer

"But he was pierced for our transgressions, he was crushed for our iniquities; the punishment that brought us peace was on him, and by his wounds we are healed." - Isaiah 53:5 (NIV)

Through His sacrificial death on the cross, Jesus not only bore the weight of our sins but also carried our pains and infirmities. He is the ultimate source of healing, both for our physical bodies and our wounded souls.

Jesus' ministry on earth was marked by countless miracles of healing. He restored sight to the blind, made the lame walk, and even raised the dead to life. But His healing went beyond the physical realm; it reached into the depths of human suffering and brought forth wholeness and restoration.

As believers, we have the privilege of experiencing Jesus as our Healer in our lives today. Whether we are grappling with sickness, emotional wounds, or spiritual struggles, Jesus offers us His healing touch. He invites us to come to Him with our burdens and lay them at His feet, trusting in His power to bring healing and restoration.

Heavenly Father, we thank You for the gift of Jesus, our Healer. We praise You for His sacrificial love and His power to bring healing and restoration into our lives. Today, we bring before You our needs and struggles, asking for Your healing touch to be upon us. May Your grace flow abundantly, bringing wholeness to every area of our lives. In Jesus' name, we pray. Amen.

DAY 73

Jesus as Redeemer

"In him we have redemption through his blood, the forgiveness of sins, in accordance with the riches of God's grace." - Ephesians 1:7 (NIV)

His blood, shed out of love, became the ultimate payment for our freedom from sin and reconciliation with God.

The concept of redemption is deeply personal and profoundly transformative. It speaks to the reality of our brokenness and the boundless grace of God. In Jesus, we find forgiveness for our past mistakes, healing for our wounded hearts, and restoration for our broken lives. He doesn't just offer a second chance; He offers a new beginning, a fresh start made possible by His redeeming love.

As we embrace Jesus as our Redeemer, we are invited into a journey of healing and restoration. It's a journey marked by grace, mercy, and the transformative power of God's love. No matter how far we've wandered or how deep our sins may seem, Jesus stands ready to redeem and restore us, to wash us clean and make us whole.

Heavenly Father, thank You for the gift of redemption through Your Son, Jesus Christ. Thank You for His sacrificial love that paid the price for our sins and secured our freedom. Help us to fully embrace His redemption in our lives, to walk in the freedom and grace that He offers. May we live each day as grateful recipients of Your redeeming love. In Jesus' name, we pray. Amen.

DAY 74

Jesus as Lord

"Therefore God exalted him to the highest place and gave him the name that is above every name, that at the name of Jesus every knee should bow, in heaven and on earth and under the earth, and every tongue acknowledge that Jesus Christ is Lord, to the glory of God the Father." - Philippians 2:9-11 (NIV)

As believers, we affirm that Jesus is not just a great teacher or moral example, but He is the Lord of all creation. His lordship encompasses every aspect of our lives, and acknowledging Him as Lord is central to our faith.

To declare Jesus as Lord is to recognize His authority, supremacy, and sovereignty over all things. It is to submit our will, our desires, and our plans to His divine rule. When we acknowledge Jesus as Lord, we willingly surrender control of our lives to Him, trusting in His wisdom and guidance above our own.

Jesus as Lord is not just a title; it's a relationship. It's about walking in intimacy and obedience with the One who loved us enough to lay down His life for us. It's about allowing His lordship to transform us from the inside out, shaping our thoughts, words, and actions to reflect His love and grace.

Lord Jesus, we declare that You are Lord of all. Help us to surrender our lives completely to Your lordship, trusting in Your wisdom and guidance. May Your will be done in our lives, and may Your name be glorified in all that we say and do. Thank You for the privilege of knowing You as Lord and Savior. In Your mighty name, we pray. Amen.

DAY 75

God's Faithfulness

"The steadfast love of the Lord never ceases; his mercies never come to an end; they are new every morning; great is your faithfulness." - Lamentations 3:22-23 (ESV)

Despite the trials and tribulations we may face, His love remains steadfast and His mercies never run dry. The faithfulness of God is not dependent on our circumstances or actions; it is a fundamental aspect of His character.

God's faithfulness is a beacon of hope in the midst of life's storms. It is a reassuring promise that we can cling to when we feel overwhelmed or discouraged. His faithfulness extends beyond our past, present, and future, spanning generations and reaching into eternity.

As we reflect on God's faithfulness, let us also consider our response. How do we live in light of this incredible truth? One action plan is to cultivate a spirit of gratitude and trust. Take time each day to thank God for His faithfulness and to meditate on His promises. Allow His faithfulness to inspire confidence in His ability to guide, provide, and sustain us through every season of life.

Heavenly Father, we thank You for Your unwavering faithfulness and steadfast love. Help us to trust in Your promises and to lean on Your strength in times of uncertainty. Give us hearts that are grateful for Your faithfulness and minds that are focused on Your goodness. May Your faithfulness inspire us to live lives that honor and glorify You. In Jesus' name, we pray. Amen.

DAY 76

The Covenant of Grace

"For it is by grace you have been saved, through faith—and this is not from yourselves, it is the gift of God—not by works, so that no one can boast." - Ephesians 2:8-9 (NIV)

This covenant, established by God's unmerited favor and love, is the foundation of our salvation. It is a covenant not based on our own efforts or merits, but on the boundless grace of our Heavenly Father.

The Covenant of Grace reveals God's relentless pursuit of relationship with His people. Despite our sinfulness and shortcomings, God extends His grace freely to all who believe in Him. Through the sacrifice of His Son, Jesus Christ, God offers forgiveness, redemption, and eternal life to all who accept His gift with faith.

This covenant is a testament to God's faithfulness and love. It is a promise that He will never give up on us, no matter how many times we stumble or fall. His grace is inexhaustible, His mercy endless. In the Covenant of Grace, we find hope, restoration, and unending joy.

Heavenly Father, thank You for the gift of Your grace, poured out abundantly through the sacrifice of Your Son, Jesus Christ. Help us to fully grasp the depth of Your love and the richness of Your mercy. May Your grace transform our hearts and empower us to live lives that reflect Your love to the world. In Jesus' name, we pray. Amen.

DAY 77

God's Unfailing Love

"The Lord your God is with you, the Mighty Warrior who saves. He will take great delight in you; in his love he will no longer rebuke you, but will rejoice over you with singing." - Zephaniah 3:17 (NIV)

It portrays a God who not only saves and protects but also delights in us with boundless love and joy. God's love is not dependent on our performance or worthiness; it is unconditional, unwavering, and eternal.

God's love is unfailing because it is rooted in His very nature. He is the source of all love, and His love knows no bounds. It reaches into the deepest depths of our brokenness and lifts us up with grace and compassion. Even in our darkest moments, when we feel unworthy or unlovable, God's love shines brightly, offering hope and healing.

No matter what we may face in life—pain, disappointment, or failure—we can take refuge in the unchanging love of God. His love never gives up on us, never grows weary, and never fades away. It is a love that pursues us relentlessly, drawing us close to Him and filling us with peace and joy.

Heavenly Father, thank You for Your unfailing love that never gives up on us. Help us to fully grasp the depth and breadth of Your love for us. Empower us to love others as You have loved us, with grace, compassion, and forgiveness. May Your love shine through us, bringing hope and healing to a world in need. In Jesus' name, we pray. Amen.

DAY 78

Living by Faith

"Now faith is confidence in what we hope for and assurance about what we do not see." - Hebrews 11:1 (NIV)

Faith is not just believing in something we can see or understand; it's about trusting in God's promises and stepping out with confidence even when the path ahead is uncertain. Living by faith means anchoring our lives in the unshakable truth of God's Word and allowing His promises to guide our every step.

When we choose to live by faith, we embrace a journey of surrender and reliance on God's wisdom and provision. It's a radical shift from relying on our own strength and understanding to entrusting our lives entirely to God's care. Living by faith requires us to let go of fear and doubt, and to embrace a posture of trust and obedience.

Faith isn't passive; it's an active response to God's calling in our lives. It's about courageously stepping out of our comfort zones and into the unknown, knowing that God is faithful to lead us and sustain us every step of the way. As we walk by faith, we experience the miraculous unfolding of God's plans and purposes in our lives, far beyond what we could ever imagine or accomplish on our own.

Heavenly Father, thank You for the gift of faith that enables us to trust in Your promises and step out into the unknown with confidence. Help us to live each day with faith-filled hearts, knowing that You are always with us, guiding us and providing for us. Give us the courage to step out in faith, even when the path ahead seems uncertain. May our lives be a testimony to Your faithfulness and grace. In Jesus' name, we pray. Amen.

DAY 79

Walking in the Spirit

"But I say, walk by the Spirit, and you will not gratify the desires of the flesh." - Galatians 5:16 (ESV)

This call challenges us to live in constant communion with the Holy Spirit, allowing His presence to guide our thoughts, words, and actions. To walk in the Spirit is to surrender our will to His, trusting His leading in every aspect of our lives.

Walking in the Spirit means aligning ourselves with God's purposes and priorities rather than gratifying the selfish desires of our flesh. It involves seeking His wisdom and direction in every decision, relying on His strength to overcome temptation, and allowing His love to flow through us to others. When we walk in the Spirit, we experience the fruit of His presence: love, joy, peace, patience, kindness, goodness, faithfulness, gentleness, and self-control (Galatians 5:22-23).

However, walking in the Spirit is not always easy. It requires intentional effort and a willingness to surrender control to God. It means letting go of our own agendas and trusting in His perfect plan for our lives. But the rewards far outweigh the challenges. As we walk in the Spirit, we experience a deeper intimacy with God, a greater sense of purpose, and a peace that surpasses all understanding.

Heavenly Father, thank You for the precious gift of Your Holy Spirit. Fill us with Your love, joy, and peace as we abide in You. May our lives be a testimony to Your power and grace as we walk in the Spirit each day. In Jesus' name, we pray. Amen.

DAY 80

Bearing Fruit

"I am the vine; you are the branches. If you remain in me and I in you, you will bear much fruit; apart from me you can do nothing."
- John 15:5 (NIV)

He is the vine, the source of our spiritual nourishment and life, and we are the branches, connected to Him. As we remain in Him, rooted and grounded in His love and truth, we bear fruit—fruit that glorifies God and blesses others.

But what does it mean to bear fruit? Spiritual fruit is the outward manifestation of our relationship with Christ. It encompasses qualities such as love, joy, peace, patience, kindness, goodness, faithfulness, gentleness, and self-control (Galatians 5:22-23). When we abide in Christ, His Spirit works within us, transforming our character and producing these fruits in our lives.

Bearing fruit is not just about personal growth; it's also about impacting the world around us. As we reflect the love and character of Christ, we become His ambassadors, sharing His light and truth with others. Our actions, words, and attitudes become a testimony of God's grace and power at work in our lives.

Heavenly Father, thank You for the privilege of being connected to Christ, the true vine. Help us to abide in Him daily, drawing strength and nourishment from His presence. May our lives bear fruit that brings glory to Your name and blesses those around us. Empower us by Your Spirit to walk in love, joy, peace, and all the fruits of the Spirit, reflecting the character of Christ to the world. In Jesus' name, we pray. Amen.

DAY 81

Abiding in Christ

"Remain in me, as I also remain in you. No branch can bear fruit by itself; it must remain in the vine. Neither can you bear fruit unless you remain in me." - John 15:4 (NIV)

To abide in Christ is to dwell in His presence, to walk closely with Him in every moment of our lives. It's not merely about occasional encounters or fleeting moments of connection, but a continuous, steadfast commitment to remain rooted and grounded in Him.

Abiding in Christ is the key to a fruitful and fulfilling Christian life. When we abide in Him, we draw strength, nourishment, and guidance from the true Vine. Like branches connected to a vine, we are sustained by His life-giving power, enabling us to bear fruit that glorifies God and blesses others. Without this connection, we wither and become ineffective in our faith.

Abiding in Christ requires intentional effort and a heart surrendered to His will. It means prioritizing time spent in prayer, meditation on His Word, and fellowship with other believers. It means allowing His Spirit to dwell richly within us, transforming our thoughts, desires, and actions to reflect His likeness.

Lord Jesus, thank You for the privilege of abiding in You and experiencing Your presence in our lives. Help us to remain steadfast and faithful, drawing strength and nourishment from You each day. May our lives bear fruit that brings glory to Your name and blesses those around us. In Your precious name, we pray. Amen.

DAY 82

The Narrow Path

"Enter through the narrow gate. For wide is the gate and broad is the road that leads to destruction, and many enter through it. But small is the gate and narrow the road that leads to life, and only a few find it." - Matthew 7:13-14 (NIV)

This imagery illustrates the journey of faith and the choices we make along the way. The wide gate represents the allure of worldly pleasures and the easy path that leads to destruction, while the narrow gate symbolizes the challenging yet rewarding journey of following Christ.

The narrow path is not always popular or comfortable. It requires sacrifice, self-discipline, and a willingness to go against the flow of society. It means choosing obedience to God's Word over the fleeting pleasures of sin, and prioritizing His kingdom above earthly treasures. It's a path marked by trials and tribulations, but also by the assurance of eternal life with our Savior.

While the wide gate may seem inviting with its promises of immediate gratification, it ultimately leads to emptiness and destruction. In contrast, the narrow path leads to abundant life and eternal joy in the presence of God.

Heavenly Father, thank You for the gift of salvation and the opportunity to walk the narrow path with You. Give us the strength and courage to resist the temptations of the wide gate and to follow You wholeheartedly. May we walk in Your light and experience the abundant life You have promised. In Jesus' name, we pray. Amen.

DAY 83

The Broad Path

"Enter through the narrow gate. For wide is the gate and broad is the road that leads to destruction, and many enter through it." - Matthew 7:13 (NIV)

The broad path represents the allure of worldly pleasures, the pursuit of selfish desires, and the temptation to follow the crowd rather than God's calling.

Choosing the broad path may seem easier at first, promising instant gratification and temporary happiness. But in reality, it leads to emptiness, despair, and spiritual death. It's a path marked by self-indulgence, greed, and moral compromise, ultimately separating us from God's abundant life and eternal blessings.

On the other hand, Jesus invites us to walk the narrow path, a road less traveled but one that leads to true fulfillment and everlasting joy. This path requires sacrifice, discipline, and obedience to God's word. It's a journey of faith, characterized by humility, love, and a wholehearted commitment to following Jesus Christ.

Heavenly Father, thank You for Your guidance and wisdom. Help us to discern between the broad path that leads to destruction and the narrow path that leads to life. Give us the courage to choose the path of faith, even when it's difficult or unpopular. May our hearts be aligned with Your will, and may we walk in obedience to Your word, following Jesus Christ, our Savior and Lord. In His name, we pray. Amen.

DAY 84

Being Salt and Light

"You are the salt of the earth. But if the salt loses its saltiness, how can it be made salty again? It is no longer good for anything, except to be thrown out and trampled underfoot. You are the light of the world. A town built on a hill cannot be hidden. Neither do people light a lamp and put it under a bowl. Instead, they put it on its stand, and it gives light to everyone in the house." - Matthew 5:13-15 (NIV)

Salt serves as a preservative, adding flavor and preventing decay. Similarly, as salt of the earth, we are called to bring flavor and life to the world around us. We are to live in such a way that our presence makes a positive impact, preserving moral values, spreading kindness, and bringing out the beauty in others.

Likewise, light dispels darkness and illuminates the path ahead. As lights of the world, we are called to shine the light of Christ in the midst of darkness.

As we embrace our identity as salt and light, we have the opportunity to make a difference in our communities and beyond. We can choose to live authentically, love sacrificially, and serve selflessly, knowing that our actions have the power to influence and inspire others for the glory of God.

Heavenly Father, thank You for calling us to be salt and light in the world. Give us the courage and wisdom to shine brightly in the midst of darkness, and may our lives be a testimony to Your grace and truth. In Jesus' name, we pray. Amen.

DAY 85

The New Covenant

"For this is the covenant that I will make with the house of Israel after those days, declares the Lord: I will put my law within them, and I will write it on their hearts. And I will be their God, and they shall be my people." - Jeremiah 31:33 (ESV)

Unlike the old covenant, which was based on obedience to the law, the New Covenant is founded on grace, mercy, and a personal relationship with God. It is a covenant of the heart, where God's law is not merely written on tablets of stone but inscribed within us, transforming our desires and guiding our actions.

Through the sacrifice of Jesus Christ, we have been brought into this New Covenant. His blood shed on the cross is the seal of this eternal agreement between God and humanity. In Christ, we find forgiveness for our sins and reconciliation with our Heavenly Father. We are no longer bound by the demands of the law but set free to live in the fullness of God's grace.

The New Covenant is a testament to God's unfailing love and faithfulness. It is a promise of redemption, restoration, and eternal life for all who believe in Jesus Christ. As recipients of this covenant, we are called to embrace its truth and live in accordance with its principles.

Help us to fully grasp the depth of Your love and the freedom we have in Him. Empower us to live as faithful recipients of this covenant, bearing witness to Your grace and sharing Your love with the world. May Your Spirit guide us in all we do, to the glory of Your name. In Jesus' precious name, we pray. Amen.

DAY 86

The Tribulation

"For then there will be great distress, unequaled from the beginning of the world until now—and never to be equaled again."
- Matthew 24:21 (NIV)

Matthew 24:21 speaks of a time of great distress, unparalleled in human history. This period, often associated with the end times, is characterized by intense persecution, turmoil, and suffering.

While the idea of the tribulation may evoke fear or anxiety, it's important to remember that as followers of Christ, we are not called to live in fear but in faith. The tribulation serves as a reminder of the reality of spiritual warfare and the ultimate victory we have in Jesus Christ. It is a time when the forces of darkness will wage war against the people of God, but it is also a time when God's power and faithfulness will be revealed in miraculous ways.

As we contemplate the tribulation, let us be reminded of the importance of spiritual preparedness. Just as a soldier prepares for battle, we must equip ourselves with the armor of God: truth, righteousness, faith, salvation, and the Word of God. We must stand firm in our faith, knowing that God is with us always, even in the midst of trials and tribulations.

Heavenly Father, we acknowledge that we live in a world filled with tribulation and trials. Give us the courage and faith to stand firm in the face of adversity, knowing that You are with us always. May Your peace that surpasses all understanding guard our hearts and minds in Christ Jesus. In His name, we pray. Amen.

DAY 87

The Day of the Lord

"The day of the Lord will come like a thief. The heavens will disappear with a roar; the elements will be destroyed by fire, and the earth and everything done in it will be laid bare." - 2 Peter 3:10 (NIV)

God will intervene decisively in human history to bring about His final judgment and establish His eternal kingdom. This day is not to be taken lightly; it will be a time of reckoning and divine justice.

As believers, we are called to live in anticipation of the Day of the Lord. It serves as a reminder of the reality of eternity and the urgency of our faith. While we do not know the exact timing of this event, we are exhorted to be vigilant and prepared, living holy and righteous lives in light of its coming.

The Day of the Lord is not just a distant event; it has implications for how we live today. It challenges us to examine our priorities, aligning them with God's kingdom purposes. It compels us to share the hope of salvation with others, knowing that time is short and eternity is at stake.

Heavenly Father, we acknowledge Your sovereignty and the certainty of the Day of the Lord. Help us to live with hearts prepared and minds alert, eagerly awaiting the return of Your Son, Jesus Christ. Give us the courage to boldly proclaim the gospel and the wisdom to live in accordance with Your will each day. May our lives be a testimony to Your grace and glory as we await the blessed hope of Your coming kingdom. In Jesus' name, we pray. Amen.

DAY 88

The Judgment Seat of Christ

"For we must all appear before the judgment seat of Christ, so that each of us may receive what is due us for the things done while in the body, whether good or bad." - 2 Corinthians 5:10 (NIV)

In 2 Corinthians 5:10, Paul reminds us that all believers will one day stand before the judgment seat of Christ to give an account of our lives.

The judgment seat of Christ is not a place of condemnation for believers but a time of evaluation and reward. It is where our works, motives, and actions will be examined in the light of eternity. While our salvation is secure in Christ, the judgment seat is an opportunity for us to receive rewards based on how we have lived our lives for Him.

As we reflect on the reality of the judgment seat of Christ, let it serve as a motivation for living a life that honors God. Let us strive to steward our time, talents, and resources wisely, investing them in things of eternal value. May our hearts be filled with a sense of urgency to share the love of Christ with others and to make a difference in the world around us.

Heavenly Father, thank You for the assurance of salvation we have in Christ Jesus. Help us to live each day with a sense of eternity in mind, knowing that one day we will stand before Your judgment seat. May our lives bring glory to Your name and may we hear the words, "Well done, good and faithful servant," when we stand before You. In Jesus' name, we pray. Amen.

DAY 89

The Great White Throne Judgment

"Then I saw a great white throne and him who was seated on it. The earth and the heavens fled from his presence, and there was no place for them. And I saw the dead, great and small, standing before the throne, and books were opened. Another book was opened, which is the book of life. The dead were judged according to what they had done as recorded in the books." - Revelation 20:11-12 (NIV)

This judgment is not based on outward appearances or human standards of righteousness but on the truth and justice of God's Word.

As believers, we can find comfort in knowing that our sins have been forgiven through the sacrifice of Jesus Christ, and our names are written in the Lamb's Book of Life. However, the Great White Throne Judgment serves as a reminder of the reality of judgment for those who have rejected God's offer of salvation.

In that moment, every knee will bow, and every tongue will confess that Jesus Christ is Lord. There will be no hiding from His presence, no excuses or justifications. It will be a time of reckoning, where the secrets of every heart are laid bare before the righteous Judge.

Heavenly Father, we acknowledge Your sovereignty and righteousness as the Judge of all the earth. Help us to live our lives in a manner pleasing to You, knowing that one day we will stand before Your Great White Throne. Thank You for the assurance of salvation through Jesus Christ. In His name, we pray. Amen.

DAY 90

Overcoming by the Blood of the Lamb

"They triumphed over him by the blood of the Lamb and by the word of their testimony; they did not love their lives so much as to shrink from death." - Revelation 12:11 (NIV)

The blood of the Lamb symbolizes the sacrificial death of Jesus on the cross, which has the power to conquer sin, defeat Satan, and bring eternal life to all who put their faith in Him.

As Christians, we are called to walk in the victory secured for us by the blood of the Lamb. This victory is not just a future hope but a present reality that empowers us to overcome the challenges and trials of this world. Through the blood of Jesus, we are set free from the bondage of sin, liberated from guilt and shame, and given the strength to live victoriously.

Our testimony, our story of how Jesus has transformed our lives, is a powerful weapon in the battle against the forces of darkness. By sharing our experiences of redemption, healing, and restoration, we not only encourage others but also declare the triumph of the blood of the Lamb over every obstacle and enemy.

Lord Jesus, thank You for the victory we have through Your precious blood shed for us on the cross. Help us to walk in the reality of this victory every day, trusting in Your strength to overcome every obstacle and challenge we face. Give us boldness to share our testimony of Your saving grace with others, that they too may experience the power of Your love and redemption. In Your name, we pray. Amen.

DAY 91

The Bride of Christ

"For the husband is the head of the wife as Christ is the head of the church, his body, of which he is the Savior." - Ephesians 5:23 (NIV)

This metaphor captures the depth of intimacy and love that exists between Christ and His followers. As the Bride of Christ, we are more than just His followers; we are His beloved, cherished and adored.

The relationship between Christ and His Church mirrors the covenant of marriage, where love, commitment, and sacrifice are central. Christ's love for His bride is unconditional, sacrificial, and unwavering. He gave Himself up for her, laying down His life to redeem and sanctify her. In return, the Church is called to respond with wholehearted devotion, loyalty, and submission to her Bridegroom.

As the Bride of Christ, we are called to cultivate a deep, intimate relationship with Him. This relationship is built on prayer, worship, and the study of God's Word. It is sustained through fellowship with other believers and obedience to His commands.

Dear Jesus, thank You for loving us with an everlasting love and for calling us Your beloved Bride. May we respond to Your love with wholehearted devotion and obedience, eagerly anticipating Your glorious return. May our lives reflect the beauty of Your love for the world to see. In Your precious name, we pray. Amen.

DAY 92

The Household of Faith

"So then, as we have opportunity, let us do good to everyone, and especially to those who are of the household of faith." - Galatians 6:10 (ESV)

This concept of the household of faith encompasses more than just a physical gathering of believers; it represents a spiritual family united by our common faith in Jesus Christ.

As members of the household of faith, we are bound together by a bond that transcends blood ties or cultural differences. We are brothers and sisters in Christ, sharing in the joys and burdens of life together. This community of believers provides support, encouragement, and accountability as we journey through life's ups and downs.

The household of faith is a place of belonging, acceptance, and love. It's a refuge where we can find comfort in times of distress, strength in times of weakness, and celebration in times of victory. It's a place where our faith is nurtured, our gifts are valued, and our lives are transformed by the power of God's Spirit working within us.

Heavenly Father, thank You for the gift of the household of faith, where we find belonging and support as we journey together in faith. Help us to cherish and nurture the relationships within our spiritual family, fostering unity, love, and mutual care. May our lives be a reflection of Your grace and goodness, drawing others into the warmth of Your embrace. In Jesus' name, we pray. Amen.

DAY 93

The Ministry of Angels

"Are not all angels ministering spirits sent to serve those who will inherit salvation?" - Hebrews 1:14 (NIV)

Angels are not merely mystical beings of folklore; they are real, spiritual beings created by God to serve and protect His children. Their ministry is a testament to God's care and provision for His people, offering comfort, guidance, and protection in times of need.

Throughout the Bible, we see angels playing pivotal roles in God's divine plan. From announcing the birth of Jesus to comforting Jesus in the Garden of Gethsemane, their presence is a tangible expression of God's love and watchful care. Angels are God's messengers, delivering His word and carrying out His will with unwavering obedience and devotion.

As believers, we can take comfort in knowing that we are never alone. God has assigned His angels to watch over us and minister to our needs, both seen and unseen. They stand ready to offer assistance and protection, fighting battles on our behalf in the spiritual realm.

Heavenly Father, we thank You for the ministry of angels in our lives. Thank You for assigning them to watch over us and to serve us according to Your will. Help us to be aware of their presence and to trust in Your divine protection. May we take comfort in knowing that Your angels are fighting for us and that we are never alone. In Jesus' name, we pray. Amen.

DAY 94

The Power of the Gospel

"For I am not ashamed of the gospel, because it is the power of God that brings salvation to everyone who believes: first to the Jew, then to the Gentile." - Romans 1:16 (NIV)

The gospel holds the transformative power to change lives, heal brokenness, and bring salvation to all who embrace it.

At its core, the gospel is the good news of Jesus Christ—His life, death, and resurrection. It is the story of God's relentless love for humanity, demonstrated through the sacrificial death of His Son on the cross. Through His resurrection, Jesus conquered sin and death, offering forgiveness and eternal life to all who repent and believe in Him.

The power of the gospel is evident throughout history and across cultures. It has the capacity to break down barriers, reconcile relationships, and bring hope to the hopeless. From the moment we first encounter the gospel message, our lives are forever changed as we experience the saving grace of Jesus Christ.

Heavenly Father, thank You for the power of the gospel that brings salvation to all who believe. Give us boldness and compassion as we share this life-changing message with others. Open hearts and minds to receive Your love and grace, and may Your kingdom advance through the proclamation of the gospel. In Jesus' name, we pray. Amen.

DAY 95

The Power of the Resurrection

"He is not here; he has risen, just as he said. Come and see the place where he lay." - Matthew 28:6 (NIV)

In Matthew 28:6, we hear the angel's proclamation to the women at the empty tomb: "He is not here; he has risen, just as he said." These words echo through history, resonating with hope and triumph for believers around the world.

The resurrection of Jesus is not merely a historical event; it is a living reality that continues to shape our lives today. It is a reminder that death has been conquered, and new life is available to all who believe. Through His resurrection, Jesus offers forgiveness, redemption, and eternal life to all who place their faith in Him.

The power of the resurrection transforms our lives in profound ways. It gives us hope in the midst of despair, strength in times of weakness, and purpose in our journey on earth. It reminds us that we serve a living Savior who is actively at work in our lives, bringing beauty out of ashes and victory out of defeat.

Heavenly Father, we thank You for the power of the resurrection and the hope it brings to our lives. Help us to fully grasp the significance of Jesus' victory over sin and death. May His resurrection power transform us from the inside out, giving us strength to overcome every obstacle and joy to face each day with confidence. In Jesus' name, we pray. Amen.

DAY 96

The Glory of God

"For from him and through him and for him are all things. To him be the glory forever! Amen." - Romans 11:36 (NIV)

he very essence of existence is intertwined with His majesty. The glory of God is not merely a concept to be grasped; it is a reality to be experienced and celebrated.

Consider the sunrise, painting the sky with hues of pink and gold, or the vast expanse of the ocean, echoing His power and depth. These are glimpses of His glory manifested in the world around us. But His glory extends far beyond the natural world. It is revealed in His grace, His mercy, His justice, and His love. It shines brightly in the face of Jesus Christ, who embodies the fullness of God's glory.

To fully appreciate the glory of God is to recognize our place in His story. We are not just bystanders but participants in His divine plan. Our lives are meant to reflect His glory, like mirrors catching the light of the sun. Every thought, every word, and every action should point back to Him, drawing attention not to ourselves but to the One who deserves all honor and praise.

Heavenly Father, we stand in awe of Your glory, which fills the heavens and the earth. Help us to recognize Your presence in every aspect of our lives and to live in a way that brings honor and glory to Your name. May we reflect Your light to a world in need of Your love and grace. In Jesus' name, we pray. Amen.

DAY 97

Created in God's Image

"So God created mankind in his own image, in the image of God he created them; male and female he created them." - Genesis 1:27 (NIV)

This truth forms the foundation of our understanding of ourselves and our relationship with our Creator. To be created in God's image is to bear His likeness, reflecting His character, attributes, and nature.

What does it mean to be created in God's image? It means that we are endowed with inherent value and dignity. Our worth is not derived from our accomplishments, appearance, or possessions, but from the fact that we are fearfully and wonderfully made by the hand of God Himself. It means that we possess the capacity for love, compassion, creativity, and reason, mirroring the qualities of our Heavenly Father.

Understanding our identity as image-bearers of God should profoundly impact the way we view ourselves and others. It calls us to treat ourselves and those around us with reverence and respect, recognizing the divine imprint upon each person we encounter. It also reminds us of our responsibility to steward our lives and the world around us in a manner that honors God.

Heavenly Father, thank You for creating us in Your image and for bestowing upon us inherent value and dignity Guide us in stewarding our lives and the world around us in a manner that brings glory to Your name. In Jesus' name, we pray. Amen.

DAY 98

The Fall of Man

"Therefore, just as sin entered the world through one man, and death through sin, and in this way death came to all people, because all sinned." - Romans 5:12 (NIV)

The fall of man shattered this idyllic union. Romans 5:12 reminds us that sin entered the world through one man, Adam, and with it came the devastating consequences of death and separation from God.

The fall of man is a pivotal moment in human history, marking the beginning of our struggle with sin and brokenness. Adam and Eve's disobedience in the Garden of Eden unleashed a chain reaction of sin and suffering that continues to impact us today. Every act of injustice, every broken relationship, and every heartache can be traced back to that fateful choice to rebel against God's perfect will.

Yet, even in the midst of our fallenness, there is hope. For God did not abandon us to our own devices. He sent His Son, Jesus Christ, to redeem us from the consequences of sin and to restore what was lost in the fall. Through His death and resurrection, Jesus offers us forgiveness, reconciliation, and the promise of eternal life.

Heavenly Father, we confess that we have fallen short of Your glory and have been marred by sin. Thank You for sending Your Son, Jesus Christ, to redeem us and to restore our relationship with You. Help us to live in the freedom and victory that He has won for us, and to be agents of Your grace and reconciliation in a broken world. In Jesus' name, we pray. Amen.

DAY 99

The Great Awakenings

"And do not be conformed to this world, but be transformed by the renewing of your mind, so that you may prove what the will of God is, that which is good and acceptable and perfect." - Romans 12:2 (NASB)

Just as Romans 12:2 urges us not to conform to the patterns of this world but to be transformed by the renewing of our minds, the Great Awakenings serve as powerful reminders of God's ability to bring about radical transformation in individuals and societies.

The Great Awakenings are characterized by the outpouring of the Holy Spirit, igniting a passion for God's Word, prayer, and worship. During these times, people are awakened to the reality of their spiritual condition and their need for salvation. Lives are transformed, families are restored, and communities are impacted as the light of Christ shines brightly in the midst of darkness.

While the Great Awakenings of the past hold a special place in history, we are called to seek a fresh awakening in our own lives and in our generation. We are not merely spectators of revival; we are participants, called to fervent prayer, humble repentance, and bold proclamation of the Gospel.

Heavenly Father, we thank You for the times throughout history when You have moved in power and brought about spiritual awakening. May we be transformed by Your Spirit, living as lights in a dark world, and proclaiming the good news of Jesus Christ with boldness and love. In Jesus' name, we pray. Amen.

DAY 100

The Persecuted Church

"Blessed are those who are persecuted because of righteousness, for theirs is the kingdom of heaven." - Matthew 5:10 (NIV)

Matthew 5:10 reminds us that persecution is not a sign of failure but a badge of honor for those who stand firm in righteousness.

The persecuted Church is a poignant reminder of the price of discipleship. In countries where Christianity is restricted or outlawed, believers face discrimination, imprisonment, and even death for their faith. Their courage and steadfastness in the face of such adversity serve as a powerful testimony to the transformative power of the gospel.

As we reflect on the plight of the persecuted Church, we are called to solidarity and action. We cannot turn a blind eye to the suffering of our fellow believers. Instead, we are called to lift them up in prayer, to advocate for their rights, and to support them practically and financially.

Lord Jesus, we lift up our persecuted brothers and sisters who suffer for their faith in You. Strengthen them with Your presence, comfort them in their affliction, and grant them courage to stand firm in the face of persecution. May Your Church around the world be united in love and support for one another, and may Your kingdom come and Your will be done on earth as it is in heaven. In Your holy name, we pray. Amen.

DAY 101

Martyrdom

"Blessed are those who are persecuted because of righteousness, for theirs is the kingdom of heaven." - Matthew 5:10 (NIV)

Matthew 5:10 reminds us that persecution for the sake of righteousness is not only a reality but also a pathway to the kingdom of heaven. Martyrdom, though often associated with physical death, encompasses a broader spectrum of sacrifice for the cause of Christ.

To understand martyrdom is to delve into the essence of discipleship. It is a willingness to lay down one's life, not only in the face of physical threats but also in the daily crucifixion of self. Martyrdom calls us to surrender our ambitions, desires, and comforts at the feet of Jesus, embracing His mission with unwavering devotion. It is a call to stand firm in the face of opposition, trusting in the promises of God even when the cost is great.

The stories of martyrs throughout history serve as a testament to the enduring power of faith. From the early disciples who faced persecution in the Roman Empire to modern-day believers who endure imprisonment and torture for their beliefs, the legacy of martyrdom continues to inspire and challenge us.

Heavenly Father, we thank You for the example of martyrs who have laid down their lives for the sake of Your kingdom. Give us the courage to follow in their footsteps, trusting in Your strength and grace. In Jesus' name, we pray. Amen.

DAY 102

Christian Unity

"Behold, how good and pleasant it is when brothers dwell in unity!" - Psalm 133:1 (ESV)

Unity among Christians is not merely a nice sentiment; it is a reflection of the very heart of God. Jesus prayed for unity among His followers, knowing that it is through our unity that the world would recognize the truth of His message.

Christian unity is not about uniformity; it's about embracing diversity within the body of Christ. We are all uniquely gifted and called, yet we are bound together by our common identity as children of God. When we set aside our differences and come together in love and mutual respect, we become a powerful testimony to the transformative power of Christ.

However, achieving and maintaining unity requires intentional effort. It means extending grace to one another, practicing humility, and prioritizing love above all else. It means seeking reconciliation when conflicts arise and striving for understanding amidst disagreements. But the beauty of Christian unity is that it is not something we achieve on our own strength; it is a gift from God, made possible by the Holy Spirit working within us.

Heavenly Father, we thank You for the gift of Christian unity, which binds us together as one body in Christ. Fill us with Your Holy Spirit, that we may be agents of love and unity in a world that is often divided. May our unity bring glory to Your name and draw others into Your kingdom. In Jesus' name, we pray. Amen.

DAY 103

Rest and Renewal

"Come to me, all you who are weary and burdened, and I will give you rest." - Matthew 11:28 (NIV)

Yet, in Matthew 11:28, Jesus extends a gentle invitation to all who are weary and burdened: "Come to me, and I will give you rest." This invitation is not just a promise of physical relaxation but a beckoning to find deep, soulful renewal in His presence.

Rest and renewal are essential aspects of our spiritual journey. Just as our bodies require sleep to rejuvenate, our souls long for moments of quiet retreat with our Heavenly Father. In the hustle and bustle of life, it's easy to neglect this need, but when we prioritize rest, we open ourselves to experience the peace and restoration that only God can provide.

True rest goes beyond simply ceasing from physical labor; it involves surrendering our worries, fears, and anxieties at the feet of Jesus. It's about entrusting our burdens to Him and allowing His love to wash over us, filling us with His peace that surpasses all understanding. In these moments of rest, we find strength to face the challenges of life with courage and resilience.

Gracious Father, thank You for the invitation to find rest in Your presence. Help us to heed Your call and come to You with our burdens, knowing that You are faithful to provide the renewal we desperately need. May we find solace in Your arms and strength for the journey ahead. In Jesus' name, we pray. Amen.

DAY 104

Fasting

"But when you fast, put oil on your head and wash your face, so that it will not be obvious to others that you are fasting, but only to your Father, who is unseen; and your Father, who sees what is done in secret, will reward you." - Matthew 6:17-18 (NIV)

Fasting involves abstaining from food or other physical necessities for a period of time, often to seek God's guidance, repentance, or spiritual breakthrough.

While fasting involves denying ourselves of physical comforts, its true essence lies in the spiritual journey it initiates. It's not merely about going without food; it's about drawing closer to God, aligning our hearts with His will, and deepening our dependence on Him. Fasting creates a space for spiritual intimacy, allowing us to set aside distractions and focus wholeheartedly on seeking God's presence.

During times of fasting, we are called to engage in self-examination, repentance, and prayer. It's a time to surrender our desires and agendas to God, inviting His guidance and transformation into our lives. As we humble ourselves before Him, He meets us with His grace, comfort, and strength.

Heavenly Father, as we embark on this journey of fasting, we acknowledge our need for You. Help us to surrender our desires and distractions, and to draw closer to You with open hearts. May this time of fasting be a catalyst for spiritual growth and renewal in our lives. In Jesus' name, we pray. Amen.

DAY 105

Spiritual Retreats

"But Jesus often withdrew to lonely places and prayed." - Luke 5:16 (NIV)

Jesus Himself set this example, frequently withdrawing to solitary places to commune with His Father. Spiritual retreats provide us with the opportunity to follow in His footsteps, to pause, reflect, and deepen our relationship with God.

A spiritual retreat is more than just a vacation or a getaway; it is a deliberate and intentional time set apart for spiritual renewal and growth. It is a sacred space where we can disconnect from the distractions of the world and reconnect with the voice of God speaking to our hearts. Whether it's a day-long retreat at a local retreat center or a longer, more immersive experience in a serene natural setting, the purpose remains the same: to draw near to God and allow Him to minister to our souls.

During a spiritual retreat, we have the chance to engage in practices that nourish our spirit, such as prayer, meditation, journaling, and studying Scripture. It's a time to listen attentively to the whispers of the Holy Spirit, to discern His direction for our lives, and to surrender our worries and burdens at His feet.

Heavenly Father, we thank You for the gift of spiritual retreats, where we can draw near to You and find rest for our souls. As we set aside time to seek Your face, may Your presence fill every moment, renewing and refreshing us. Guide us as we listen for Your voice and grant us the grace to follow where You lead. In Jesus' name, we pray. Amen.

DAY 106

Gender Equality

"So God created mankind in his own image, in the image of God he created them; male and female he created them." - Genesis 1:27 (NIV)

Genesis 1:27 beautifully captures this truth, affirming that both male and female reflect the divine image of God. Yet, throughout history, the concept of gender equality has been distorted, leading to discrimination, oppression, and injustice.

As followers of Christ, we are called to uphold the inherent worth and dignity of every individual, regardless of gender. Gender equality is not merely a social or political issue; it is a matter of justice rooted in the character of God. Jesus Himself demonstrated a radical inclusivity, welcoming women as disciples, and treating them with dignity and respect in a society that often marginalized them.

To embrace gender equality is to recognize the unique gifts and contributions of both men and women in the Kingdom of God. It is to affirm the equal value of their voices, their talents, and their leadership. It is to dismantle harmful stereotypes and systems of oppression that perpetuate inequality.

Heavenly Father, we thank You for creating us in Your image, male and female. Help us to honor the inherent worth and dignity of every person, regardless of gender. May Your Kingdom come, where all are valued and celebrated as equal heirs to Your promises. In Jesus' name, we pray. Amen.

DAY 107

Religious Freedom

"So if the Son sets you free, you will be free indeed." - John 8:36
(NIV)

John 8:36 reminds us that true freedom is found in Christ. It is a freedom that transcends earthly circumstances and extends to the very core of our souls. But alongside this spiritual freedom, there is also a precious gift bestowed upon us: religious freedom.

Religious freedom is a fundamental human right, recognized and cherished by many nations around the world. It is the freedom to practice one's faith without coercion or persecution, to gather with fellow believers, and to live out one's convictions openly and without fear. This freedom is not merely a privilege but a sacred responsibility entrusted to us by God.

As Christians, we are called to defend and uphold religious freedom, not just for ourselves but for all people, regardless of their beliefs. We do this not out of selfish ambition or personal gain but out of love for our neighbors and obedience to God's commandments. Just as we desire to worship freely, so too should we advocate for the rights of others to do the same.

Heavenly Father, we thank You for the gift of religious freedom, which allows us to worship You without fear. Help us to cherish this freedom and to advocate for it with courage and compassion. Strengthen those who are persecuted for their faith and grant them Your peace and protection. May Your love shine brightly through us as we stand up for what is right. In Jesus' name, we pray. Amen.

DAY 108

The Trinity

"Go therefore and make disciples of all nations, baptizing them in the name of the Father and of the Son and of the Holy Spirit." - Matthew 28:19 (ESV)

In Matthew 28:19, Jesus commissions His disciples to baptize new believers in the name of the Father, the Son, and the Holy Spirit. This verse offers a glimpse into the triune nature of God, three distinct persons existing in perfect unity and harmony.

God the Father, the Creator of all things, is the source of life and love. He is the one who spoke the world into existence and sustains it by His power. God the Son, Jesus Christ, is the Savior of humanity, who willingly laid down His life to redeem us from sin and death. God the Holy Spirit is the Comforter and Guide who dwells within every believer, empowering us to live according to God's will.

The Trinity reveals to us the relational nature of God. Just as the Father, Son, and Holy Spirit exist in perfect communion, so too are we invited into relationship with God and with one another. We are called to love one another as God loves us, to live in unity and harmony as members of the body of Christ.

Gracious God, we thank You for the mystery and beauty of the Trinity, three persons in one divine essence. Help us to understand and embrace this truth more fully, that we may live in loving relationship with You and with one another. May our lives reflect the unity and harmony of the Trinity, bringing glory to Your name. In Jesus' name, we pray. Amen.

DAY 109

The Power of the Gospel

"For I am not ashamed of the gospel, because it is the power of God that brings salvation to everyone who believes: first to the Jew, then to the Gentile." - Romans 1:16 (NIV)

The gospel is not merely a message; it is the very power of God at work in the hearts and lives of those who believe. It is the proclamation of salvation, redemption, and reconciliation with God, made possible through the sacrificial death and resurrection of Jesus Christ.

The gospel has the power to break chains of bondage, to heal broken hearts, and to set captives free. It is a message of hope for the lost, comfort for the brokenhearted, and joy for the despairing. The gospel transcends barriers of race, ethnicity, and culture, offering salvation to all who will receive it with open hearts.

As followers of Christ, we have the privilege and responsibility of sharing the life-changing power of the gospel with others. Whether through our words, actions, or lifestyles, we are called to be ambassadors of Christ, proclaiming the good news to a world in need of hope and salvation.

Heavenly Father, we thank You for the power of the gospel to transform lives and bring salvation to all who believe. Give us boldness and compassion as we share this message with others. Use us as vessels of Your grace and love, Lord, as we proclaim the good news of Jesus Christ to a world in need. In His name, we pray. Amen.

DAY 110

The Image of God

"So God created mankind in his own image, in the image of God he created them; male and female he created them." - Genesis 1:27 (NIV)

To be made in God's image means that we bear His likeness, reflecting His attributes and character in our lives. It is a mark of dignity and worth bestowed upon every individual, regardless of race, gender, or status.

Consider the implications of this truth. We are not merely products of chance or evolution but intentional creations of a loving and purposeful God. In each of us resides a spark of the divine, a reflection of His glory waiting to be revealed. This understanding should transform the way we view ourselves and others, instilling a sense of reverence for the sanctity of human life.

The image of God within us is not something to be taken lightly or neglected. It calls us to live lives of holiness and righteousness, reflecting His love and grace to the world around us. It reminds us of our responsibility to steward His creation with wisdom and care, to seek justice and mercy, and to pursue reconciliation and unity.

Heavenly Father, thank You for creating us in Your image and likeness. Help us to recognize the inherent worth and dignity You have bestowed upon every human being. May Your image shine brightly in us, drawing others to know and love You. In Jesus' name, we pray. Amen.

DAY 111

The Fall of Man

"For all have sinned and fall short of the glory of God." - Romans 3:23 (NIV)

In Genesis, we read of Adam and Eve's disobedience in the Garden of Eden, a choice that introduced sin and brokenness into the world. Romans 3:23 reminds us that this act of rebellion affected all of humanity, leading us away from the glory of God and into a state of separation.

The Fall represents more than just a historical event; it reveals the universal truth of human nature. We are all prone to wander, to choose our own desires over God's will. The consequences of this rebellion are evident in the brokenness and suffering that surround us. God's love and grace extend beyond our failures, offering redemption and restoration to all who turn to Him.

Recognizing the reality of the Fall prompts us to confront our own sinfulness and need for a Savior. It humbles us, reminding us of our dependence on God's mercy and forgiveness. But it also invites us to respond with repentance and faith, turning away from sin and embracing the abundant life that Jesus offers.

Lord, we confess our sinfulness and acknowledge our need for Your grace. Thank You for the redemption that is found in Jesus Christ, who has made a way for us to be reconciled to You. Help us to walk in obedience and humility, relying on Your strength to overcome sin and live in the fullness of Your love. In Jesus' name, we pray. Amen.

DAY 112

God's Plan of Redemption

"For God so loved the world that he gave his one and only Son,
that whoever believes in him shall not perish but have eternal life."
- John 3:16 (NIV)

God's plan of redemption is the ultimate expression of His unfailing love for humanity. It is the story of hope restored, brokenness healed, and eternal life offered freely to all who believe.

From the moment sin entered the world, God set in motion His plan to reconcile us to Himself. Throughout history, He revealed glimpses of this plan through prophecies, promises, and foreshadowings. And in the fullness of time, He sent His Son, Jesus Christ, to be the embodiment of His redemption. Through Jesus' life, death, and resurrection, God's plan was fulfilled in its entirety.

The beauty of God's plan of redemption lies not only in its scope but also in its accessibility. It is not limited to a select few but is offered to all who would receive it. No sin is too great, no heart too broken, no life too far gone for the redeeming power of God's love to reach.

Heavenly Father, thank You for Your incredible plan of redemption, demonstrated through the gift of Your Son, Jesus Christ. Help us to grasp the depth of Your love and the magnitude of Your sacrifice on our behalf. May we live each day in the freedom and joy of Your redemption, sharing Your love with others and pointing them to the hope found in Christ alone. In His name, we pray. Amen.

DAY 113

The Lord's Day

*"Remember the Sabbath day by keeping it holy." - Exodus 20:8
(NIV)*

Exodus 20:8 reminds us of the importance of setting aside this day for rest and worship. It is a day set apart from the busyness of the world, a day dedicated to honoring God and renewing our spirits.

In our fast-paced society, where schedules are packed and priorities constantly shifting, the Lord's Day serves as an anchor for our souls. It is a day of spiritual rejuvenation, a time to pause and reflect on God's goodness and faithfulness. Just as God rested on the seventh day after creating the world, we too are called to rest and find restoration in Him.

The Lord's Day is not merely about abstaining from work; it is about delighting in the presence of God. It is an opportunity to gather with fellow believers, to worship Him in spirit and in truth, and to draw near to Him through prayer, study, and fellowship. It is a day to be filled with joy and gratitude for the blessings He has bestowed upon us.

Heavenly Father, we thank You for the gift of the Lord's Day, a day set apart for rest and worship. Help us to honor You with our time and our hearts, and to find renewal and refreshment in Your presence. May this day be a foretaste of the eternal rest we will find in You. In Jesus' name, we pray. Amen.

DAY 114

The Sanctity of Life

"So God created mankind in his own image, in the image of God he created them; male and female he created them." - Genesis 1:27 (NIV)

This truth forms the foundation of the sanctity of life. Every person, from the moment of conception to natural death, bears the imprint of the divine. Each life is precious, unique, and irreplaceable, deserving of reverence and protection.

Yet, in a world marked by brokenness and sin, the sanctity of life is often disregarded. From the unborn child in the womb to the elderly nearing the end of their journey, countless lives are threatened and devalued. But as followers of Christ, we are called to uphold the sanctity of life in all its forms. We are called to be champions for the vulnerable, the marginalized, and the voiceless.

To honor the sanctity of life is to recognize the inherent dignity and worth of every person. It is to stand against injustice, oppression, and violence. It is to extend compassion and support to those in need, offering love and hope in the face of despair.

Gracious God, we thank You for the precious gift of life, bestowed upon us in Your image. Give us eyes to see the sanctity of every person and hearts to defend the vulnerable. May we be instruments of Your love and mercy in a world that often fails to recognize the value of life. Strengthen us to be voices for the voiceless and advocates for the marginalized. In Jesus' name, we pray. Amen.

DAY 115

Practicing Gratitude

"Give thanks in all circumstances; for this is God's will for you in Christ Jesus." - 1 Thessalonians 5:18 (NIV)

This doesn't mean we deny the challenges or difficulties we face; rather, it means choosing to find reasons to be thankful even in the midst of trials.

Practicing gratitude is a transformative discipline that shifts our focus from what we lack to what we have been given. It opens our eyes to the countless blessings that surround us each day, both big and small. When we cultivate a spirit of gratitude, we discover that even in the darkest moments, there is always something to be grateful for - whether it's the love of family and friends, the beauty of creation, or the hope we have in Christ.

Gratitude also deepens our relationship with God. When we acknowledge His goodness and faithfulness in our lives, our hearts overflow with praise and adoration. We recognize that every good and perfect gift comes from Him, and we respond with thanksgiving and worship.

Heavenly Father, thank You for the countless blessings You pour into our lives each day. Help us to cultivate a spirit of gratitude that transcends our circumstances and draws us closer to You. Teach us to give thanks in all things, knowing that Your love never fails and Your mercies are new every morning. In Jesus' name, we pray. Amen.

DAY 116

Seeking Wisdom

"For the Lord gives wisdom; from his mouth come knowledge and understanding." - Proverbs 2:6 (NIV)

It is not merely intellectual knowledge but a deep understanding rooted in God's truth and guided by His Spirit. To seek wisdom is to seek God Himself, for He is the source of all wisdom and understanding.

Seeking wisdom is a journey, a lifelong pursuit of aligning our hearts and minds with God's will. It involves humility, recognizing our limitations and acknowledging our need for His guidance. As we delve into His Word, we discover timeless principles and insights that illuminate our path and empower us to make wise decisions.

Wisdom is not just about making smart choices; it's about living a life that reflects God's character and glorifies Him in all we do. It's about cultivating virtues such as patience, kindness, and compassion, even in the face of challenges and uncertainties. Wisdom enables us to navigate the complexities of life with grace and discernment, drawing closer to God with each step we take.

Heavenly Father, we thank You for the gift of wisdom that comes from You alone. As we seek Your face and delve into Your Word, guide us by Your Spirit and grant us discernment to walk in Your ways. May our lives be a reflection of Your wisdom and grace, shining brightly in a world that desperately needs Your light. In Jesus' name, we pray. Amen.

DAY 117

The Holy Spirit's Guidance

"But when he, the Spirit of truth, comes, he will guide you into all the truth. He will not speak on his own; he will speak only what he hears, and he will tell you what is yet to come." - John 16:13 (NIV)

In a world filled with uncertainty and confusion, the Holy Spirit serves as our compass, directing our steps and whispering words of wisdom and clarity into our hearts.

When we surrender to the guidance of the Holy Spirit, we open ourselves to a divine partnership. It's not about relying solely on our own understanding but trusting in the wisdom and discernment that comes from God. The Holy Spirit speaks to us through the Scriptures, through prayer, and through the still, small voice within us. His guidance may come in unexpected ways – a gentle nudge, a timely word from a friend, or a sudden clarity of thought – but it is always faithful and true.

As we walk in step with the Holy Spirit, we are empowered to live lives that reflect the character of Christ. His guidance shapes our decisions, molds our attitudes, and transforms our hearts. We become vessels of His love, channels of His grace, and beacons of His light in a world that desperately needs His touch.

Holy Spirit, we thank You for Your constant presence and guidance in our lives. Open our ears to hear Your voice and our hearts to receive Your wisdom. Lead us into all truth and empower us to walk in obedience to Your will. May Your guidance shape every aspect of our lives and bring glory to Your name. In Jesus' name, we pray. Amen.

DAY 118

Strength in Weakness

"But he said to me, 'My grace is sufficient for you, for my power is made perfect in weakness.' Therefore I will boast all the more gladly about my weaknesses, so that Christ's power may rest on me." - 2 Corinthians 12:9 (NIV)

God's power shines brightest in our moments of weakness. It is in our vulnerability and dependence on Him that His strength is made perfect.

Our weaknesses can take many forms—physical limitations, emotional struggles, spiritual doubts—but whatever shape they may assume, they serve as opportunities for God to demonstrate His faithfulness and provision. When we reach the end of our own strength, we discover the limitless reservoir of grace that God offers to sustain us.

Paul, the author of Corinthians, understood this truth intimately. Despite facing various trials and hardships, he embraced his weaknesses as opportunities for God's power to be revealed. Instead of hiding his flaws or pretending to be self-sufficient, he boasted in his weaknesses, knowing that they were the very places where God's strength could be most clearly seen.

Heavenly Father, thank You for the assurance that Your grace is sufficient for us, even in our moments of weakness. Help us to trust in Your power and to find strength in surrendering to You. May Your grace be our comfort and Your strength our support in every trial we face. In Jesus' name, we pray. Amen.

DAY 119

Living by Faith

"For we live by faith, not by sight." - 2 Corinthians 5:7 (NIV)

2 Corinthians 5:7, Paul reminds us that our lives are not dictated by what we can see or touch but by our unwavering belief in God's faithfulness. It's a call to step out in courage, to relinquish control, and to embrace the unknown with confidence in God's sovereignty.

Faith is not just a passive belief; it's an active, intentional choice to trust God in every circumstance. It's about surrendering our doubts and fears at the feet of Jesus and allowing His peace to reign in our hearts. Living by faith means daring to dream God-sized dreams, even when the world tells us they're impossible. It means holding onto hope in the midst of adversity, knowing that God is working all things together for our good.

But living by faith isn't always easy. It requires us to step out of our comfort zones, to take risks, and to persevere through trials. Yet, it's in those moments of uncertainty that our faith is refined and strengthened. It's when we choose to trust God in the darkest of nights that His light shines brightest in our lives.

Heavenly Father, help us to live by faith, trusting in Your goodness and sovereignty in every aspect of our lives. Give us the courage to step out in obedience, even when the path ahead is uncertain. May our lives be a testimony to Your faithfulness, as we walk confidently in the promises of Your Word. In Jesus' name, we pray. Amen.

DAY 120

God's Promises

"For no matter how many promises God has made, they are 'Yes' in Christ. And so through him the 'Amen' is spoken by us to the glory of God." - 2 Corinthians 1:20 (NIV)

His word is a testament to His faithfulness, a beacon of hope in a world filled with uncertainty. As we journey through life, it's easy to be overwhelmed by doubts and fears, but God's promises stand as a firm foundation beneath our feet.

God's promises are not empty words; they are declarations of His love and provision for His children. From the promise of salvation to the assurance of His presence with us always, His word is filled with countless assurances of His goodness and grace. Even in the midst of trials and tribulations, we can cling to His promises with confidence, knowing that He who promised is faithful.

As believers, it is our privilege and responsibility to hold fast to God's promises. We are called to anchor our faith in His word, trusting in His unfailing love and unwavering faithfulness. But our faith is not passive; it requires action. We must actively pursue God's promises, seeking His guidance and wisdom as we navigate the ups and downs of life.

Heavenly Father, thank You for Your faithful promises, which are a source of hope and strength for us. Help us to trust in Your word and to live in obedience to Your commands. May Your promises guide our steps and sustain us through every trial and triumph. In Jesus' name, we pray. Amen.

DAY 121

The Joy of Salvation

"Restore to me the joy of your salvation and grant me a willing spirit, to sustain me." - Psalm 51:12 (NIV)

It speaks of a deep longing to experience the fullness of God's saving grace and to be filled with an uncontainable joy that can only come from Him. The joy of salvation is not just a fleeting emotion but a profound reality that transforms our lives from the inside out.

When we accept Jesus Christ as our Savior, we are set free from the bondage of sin and welcomed into a new life of redemption and hope. It's a joy that surpasses any earthly pleasure or circumstance because it is rooted in the unchanging love and faithfulness of God. It's a joy that sustains us through trials and tribulations, reminding us that we are never alone and that nothing can separate us from the love of Christ.

But sometimes, amidst the busyness of life or the struggles we face, we may find ourselves losing sight of the joy of salvation. We become weighed down by worries, doubts, and distractions, forgetting the incredible gift that has been freely given to us. In those moments, we need to echo the psalmist's plea and ask God to restore to us the joy of His salvation.

Heavenly Father, thank You for the incredible gift of salvation through Your Son, Jesus Christ. Restore to us the joy of Your salvation and fill us with Your Holy Spirit, that we may live each day with grateful hearts and overflowing joy. Help us to share this joy with others and to be a beacon of hope in a world that desperately needs Your love. In Jesus' name, we pray. Amen.

DAY 122

Forgiveness and Grace

"Be kind and compassionate to one another, forgiving each other, just as in Christ God forgave you." - Ephesians 4:32 (NIV)

Ephesians 4:32 reminds us of the profound example set by Christ Himself. In His life, Jesus demonstrated radical forgiveness and boundless grace, even in the face of betrayal and suffering. As followers of Christ, we are called to embody this same spirit of compassion and forgiveness toward others.

Forgiveness is not always easy. It requires us to release feelings of anger, resentment, and hurt, and instead, extend love and understanding. But in doing so, we mirror the incredible forgiveness we have received from God. His grace knows no bounds; it covers our sins and offers us a new beginning. How can we, then, withhold forgiveness from others when we ourselves have been forgiven so much?

Grace goes hand in hand with forgiveness. It is the unmerited favor and kindness bestowed upon us by God, despite our shortcomings. Just as we have received grace abundantly, we are called to extend it generously to those around us. It is through grace that we can break the chains of bitterness and resentment, and embrace the freedom found in forgiveness.

Gracious God, we thank You for the forgiveness and grace that You lavish upon us each day. Help us to forgive others as You have forgiven us, and to extend grace to those who need it most. Fill our hearts with Your love, that we may reflect Your mercy and compassion in all that we do. In Jesus' name, we pray. Amen.

DAY 123

Serving Others

"For even the Son of Man did not come to be served, but to serve, and to give his life as a ransom for many." - Mark 10:45 (NIV)

Jesus, the very Son of God, humbled Himself to serve humanity, demonstrating the ultimate act of selflessness by giving His life for our salvation. His example challenges us to follow in His footsteps, to embrace the call to serve others with love and compassion.

Serving others is not merely an optional virtue for Christians; it is a fundamental expression of our faith. It is through service that we reflect the character of Christ and fulfill His commandment to love one another as He has loved us. When we serve others, we emulate the sacrificial love of Jesus, pouring out ourselves for the well-being of those around us.

True service goes beyond acts of charity or kindness; it requires a heart posture of humility and genuine concern for others. It means putting the needs of others before our own, seeking opportunities to uplift and encourage, and being willing to step out of our comfort zones to meet the needs of those around us.

Gracious God, thank You for the example of Jesus, who came not to be served but to serve. Help us to follow His example and to be instruments of Your love and compassion in the world. Open our eyes to the needs of those around us and give us the courage to act with humility and kindness. May our lives be a reflection of Your grace and mercy. In Jesus' name, we pray. Amen.

DAY 124

Patience in God's Timing

"But do not forget this one thing, dear friends: With the Lord a day is like a thousand years, and a thousand years are like a day." - 2 Peter 3:8 (NIV)

His perspective transcends our understanding, and His timing is perfect, even when it may not align with our own desires or expectations.

Patience in God's timing requires trust and surrender. It means relinquishing our need for control and embracing the divine timing of the One who sees the beginning from the end. Though we may grow weary in waiting, we can take comfort in knowing that God is faithful and His promises never fail. What may seem like delay to us is simply an opportunity for God to work all things together for our good and His glory.

As we wait upon the Lord, we are called to actively cultivate patience in our hearts. This means remaining steadfast in prayer, holding fast to hope, and seeking His guidance in all things. It also involves trusting in His sovereignty, knowing that He is orchestrating every detail according to His perfect plan.

Heavenly Father, teach us to wait upon You with patience and trust. Help us to surrender our desires and plans to Your sovereign will, knowing that Your timing is always perfect. Strengthen our faith as we wait expectantly for Your promises to be fulfilled in our lives. May we find peace in Your presence and confidence in Your unfailing love. In Jesus' name, we pray. Amen.

DAY 125

Walking in the Light

"But if we walk in the light, as he is in the light, we have fellowship with one another, and the blood of Jesus, his Son, purifies us from all sin." - 1 John 1:7 (NIV)

To walk in the light is to live in alignment with the truth and righteousness of God. It is to step out of the darkness of sin and into the radiant presence of His love and grace. When we walk in the light, we experience fellowship with God and with one another, and we are purified by the cleansing power of Jesus' sacrifice.

Walking in the light requires intentionality and surrender. It means allowing God's truth to illuminate every corner of our hearts and minds, exposing and dispelling the darkness within. It means living transparently and authentically, with nothing hidden or concealed. It means actively pursuing holiness and righteousness in our thoughts, words, and actions.

As we walk in the light, we become beacons of hope and love in a world shrouded in darkness. Our lives become a testimony to the transformative power of God's grace, inviting others to experience the same freedom and redemption that we have found in Christ.

Heavenly Father, thank You for the gift of Your light that shines brightly in our lives. Help us to walk in the light, to live in alignment with Your truth and righteousness. Shine Your light into every corner of our hearts, exposing and purifying us from all sin. May our lives be a reflection of Your glory, drawing others into fellowship with You. In Jesus' name, we pray. Amen.

DAY 126

Spiritual Discernment

"But solid food is for the mature, who by constant use have trained themselves to distinguish good from evil." - Hebrews 5:14 (NIV)

Just as physical maturity enables us to distinguish between healthy and unhealthy food, spiritual maturity empowers us to discern between good and evil, truth and falsehood. Spiritual discernment is not merely a skill to be acquired but a gift of the Holy Spirit, cultivated through prayer, study of Scripture, and a deepening relationship with God.

In a world filled with conflicting voices and ideologies, spiritual discernment is more crucial than ever. It enables us to navigate the complexities of life with wisdom and clarity, to recognize the prompting of the Holy Spirit amidst the noise of the world.

Developing spiritual discernment requires intentionality and discipline. It involves surrendering our own desires and biases to the leading of the Holy Spirit, allowing Him to guide and illuminate our understanding. It also requires a commitment to truth, seeking wisdom from God's Word and seeking counsel from mature believers who can offer godly insight and perspective.

Heavenly Father, we thank You for the gift of spiritual discernment, which enables us to distinguish between good and evil. Grant us wisdom and insight as we seek to walk in Your ways and to discern Your will for our lives. May our lives be a reflection of Your wisdom and grace. In Jesus' name, we pray. Amen.

DAY 127

The Armor of God

"Put on the full armor of God, so that you can take your stand against the devil's schemes." - Ephesians 6:11 (NIV)

Just as a soldier prepares for war by donning armor, we are called to put on the full armor of God to stand firm against the schemes of the enemy. This armor is not physical but spiritual, designed to equip us for the challenges of life and the attacks of the enemy.

Each piece of the armor described in Ephesians 6 serves a specific purpose in our spiritual defense. The belt of truth holds everything together, reminding us to stand firm in God's Word and live lives of integrity. The breastplate of righteousness guards our hearts, protecting us from the accusations of the enemy. The shoes of peace enable us to walk confidently in the midst of turmoil, rooted in the peace that surpasses all understanding.

The shield of faith extinguishes the fiery darts of doubt and fear, allowing us to trust in God's promises and provision. The helmet of salvation protects our minds, reminding us of our identity as children of God and heirs of eternal life.

Heavenly Father, thank You for equipping us with the armor of God to stand firm in the face of spiritual battle. Help us to be diligent in putting on this armor daily, relying on Your strength and protection. Give us wisdom to recognize the enemy's schemes and courage to resist him. May we walk in victory, knowing that You are with us always. In Jesus' name, we pray. Amen.

DAY 128

The Fruit of the Spirit

"But the fruit of the Spirit is love, joy, peace, forbearance, kindness, goodness, faithfulness, gentleness and self-control. Against such things there is no law." - Galatians 5:22-23 (NIV)

These verses describe the "fruit of the Spirit," which are the qualities that flow from a life surrendered to God. As Christians, we are called to bear this fruit, allowing it to manifest in our thoughts, words, and actions.

The fruit of the Spirit is not something we can manufacture on our own; it is the natural outgrowth of a life rooted in relationship with God. Love, joy, peace, patience, kindness, goodness, faithfulness, gentleness, and self-control—they are the evidence of God's presence in our lives, His Spirit at work within us.

When we cultivate these qualities, we become more like Christ, who embodied each one perfectly. Love motivates us to sacrificially serve others. Joy fills our hearts despite circumstances, knowing our hope is in Him. Peace guards our minds and hearts, even in the midst of turmoil. Patience enables us to endure trials with grace. Kindness and goodness flow from hearts transformed by grace. Faithfulness keeps us steadfast in our commitment to God.

Heavenly Father, thank You for the gift of Your Spirit, who produces within us the fruit of love, joy, peace, and so much more. Help us to abide in You, allowing Your Spirit to work in and through us, transforming us into vessels of Your grace and truth. Give us the strength and wisdom to bear fruit that glorifies Your name and blesses those around us. In Jesus' name, we pray. Amen.

DAY 129

Trust in God's Provision

"And my God will meet all your needs according to the riches of his glory in Christ Jesus." - Philippians 4:19 (NIV)

He will abundantly meet all our needs according to His riches in glory. Yet, trusting in God's provision is not always easy, especially when we are faced with uncertainty or challenges. However, the Bible is filled with stories of God's faithfulness to His people, providing for them in miraculous ways, even in the midst of trials.

Trusting in God's provision means surrendering our worries and fears to Him and placing our faith in His promises. It is about acknowledging that He is our ultimate provider, the source of all good things. When we trust in God's provision, we can find peace and security knowing that He is in control and will never leave us nor forsake us.

As we cultivate a spirit of trust in God's provision, we can also be inspired to live lives of generosity and gratitude. When we recognize that everything we have comes from God, we can freely give of our time, talents, and resources to bless others and further His kingdom on earth.

Heavenly Father, thank You for Your abundant provision and faithfulness. Give us the courage to surrender our worries to You and to live lives of faith, generosity, and gratitude. May Your provision in our lives be a testimony to Your goodness and grace. In Jesus' name, we pray. Amen.

DAY 130

Living a Life of Worship

"Therefore, I urge you, brothers and sisters, in view of God's mercy, to offer your bodies as a living sacrifice, holy and pleasing to God—this is your true and proper worship." - Romans 12:1 (NIV)

To live a life of worship is to recognize the mercy of God and respond with hearts surrendered to His will. It's an acknowledgment that every moment, every action, every thought can be an offering unto Him.

Living a life of worship means viewing every aspect of our existence as an opportunity to honor God. Whether we're at work, at home, or in our communities, our lives should reflect His glory. Our daily activities become acts of worship when they are infused with love, integrity, and devotion to God. Even the simplest tasks, when done with a heart of gratitude and obedience, can become offerings pleasing to Him.

Worship isn't just about what we do; it's about who we are becoming. As we surrender ourselves to God, allowing Him to transform us from the inside out, our lives become a living testimony to His grace and power.

Heavenly Father, thank You for the privilege of worshiping You with our lives. Help us to offer ourselves to You as living sacrifices, holy and pleasing in Your sight. May every aspect of our existence be a reflection of Your goodness and grace. Empower us to live with hearts surrendered to Your will, that Your name may be glorified through us. In Jesus' name, we pray. Amen.

DAY 131

God's Unchanging Nature

"Jesus Christ is the same yesterday and today and forever." -
Hebrews 13:8 (NIV)

Hebrews 13:8 assures us that Jesus Christ remains consistent throughout all time—yesterday, today, and forever. His character, His promises, and His love are eternal and unwavering, providing us with comfort and assurance in every season of life.

God's unchanging nature is a source of great hope and security for believers. In a world where circumstances can shift in an instant, we can trust in the unchanging nature of our God. His faithfulness endures through every trial, His love remains constant in every storm, and His grace sustains us through every challenge we face.

Knowing that God does not change also gives us confidence in His promises. The same God who has been faithful in the past will continue to be faithful in the present and in the future. His word stands firm, His purposes remain steadfast, and His plans for us are sure. We can rest in the assurance that He who began a good work in us will carry it on to completion.

Faithful God, we thank You for Your unchanging nature and Your steadfast love. In a world of uncertainty, You remain our rock and our refuge. Help us to trust in Your faithfulness and to find peace in Your unchanging character. May Your presence sustain us through every season of life. In Jesus' name, we pray. Amen.

DAY 132

Peace in Christ

"Peace I leave with you; my peace I give you. I do not give to you as the world gives. Do not let your hearts be troubled and do not be afraid." - John 14:27 (NIV)

John 14:27 reminds us that the peace offered by Jesus is unlike anything the world can provide. It is a peace that transcends circumstances, a peace that surpasses understanding, a peace that anchors our souls in the midst of life's storms.

Peace in Christ is not the absence of conflict or difficulty but the presence of His comforting and reassuring presence. It is knowing that no matter what challenges we face, we are held secure in the arms of our Savior. This peace is not dependent on external factors but springs from our relationship with Jesus. It is a peace that flows from knowing that we are loved, forgiven, and eternally secure in Him.

When we abide in Christ, His peace becomes a shield that guards our hearts and minds against fear and anxiety. It empowers us to face life's trials with courage and confidence, knowing that we are never alone. Even in the darkest valleys, His peace shines as a guiding light, leading us safely through.

Heavenly Father, we thank You for the gift of peace that surpasses all understanding, a peace that is found only in Christ Jesus. Help us to abide in Him daily, trusting in His unfailing love and unwavering faithfulness. May His peace guard our hearts and minds, and may we be vessels of His peace to a world in desperate need. In Jesus' name, we pray. Amen.

DAY 133

Overcoming Temptation

"No temptation has overtaken you except what is common to mankind. And God is faithful; he will not let you be tempted beyond what you can bear. But when you are tempted, he will also provide a way out so that you can endure it." - 1 Corinthians 10:13 (NIV)

He understands our struggles intimately and promises to provide a way out, empowering us to overcome.

Temptation comes in many forms, often appealing to our deepest desires and weaknesses. It can be subtle, creeping into our thoughts and tempting us to compromise our values and convictions. Yet, God's Word reminds us that we are not helpless in the face of temptation. Through His strength and guidance, we can resist and overcome.

One key aspect of overcoming temptation is to recognize that we are not alone in our struggle. God is with us, offering His grace and wisdom to navigate through the temptations that we face. He provides us with the strength to resist and the discernment to recognize the way out that He has graciously provided.

Heavenly Father, thank You for Your faithfulness in the midst of temptation. Give us the strength to resist and the wisdom to discern Your way out. Help us to rely on Your grace and to trust in Your promises. May Your Spirit empower us to overcome temptation and live lives that honor and glorify You. In Jesus' name, we pray. Amen.

DAY 134

The Value of Humility

"Do nothing out of selfish ambition or vain conceit. Rather, in humility value others above yourselves." - Philippians 2:3 (NIV)

Humility is not about diminishing ourselves or denying our worth; rather, it is about recognizing the inherent value and dignity of every individual, just as God does.

In a world that often elevates self-promotion and pride, the concept of humility may seem counter-cultural. Yet, it is precisely through humility that we embody the spirit of Christ. Jesus Himself demonstrated the ultimate act of humility by leaving the glory of heaven to dwell among us as a servant, ultimately laying down His life for our salvation.

Humility is not weakness; it is strength under control. It is the courage to acknowledge our limitations and imperfections while also recognizing the beauty and worth in others. When we humble ourselves before God and others, we open ourselves up to His grace and enable deeper connections with those around us.

Heavenly Father, teach us the value of humility as demonstrated by Jesus Christ. Help us to set aside our pride and selfish ambitions, and to value others above ourselves. May our lives be a reflection of Your love and grace, as we seek to serve others with humility and compassion. In Jesus' name, we pray. Amen.

DAY 135

Love Thy Neighbor

"Love your neighbor as yourself." - Mark 12:31b (NIV)

This directive serves as a guiding principle for our interactions with others, challenging us to extend the same love, kindness, and compassion to our neighbors that we desire for ourselves.

But who is our neighbor? Jesus answers this question through the parable of the Good Samaritan (Luke 10:25-37), illustrating that our neighbor is anyone in need, regardless of their background, beliefs, or social status. Our neighbors include the person next door, the stranger on the street, the marginalized, and the forgotten. Loving our neighbor means recognizing the inherent worth and dignity of every individual and treating them with respect and care.

This commandment is not merely a suggestion; it is a call to action. It requires us to actively seek out opportunities to demonstrate love and compassion in practical ways. It means stepping out of our comfort zones, overcoming prejudices, and embracing the diversity of God's creation. When we love our neighbors as ourselves, we mirror the love of Christ and bear witness to His transformative power in our lives.

Heavenly Father, thank You for the commandment to love our neighbors as ourselves. Give us the strength and courage to live out this commandment in our daily lives, reaching out with compassion and kindness to those around us. Help us to see others through Your eyes and to treat them with the same love and grace that You have shown us. In Jesus' name, we pray. Amen.

DAY 136

Bearing Good Fruit

"By their fruit you will recognize them. Do people pick grapes from thorn bushes, or figs from thistles? Likewise, every good tree bears good fruit, but a bad tree bears bad fruit." - Matthew 7:16-17 (NIV)

Just as a healthy tree naturally yields good fruit, a life rooted in Christ will bear the fruit of righteousness, love, joy, peace, patience, kindness, goodness, faithfulness, gentleness, and self-control (Galatians 5:22-23).

Bearing good fruit is not just about outward actions; it is about the transformation of our inner being. When we abide in Christ, allowing His Spirit to work within us, our lives become a testimony to His grace and power. Our words, our actions, and our attitudes all become channels through which His love flows to others.

As followers of Christ, we are called to be intentional about cultivating good fruit in our lives. This requires daily surrender to God's will, allowing Him to prune away anything that hinders growth and to nourish us with His Word and His Spirit. It also involves active participation in His kingdom work, using our gifts and resources to bless others and advance His purposes in the world.

Heavenly Father, thank You for the privilege of bearing fruit for Your kingdom. Help us to abide in Christ, drawing nourishment from Him so that our lives may be fruitful and pleasing to You. May our lives be a reflection of Your grace and goodness, bringing glory to Your name. In Jesus' name, we pray. Amen.

DAY 137

The Power of the Word

"For the word of God is alive and active. Sharper than any double-edged sword, it penetrates even to dividing soul and spirit, joints and marrow; it judges the thoughts and attitudes of the heart." -
Hebrews 4:12 (NIV)

It is not merely a collection of ancient texts; it is a living, breathing expression of God's truth and love. The Word of God has the ability to penetrate deep into our souls, exposing our innermost thoughts and desires, and bringing about profound change in our lives.

The Bible is more than just a book; it is a source of wisdom, guidance, comfort, and strength. Its words have the power to heal brokenness, bring hope to the hopeless, and restore the weary. When we immerse ourselves in Scripture, we encounter the living God, who speaks to us through its pages and reveals His will for our lives.

The power of the Word lies not only in its ability to convict and challenge us but also in its capacity to transform us from the inside out. As we meditate on Scripture and allow its truths to take root in our hearts, we are renewed and transformed into the likeness of Christ.

Heavenly Father, thank You for the gift of Your Word, which is alive and active. Help us to treasure and cherish Scripture as a precious gift from You. Open our hearts and minds to receive Your truth and wisdom, and empower us to live according to Your will. May Your Word be a light to guide us and a source of strength and encouragement in our daily lives. In Jesus' name, we pray. Amen.

DAY 138

The Greatness of God

"Oh, the depth of the riches of the wisdom and knowledge of God! How unsearchable his judgments, and his paths beyond tracing out!" - Romans 11:33 (NIV)

Romans 11:33 invites us to contemplate the incomprehensible greatness of God. His wisdom, knowledge, and judgments are beyond our understanding, stretching into the depths of eternity. Attempting to fathom the vastness of His greatness is like trying to measure the expanse of the universe—it is an endeavor that humbles the human heart and fills it with awe.

The greatness of God is not confined to His power or His majesty, although they are undoubtedly awe-inspiring. It encompasses every aspect of His character—His love, His grace, His mercy, and His faithfulness. It is revealed in the intricacies of creation, the beauty of redemption, and the promise of eternity. His greatness knows no bounds, reaching into every corner of existence and beyond.

As we meditate on the greatness of God, we are called to respond with reverence, gratitude, and worship. We are reminded of our smallness in comparison to His vastness, yet we are also assured of His intimate presence in our lives. In His greatness, we find comfort, strength, and hope, knowing that He holds all things in His hands and works all things for the good of those who love Him.

Heavenly Father, we stand in awe of Your greatness, which surpasses all understanding. Thank You for revealing Yourself to us and inviting us into relationship with You. In Jesus' name, we pray. Amen.

DAY 139

Walking in Humility

"He has shown you, O mortal, what is good. And what does the Lord require of you? To act justly and to love mercy and to walk humbly with your God." - Micah 6:8 (NIV)

To walk in humility is to embrace a posture of surrender and reverence before our Creator. It is a recognition of our dependence on Him and an acknowledgment of His sovereignty over our lives.

Humility is not weakness; it is strength under control. It is the quiet confidence that comes from knowing our identity and worth in Christ, yet willingly laying down our pride and self-interest for the sake of others. Jesus, our ultimate example, humbled Himself to the point of death on the cross, demonstrating the incomparable power of humility to bring about redemption and reconciliation.

Walking in humility requires a continual surrender of our own agendas and desires to align with God's will. It means valuing others above ourselves, extending grace and forgiveness even when it's difficult, and being quick to listen and slow to speak. Humility enables us to see beyond ourselves and to recognize the inherent worth and dignity of every person as fellow image-bearers of God.

Heavenly Father, teach us to walk humbly before You, recognizing Your sovereignty and our dependence on Your grace. Give us the strength to lay down our pride and self-interest, and to embrace a spirit of humility in all that we do. May our lives be a reflection of Your love and mercy, bringing glory to Your name. In Jesus' name, we pray. Amen.

DAY 140

The Call to Holiness

"But just as he who called you is holy, so be holy in all you do; for it is written: 'Be holy, because I am holy.'" - 1 Peter 1:15-16 (NIV)

1 Peter 1:15-16 reminds us that our calling as Christians is not just to believe in Christ but to be transformed by His grace into holy beings, set apart for His purposes. Holiness is not merely about adhering to a set of rules or rituals; it is about embodying the purity, righteousness, and love of God in our thoughts, words, and actions.

To be holy is to strive for moral excellence and spiritual wholeness, aligning our lives with the will of God. It requires a continual surrender of our desires and ambitions to His perfect plan, allowing His Spirit to work within us to conform us to the image of Christ. Holiness is a journey of growth and sanctification, marked by repentance, obedience, and a deepening intimacy with God.

As we respond to the call to holiness, we are called to live lives that are distinct from the patterns of the world. Our choices, our priorities, and our attitudes should reflect the values of the Kingdom of God. We are called to be a light in the darkness, demonstrating the transformative power of God's love through our holy living.

Heavenly Father, thank You for calling us to a life of holiness and righteousness. Give us the strength and courage to live as holy people, set apart for Your purposes. Help us to continually surrender ourselves to Your will and to be transformed by Your Spirit into the likeness of Christ. May our lives be a testimony to Your grace and love. In Jesus' name, we pray. Amen.

DAY 141

God's Justice

"He has shown you, O mortal, what is good. And what does the Lord require of you? To act justly and to love mercy and to walk humbly with your God." - Micah 6:8 (NIV)

Micah 6:8 beautifully encapsulates the essence of God's justice. As believers, we are called not only to acknowledge God's justice but to embody it in our lives. But what does it mean to live justly in the eyes of God?

God's justice is rooted in His character of righteousness and fairness. It is not merely about punishment for wrongdoing but also about restoration, reconciliation, and the establishment of righteousness in the world. God's justice is a manifestation of His love for His creation, ensuring that every person is treated with dignity and equity.

As followers of Christ, we are called to be agents of God's justice in the world. This means standing up against injustice, oppression, and inequality wherever we encounter it. It means advocating for the marginalized, speaking out against systems that perpetuate injustice, and working towards a society where all people are treated with fairness and compassion.

Heavenly Father, we thank You for Your justice, which upholds righteousness and mercy. Help us to live in accordance with Your will, acting justly, loving mercy, and walking humbly with You. Give us the courage to stand up for what is right and to be a voice for the voiceless. May Your justice reign in our hearts and in our world. In Jesus' name, we pray. Amen.

DAY 142

Sharing the Good News

"But you will receive power when the Holy Spirit comes on you; and you will be my witnesses in Jerusalem, and in all Judea and Samaria, and to the ends of the earth." - Acts 1:8 (NIV)

It is a reminder that the message of salvation is not meant to be kept to ourselves but shared with others, both near and far. As followers of Christ, we are called to be His witnesses, proclaiming His love, grace, and redemption to all people.

Sharing the good news is not just a duty; it is a privilege and a joy. It is the greatest story ever told, the story of God's relentless pursuit of humanity, culminating in the sacrifice of His Son for our salvation. As recipients of this incredible gift, we have the opportunity to share it with others, inviting them into the abundant life found in Jesus Christ.

But sharing the good news goes beyond mere words; it is a lifestyle characterized by love, compassion, and authenticity. It is about living out the truth of the gospel in our daily lives, being a living testimony to the transformative power of Jesus Christ.

Heavenly Father, thank You for the gift of salvation through Your Son, Jesus Christ. Help us to be bold and courageous in sharing the good news with others, both in our words and in our actions. Fill us with Your Holy Spirit, that we may be effective witnesses to Your love and grace. May Your kingdom come and Your will be done on earth as it is in heaven. In Jesus' name, we pray. Amen.

DAY 143

God's Eternal Kingdom

"But our citizenship is in heaven. And we eagerly await a Savior from there, the Lord Jesus Christ." - Philippians 3:20 (NIV)

Philippians 3:20 reminds us that as believers, our ultimate allegiance is not to any earthly kingdom or nation, but to God's eternal kingdom. This truth is both comforting and transformative. It reassures us that our identity and destiny are secure in Christ, and it challenges us to live with a kingdom mindset here on earth.

God's eternal kingdom is not a distant, abstract concept; it is a present reality that shapes our perspective and priorities. It is a kingdom marked by righteousness, peace, and joy in the Holy Spirit (Romans 14:17), where the reign of God's love knows no end. Unlike the kingdoms of this world, which rise and fall, God's kingdom is everlasting and unshakeable.

As citizens of God's kingdom, we are called to live in a manner that reflects its values and principles. We are called to love God with all our heart, soul, and mind, and to love our neighbors as ourselves (Matthew 22:37-39). We are called to seek justice, to show mercy, and to walk humbly with our God (Micah 6:8). And we are called to proclaim the good news of the kingdom, inviting others to experience the hope and salvation found in Jesus Christ.

Help us to live in a manner worthy of this calling, seeking first Your kingdom and Your righteousness in all that we do. Give us the courage to be ambassadors of Your love and grace, sharing the hope of salvation with a world in need. In Jesus' name, we pray. Amen.

DAY 144

The Power of Faith

"Now faith is confidence in what we hope for and assurance about what we do not see." - Hebrews 11:1 (NIV)

Faith is the bedrock upon which our relationship with God is built, the fuel that ignites our spiritual journey, and the antidote to fear and doubt.

Faith is what enables us to see beyond the natural circumstances of life and to embrace the supernatural possibilities that God offers. It empowers us to face challenges with courage, knowing that God is faithful to fulfill His promises. Through faith, we are able to overcome obstacles, endure trials, and experience the miraculous work of God in our lives.

The power of faith lies not in our own strength or ability but in the unwavering trust we place in God. It is the assurance that He is with us, guiding us, and working all things together for our good. Faith moves mountains, breaks chains, and transforms lives, for nothing is impossible for those who believe.

Heavenly Father, thank You for the gift of faith that enables us to trust in Your goodness and provision. Increase our faith, Lord, and help us to rely completely on You in every aspect of our lives. Give us the courage to step out in obedience and to believe for the impossible, knowing that with You, all things are possible. In Jesus' name, we pray. Amen.

DAY 145

Jesus' Teachings on Love

"A new command I give you: Love one another. As I have loved you, so you must love one another." - John 13:34 (NIV)

This command is not a suggestion or a recommendation; it is a foundational principle of Christian faith. Jesus calls us to love others with the same selfless, sacrificial love with which He has loved us.

Jesus' teachings on love are revolutionary because they challenge us to move beyond mere affection or sentimentality. His love is active, intentional, and inclusive. It transcends boundaries of race, ethnicity, social status, and even personal preference. It is a love that seeks the well-being and flourishing of others above our own desires.

When we look at the life of Jesus, we see love in action. He healed the sick, comforted the brokenhearted, and welcomed the outcast. He demonstrated compassion for the marginalized and forgiveness for the repentant. His entire ministry was a testament to the transformative power of love.

Lord Jesus, thank You for Your teachings on love, which challenge and inspire us to live lives of compassion and grace. Help us to embody Your love in all that we do, extending kindness and mercy to those around us. Fill our hearts with Your love so that we may be vessels of Your light in a world that so desperately needs it. In Your holy name, we pray. Amen.

DAY 146

The Joy of Fellowship

"How good and pleasant it is when God's people live together in unity!" - Psalm 133:1 (NIV)

There is a unique and indescribable warmth that comes from gathering together with fellow brothers and sisters in Christ. It's a joy that surpasses mere companionship; it's a deep sense of belonging, connection, and shared purpose rooted in our common faith.

The joy of fellowship extends beyond the surface level interactions. It's about experiencing God's presence in community, where hearts are united in worship, prayer, and mutual encouragement. In fellowship, we find strength for the journey, comfort in times of trial, and celebration in moments of triumph. It's a foretaste of the heavenly unity we will experience in eternity.

As we come together in fellowship, we reflect the image of God, who exists eternally in perfect unity as Father, Son, and Holy Spirit. Our unity as believers testifies to the transformative power of the gospel, breaking down barriers of division and ushering in a foretaste of God's kingdom on earth.

Heavenly Father, we thank You for the gift of fellowship among believers. Help us to cherish and nurture the bonds of unity that You have established among us. May our interactions be filled with Your love, grace, and joy, drawing others into the beauty of community. Guide us as we seek to grow together in faith and serve Your kingdom purpose. In Jesus' name, we pray. Amen.

DAY 147

God's Presence with Us

"The Lord himself goes before you and will be with you; he will never leave you nor forsake you. Do not be afraid; do not be discouraged." - Deuteronomy 31:8 (NIV)

In the hustle and bustle of life, it's easy to feel alone and overwhelmed. But Deuteronomy 31:8 reassures us of a comforting truth: God's presence is not just a concept; it's a promise. He goes before us, walks beside us, and remains with us through every trial and triumph. The omnipotent Creator of the universe chooses to dwell among His people, offering solace, guidance, and companionship.

God's presence is not limited by time or space; it transcends our circumstances and permeates every aspect of our lives. In moments of joy, He celebrates with us. In times of sorrow, He comforts us. In the midst of uncertainty, He offers peace that surpasses understanding. His presence is a source of strength, a beacon of hope, and a constant reminder that we are never alone.

As we cultivate an awareness of God's presence, we begin to see His hand at work in the world around us. We recognize His whispers in the stillness, His guidance in the chaos, and His love in every interaction.

Heavenly Father, thank You for the assurance of Your presence with us. In moments of doubt and fear, help us to cling to the promise that You will never leave us nor forsake us. May Your presence be our strength and our song, guiding us through every season of life. In Jesus' name, we pray. Amen.

DAY 148

Learning from Biblical Figures

"Now these things occurred as examples to keep us from setting our hearts on evil things as they did." - 1 Corinthians 10:6 (NIV)

Through their lives, we glean valuable lessons that resonate with us today. 1 Corinthians 10:6 reminds us that these biblical figures are not just characters in a book but examples for us to learn from. Their experiences serve as mirrors reflecting our own struggles, temptations, and victories.

Consider the faith of Abraham, who trusted God's promise even when it seemed impossible. Or the courage of Esther, who risked her life to save her people. Each of these biblical figures faced trials and tribulations, yet their unwavering faith and obedience to God offer us inspiration and guidance.

Learning from biblical figures involves more than just studying their stories; it requires us to internalize their lessons and apply them to our own lives. As we delve into their narratives, we discover timeless truths about God's faithfulness, grace, and sovereignty. We see the consequences of sin and the rewards of obedience. We learn that despite our weaknesses, God can use us to accomplish His purposes if we trust and obey Him.

Heavenly Father, thank You for the stories of faith and courage recorded in Your Word. Help us to learn from the examples of biblical figures and to apply their lessons to our own lives. Give us wisdom and discernment as we study Your Word, and empower us to live lives that honor and glorify You. In Jesus' name, we pray. Amen.

DAY 149

God's Grace in the Old Testament

"But he said to me, 'My grace is sufficient for you, for my power is made perfect in weakness.' Therefore I will boast all the more gladly about my weaknesses, so that Christ's power may rest on me." - 2 Corinthians 12:9 (NIV)

Throughout the pages of ancient scriptures, we witness God's relentless pursuit of His people, His unwavering love, and His boundless grace. From Genesis to Malachi, the Old Testament resounds with stories of redemption, forgiveness, and unmerited favor.

Consider the story of Noah, who found favor in the eyes of the Lord amidst a world consumed by wickedness. Despite the prevailing evil, God extended His grace to Noah and his family, preserving them through the floodwaters and offering a new beginning for humanity.

Despite his shortcomings, God's grace remained steadfast, offering forgiveness and restoration time and time again. David's psalms resonate with the theme of God's enduring grace, as he declares, "The Lord is gracious and compassionate, slow to anger and rich in love" (Psalm 145:8, NIV).

Heavenly Father, thank You for Your unending grace that stretches across the ages, from the beginning of time to eternity. Help us to recognize Your grace at work in the stories of the Old Testament and in our lives today. May we be conduits of Your grace, sharing Your love and mercy with a world in need. In Jesus' name, we pray. Amen.

DAY 150

The Promises of God

"Be strong and courageous. Do not be afraid or terrified because of them, for the LORD your God goes with you; he will never leave you nor forsake you." - Deuteronomy 31:6 (NIV)

In times of uncertainty, fear, or doubt, we can take solace in the assurance that God is with us every step of the way. His promises are not empty words; they are steadfast anchors for our souls, grounding us in His unchanging love and faithfulness.

The promises of God are like precious gems scattered throughout the pages of Scripture, waiting to be discovered and cherished. From His promise of salvation and eternal life to His pledge to provide for our needs and give us peace, every word spoken by God is a declaration of His unwavering commitment to His children.

When we face trials or challenges, it can be easy to lose sight of God's promises. But even in the darkest moments, His light shines bright, offering hope and comfort. As we meditate on His promises, our faith is strengthened, and our hearts are filled with courage to press on, knowing that He who promised is faithful.

Heavenly Father, thank You for Your promises that sustain us and give us hope. Help us to trust in Your faithfulness, knowing that You are always with us and that Your word never fails. Give us strength and courage to hold fast to Your promises, especially in times of uncertainty. May Your promises be a source of comfort and assurance in our lives. In Jesus' name, we pray. Amen.

DAY 151

The Role of Angels

"For he will command his angels concerning you to guard you in all your ways." - Psalm 91:11 (NIV)

God commands His angels to protect and guide us. Angels are not just ethereal beings in stories; they are active participants in God's plan, serving as messengers, protectors, and ministers to His people.

Throughout Scripture, we see angels carrying out God's commands with unwavering obedience. They announced the birth of Jesus to Mary and Joseph, provided comfort and strength to Jesus in the wilderness, and rolled away the stone from His tomb, proclaiming His resurrection. These celestial beings play a crucial role in bridging the divine with the earthly, ensuring that God's will is accomplished.

Angels are also assigned to watch over us. They guard us in our daily lives, often unseen but always present. This divine protection should fill us with a sense of awe and gratitude. Knowing that God cares so deeply for us that He sends His angels to watch over us should inspire us to live with courage and confidence, trusting in His sovereign care.

Heavenly Father, thank You for the gift of Your angels who guard and guide us. Help us to remember that we are never alone, and that Your divine protection surrounds us always. Fill our hearts with gratitude for Your constant care, and give us the faith to trust in Your provision. May we live each day with the confidence that Your angels are watching over us. In Jesus' name, we pray. Amen.

DAY 152

Endurance in Faith

"Let us run with endurance the race that is set before us, looking to Jesus, the founder and perfecter of our faith." - Hebrews 12:1-2 (ESV)

Life's race is often filled with obstacles, trials, and moments of weariness. Yet, we are called to run this race with perseverance, fixing our eyes on Jesus, who is both the author and perfecter of our faith. He endured the cross, scorning its shame, and now sits at the right hand of the throne of God. His example fuels our resolve to press on, no matter the challenges we face.

Endurance in faith is not about never feeling weak or discouraged; it's about continuing to trust God even when the road is hard and the destination seems far. It's about holding on to His promises and believing that He is working all things for our good, even when we cannot see the full picture. This kind of faith is built through trials, as we learn to rely not on our own strength, but on God's unending grace and power.

In the moments when you feel like giving up, remember that Jesus is with you, cheering you on. His Spirit empowers you to keep going, giving you strength beyond your own.

Lord Jesus, thank You for being the perfect example of endurance and faith. When we are weary and feel like giving up, help us to fix our eyes on You. Strengthen our hearts and renew our spirits with Your grace. Help us to run with perseverance the race set before us, trusting in Your promises and relying on Your power. In Your precious name, we pray. Amen.

DAY 153

The Holy Spirit's Comfort

"And I will ask the Father, and he will give you another Advocate to help you and be with you forever—the Spirit of truth." - John 14:16-17a (NIV)

Jesus reassures His disciples—and us—that He will not leave us as orphans. He promises the Holy Spirit, our Advocate and Comforter, who will be with us forever, guiding us with truth and enveloping us in God's love.

The Holy Spirit is not a distant or abstract presence. He dwells within us, offering comfort that transcends human understanding. When our hearts are heavy with grief, fear, or uncertainty, the Holy Spirit whispers peace to our souls. He reminds us of God's promises, fills us with divine strength, and reassures us that we are never alone.

Through the Holy Spirit, we experience a closeness with God that sustains us in every circumstance. He intercedes for us with groanings too deep for words, understands our deepest needs, and wraps us in the warmth of God's embrace. This divine comfort transforms our despair into hope and our pain into resilience.

Dear Holy Spirit, we thank You for being our Comforter and Advocate. In times of trouble, fill our hearts with Your peace and remind us of the Father's love. Help us to lean on Your presence and find solace in Your unfailing support. Guide us to be instruments of Your comfort to others, sharing the hope and love we have found in You. In Jesus' name, we pray. Amen.

DAY 154

Courage in the Lord

"Have I not commanded you? Be strong and courageous. Do not be afraid; do not be discouraged, for the LORD your God will be with you wherever you go." - Joshua 1:9 (NIV)

This command is not just for Joshua; it resonates with every believer who stands at the threshold of challenges and fears. God's command to be strong and courageous is rooted in the profound truth that we are not alone. His presence is our source of courage, our reason to press on despite fear and uncertainty.

Courage in the Lord is not the absence of fear but the decision to move forward in faith, trusting in God's promises and presence. It is the strength to face the giants in our lives—be they challenges, uncertainties, or deep-seated fears—with the assurance that God is with us. His words, "Do not be afraid; do not be discouraged," remind us that courage is a choice grounded in the unshakeable foundation of His love and faithfulness.

When we embrace courage in the Lord, we align our hearts with His power and grace. This courage empowers us to step into the unknown, to stand firm in our faith, and to act according to His will, even when the path ahead seems uncertain.

Heavenly Father, thank You for the promise of Your presence, which gives us the courage to face any challenge. Help us to be strong and courageous, trusting in Your unfailing love and guidance. Fill our hearts with Your peace and embolden us to take steps of faith, knowing that You go before us and will never leave us. In Jesus' name, we pray. Amen.

DAY 155

The Gift of Salvation

"For it is by grace you have been saved, through faith—and this is not from yourselves, it is the gift of God." - Ephesians 2:8 (NIV)

This profound truth is the cornerstone of our Christian faith, a divine declaration of God's boundless love and mercy. We are saved not by our efforts or good works, but by placing our faith in Jesus Christ, who paid the ultimate price for our sins on the cross.

The gift of salvation is the greatest act of love the world has ever known. Imagine the depth of God's love that would move Him to sacrifice His only Son so that we might have eternal life. This gift transforms our lives, lifting us from the depths of sin and despair to the heights of hope and eternal joy. Through Jesus, we are forgiven, redeemed, and made new.

As recipients of this incredible gift, our hearts should overflow with gratitude and a desire to live for Him. Salvation is not just a ticket to heaven; it is an invitation to a transformed life, filled with purpose and guided by the Holy Spirit. It calls us to share this good news with others, to be beacons of His love and grace in a world that desperately needs it.

Heavenly Father, thank You for the incredible gift of salvation, given through Your grace and received by faith. Help us to live in the light of this truth, filled with gratitude and a desire to share Your love with others. Empower us by Your Holy Spirit to be witnesses of Your grace, reflecting the hope and joy we have in You. In Jesus' name, we pray. Amen.

DAY 156

The Role of the Church

"And let us consider how we may spur one another on toward love and good deeds, not giving up meeting together, as some are in the habit of doing, but encouraging one another—and all the more as you see the Day approaching." - Hebrews 10:24-25 (NIV)

The role of the church extends far beyond Sunday services; it encompasses the daily lives and interactions of its members, fostering an environment where faith can flourish and love can be shared.

The church is a sanctuary where we find spiritual nourishment and strength. It is a place where we come together to worship God, to learn from His word, and to support one another in our journeys of faith. Within this sacred community, we are reminded that we are not alone. We have brothers and sisters who stand with us, pray for us, and help us bear our burdens.

Moreover, the church is called to be the hands and feet of Jesus in the world. It is through the church that we can serve others, extend grace, and shine the light of Christ into dark places. Whether it's through local outreach, global missions, or simply being there for a friend in need, the church plays a crucial role in fulfilling God's command to love our neighbors as ourselves.

Help us to appreciate the importance of coming together, encouraging one another, and working collectively to advance Your kingdom. Guide us to actively participate and contribute to our church community, using our gifts to honor You and bless others. In Jesus' name, we pray. Amen.

DAY 157

The Beatitudes

"Blessed are the poor in spirit, for theirs is the kingdom of heaven." - Matthew 5:3 (NIV)

They stand in stark contrast to the world's definitions of success and happiness, inviting us into a deeper, more meaningful way of life. Each Beatitude begins with the word "blessed," which can also be understood as "happy" or "fortunate." But this blessedness is not about superficial joy; it is about the deep, abiding joy that comes from living in alignment with God's kingdom values.

"Blessed are the poor in spirit, for theirs is the kingdom of heaven." This first Beatitude sets the tone for the rest. To be "poor in spirit" means to recognize our spiritual poverty, our need for God. It is a call to humility and dependence on Him. The promise that accompanies this Beatitude is extraordinary: the kingdom of heaven belongs to those who acknowledge their need for God.

The Beatitudes continue to describe a life marked by mourning over sin, meekness, a hunger and thirst for righteousness, mercy, purity in heart, peacemaking, and perseverance under persecution. Each of these qualities draws us closer to God and transforms our character to reflect His love and grace.

Heavenly Father, thank You for the teachings of the Beatitudes, which guide us toward true blessedness. Give us the humility to recognize our need for You, the compassion to show mercy, and the courage to pursue righteousness and peace. May our lives reflect Your kingdom values, bringing glory to Your name. In Jesus' name, we pray. Amen.

DAY 158

Walking in the Spirit

"So I say, walk by the Spirit, and you will not gratify the desires of the flesh." - Galatians 5:16 (NIV)

Galatians 5:16 encourages us to embrace this divine guidance, promising that by doing so, we will rise above the temptations and struggles of our earthly desires.

Imagine the peace and joy that comes from living in constant communion with the Holy Spirit. It means surrendering our will and desires to God's perfect plan, trusting that His Spirit within us will lead us on the path of righteousness. Walking in the Spirit transforms our lives from the inside out, producing the fruits of love, joy, peace, patience, kindness, goodness, faithfulness, gentleness, and self-control.

This journey is not always easy. The battle between our flesh and the Spirit is real and ongoing. However, when we choose to walk in the Spirit, we are not alone. The Holy Spirit is our helper, comforter, and guide, empowering us to overcome the desires of the flesh and live in a way that honors God.

Walking in the Spirit also means being attuned to His voice, responding to His promptings, and being obedient to His leading.

Heavenly Father, thank You for the gift of Your Holy Spirit who dwells within us. Help us to walk by the Spirit, living lives that reflect Your love and grace. Guide our thoughts, words, and actions, and give us the strength to overcome the desires of the flesh. May we be sensitive to Your Spirit's leading and obedient to Your will. In Jesus' name, we pray. Amen.

DAY 159

The Power of the Cross

"For the message of the cross is foolishness to those who are perishing, but to us who are being saved it is the power of God." -
1 Corinthians 1:18 (NIV)

In 1 Corinthians 1:18, Paul reminds us that while the world may see the cross as foolishness, we who believe understand it as the power of God for salvation. The cross is where Jesus, the spotless Lamb, took upon Himself the sins of the world, transforming death into the gateway to eternal life.

The power of the cross lies in its ability to reconcile us to God. Through Jesus' sacrifice, the chasm between humanity and God was bridged. It was on the cross that Jesus uttered, "It is finished," signifying the completion of His redemptive work. His death and resurrection defeated the power of sin and death, offering us forgiveness, freedom, and new life.

Reflecting on the power of the cross, we are reminded of the depth of God's love for us. It compels us to live differently, to embrace a life of gratitude and service. The cross calls us to lay down our burdens, our sins, and our fears at the feet of Jesus, trusting in the transformative power of His sacrifice.

Heavenly Father, thank You for the power of the cross and the sacrifice of Your Son, Jesus. May the message of the cross transform our hearts and compel us to live lives that honor You. Give us the courage to share this powerful message with others, so they too may experience the hope and salvation found in Jesus. In His precious name, we pray. Amen.

DAY 160

The Importance of Hope

"May the God of hope fill you with all joy and peace as you trust in him, so that you may overflow with hope by the power of the Holy Spirit." - Romans 15:13 (NIV)

Romans 15:13 beautifully encapsulates the essence of hope that comes from God—a hope that fills us with joy and peace as we place our trust in Him. This divine hope is not a fleeting feeling but a steadfast assurance rooted in the promises of our faithful Father.

In a world often filled with uncertainty and despair, hope lights our path and anchors our souls. It gives us the strength to face each day, confident that God is working all things for our good. Hope reminds us that no matter how dark the night, the dawn of God's love and mercy is always on the horizon.

The importance of hope cannot be overstated. It fuels our perseverance, inspires our dreams, and nurtures our faith. When we hold onto hope, we are declaring our trust in God's perfect plan and His unwavering love for us. This hope is not passive; it actively shapes our attitudes and actions, prompting us to look beyond our present circumstances to the glorious future God has in store.

Heavenly Father, we thank You for being the God of hope. Fill our hearts with Your joy and peace as we trust in You. Help us to overflow with hope by the power of the Holy Spirit, especially in times of difficulty. May our lives be a testimony of Your faithfulness, and may we be bearers of hope to those around us. In Jesus' name, we pray. Amen.

DAY 161

God's Healing Power

"Heal me, LORD, and I will be healed; save me and I will be saved, for you are the one I praise." - Jeremiah 17:14 (NIV)

concept of God's healing power is not merely physical; it encompasses the restoration of body, mind, and spirit. Our Heavenly Father is not only able but willing to bring healing to every aspect of our being.

God's healing power is a testament to His boundless love and compassion for His children. Throughout Scripture, we see countless examples of His miraculous healing touch, from the blind receiving sight to the lame walking again. These miracles serve as a powerful reminder that nothing is impossible for our God.

But God's healing extends beyond the physical realm. He heals the brokenhearted, comforts the grieving, and restores the weary soul. His healing touch brings peace in the midst of turmoil, strength in times of weakness, and hope in moments of despair. In His presence, there is healing balm for every wound and restoration for every brokenness.

Heavenly Father, we come before You, acknowledging our need for Your healing touch in our lives. Whether we are battling sickness, emotional pain, or spiritual brokenness, we know that You are the ultimate healer. We ask for Your healing power to flow through us, bringing restoration and wholeness to every area of our lives. May Your healing presence be felt in our hearts and minds today and always. In Jesus' name, we pray. Amen.

DAY 162

The Role of Prophets

"Surely the Sovereign LORD does nothing without revealing his plan to his servants the prophets." - Amos 3:7 (NIV)

These individuals were divinely appointed to speak on behalf of God, delivering His messages of warning, guidance, and hope to His people.

Prophets served as God's mouthpieces, calling His people to repentance, proclaiming His judgments, and foretelling future events. They were instrumental in shaping the course of history and pointing people back to God's truth and righteousness. Despite facing opposition and persecution, prophets remained faithful to their calling, unwavering in their commitment to speak God's word with boldness and conviction.

Today, while the office of prophets in the same sense as in the Old Testament may not be as prevalent, the principles of prophetic ministry still hold true. As Christians, we are called to be prophetic voices in our generation, boldly proclaiming God's truth and standing up for justice and righteousness. We are called to speak out against injustice, to challenge oppression, and to bring comfort to the brokenhearted.

Heavenly Father, thank You for the example of the prophets who faithfully spoke Your word throughout history. Help us to be bold and courageous in proclaiming Your truth in our generation. Give us wisdom and discernment to know when and how to speak out against injustice and oppression. May our lives be a testimony to Your grace and mercy. In Jesus' name, we pray. Amen.

DAY 163

The Value of Scripture

"All Scripture is God-breathed and is useful for teaching, rebuking, correcting and training in righteousness, so that the servant of God may be thoroughly equipped for every good work."
- 2 Timothy 3:16-17 (NIV)

The Bible is not merely a collection of words penned by human authors; it is the very word of God, inspired by the Holy Spirit. It serves as our guidebook for life, providing wisdom, insight, and direction for every aspect of our journey with Christ.

The value of Scripture lies not only in its divine origin but also in its practical application. It is a lamp to our feet and a light to our path, illuminating the way forward in times of darkness and confusion. Through its pages, we encounter the living God and His redemptive plan for humanity, discovering His love, grace, and truth.

Scripture is a powerful tool for transformation, shaping our minds and hearts according to God's will. It teaches us, convicts us, corrects us, and trains us in righteousness, equipping us to live lives that honor and glorify God. As we immerse ourselves in the Word, we are empowered to walk in obedience, to resist temptation, and to bear fruit that reflects the character of Christ.

Heavenly Father, we thank You for the precious gift of Your word. Help us to treasure and value Scripture as the divine revelation of Your heart and mind. May Your word dwell richly in us, guiding us, transforming us, and equipping us for every good work. In Jesus' name, we pray. Amen.

DAY 164

Embracing God's Calling

"For we are God's handiwork, created in Christ Jesus to do good works, which God prepared in advance for us to do." - Ephesians 2:10 (NIV)

We are not merely products of chance or circumstance; we are intentional creations designed by the Master Craftsman Himself. Embracing God's calling means recognizing and accepting the specific role He has ordained for us in His grand plan of redemption and restoration.

God's calling is not limited to pastors, missionaries, or spiritual leaders. It encompasses every aspect of our lives, from our careers and relationships to our daily interactions and endeavors. When we surrender to His calling, we open ourselves up to a life of meaning, fulfillment, and eternal significance.

Discovering and embracing God's calling requires openness to His leading and a willingness to step out in faith. It may involve leaving behind comfort zones, overcoming fears, and trusting in His provision and guidance.

Heavenly Father, thank You for the privilege of being called by You to participate in Your work. Give us ears to hear Your voice and hearts that are willing to obey Your leading. May our lives be a reflection of Your love and grace, bringing glory to Your name. In Jesus' name, we pray. Amen.

DAY 165

The Authority of Jesus

"Then Jesus came to them and said, 'All authority in heaven and on earth has been given to me.'" - Matthew 28:18 (NIV)

As believers, we are called to recognize and submit to His authority in every aspect of our lives. Jesus' authority extends beyond earthly realms; it encompasses the heavens and the earth. He is the King of kings and the Lord of lords, ruling with power, wisdom, and love.

Understanding the authority of Jesus is essential for our faith journey. It reminds us that He is not merely a historical figure or a moral teacher but the Son of God, who holds the keys to life and death. His authority is supreme, and His word is final. When we acknowledge His lordship, we align ourselves with His divine will and experience the abundant life He promises.

Jesus exercised His authority not through force or coercion but through humility and servanthood. He healed the sick, raised the dead, and preached the good news of the kingdom, demonstrating His power to transform lives and bring salvation.

Lord Jesus, we acknowledge Your authority over heaven and earth. Help us to submit to Your lordship in every area of our lives, trusting in Your wisdom and sovereignty. May Your authority be our source of strength and confidence as we follow You faithfully. Guide us by Your Spirit and lead us in the paths of righteousness. In Your holy name, we pray. Amen.

DAY 166

The Gift of Peace

"Peace I leave with you; my peace I give you. I do not give to you as the world gives. Do not let your hearts be troubled and do not be afraid." - John 14:27 (NIV)

This is not the fleeting, conditional peace that the world offers, but a deep, abiding peace that settles within our souls. It is the assurance that, no matter the storms we face, we are held securely in the loving arms of our Savior. This peace calms our fears, soothes our anxieties, and fills us with a profound sense of well-being.

The gift of peace from Jesus is a reminder that we are not alone. In a world filled with chaos and uncertainty, His peace stands as a beacon of hope and stability. It is the calm in the midst of the storm, the quiet confidence that God is in control, and the serene assurance that His plans for us are good. This peace is rooted in the knowledge of His presence, His promises, and His power.

To live in this peace, we must learn to trust Jesus completely, surrendering our worries and fears to Him. It means allowing His words to penetrate our hearts and letting His love cast out all fear.

Lord Jesus, thank You for the precious gift of Your peace. Help us to rest in Your presence and to trust in Your unfailing love. Calm our hearts and minds, and let Your peace reign in every area of our lives. Teach us to cast our cares upon You, knowing that You care for us. May Your peace flow through us, bringing comfort and hope to those around us. In Your holy name, we pray. Amen.

DAY 167

Spiritual Contentment

"I have learned to be content whatever the circumstances. I know what it is to be in need, and I know what it is to have plenty. I have learned the secret of being content in any and every situation, whether well fed or hungry, whether living in plenty or in want." - Philippians 4:11-12 (NIV)

The apostle Paul shares his journey of learning to find contentment in every circumstance, regardless of whether he had an abundance or was in need. This spiritual contentment is not dependent on external factors but is rooted in a deep trust in God's provision and sovereignty.

Spiritual contentment is the state of being satisfied and at peace with what we have and where we are in life, knowing that our ultimate fulfillment comes from our relationship with God. It is a contentment that transcends material possessions, worldly achievements, or fleeting pleasures. Instead, it stems from a heart that is anchored in faith, gratitude, and a sense of purpose in God's kingdom.

In a culture that constantly bombards us with messages of dissatisfaction and the pursuit of more, cultivating spiritual contentment becomes a counter-cultural act of defiance.

Heavenly Father, thank You for the gift of spiritual contentment that comes from knowing You. Teach us to find our satisfaction in You alone, rather than in the things of this world. May we learn, like Paul, the secret of being content in every situation. In Jesus' name, we pray. Amen.

DAY 168

The Lord's Prayer

"This, then, is how you should pray: 'Our Father in heaven, hallowed be your name, your kingdom come, your will be done, on earth as it is in heaven.'" - Matthew 6:9-10 (NIV)

The Lord's Prayer, given to us by Jesus in Matthew 6:9-13, is a profound and powerful template for our daily conversations with God. It begins with addressing God as "Our Father," reminding us of the intimate relationship we have with Him. He is not a distant deity but a loving Father who desires to be close to His children.

"Hallowed be your name" calls us to worship and revere God, recognizing His holiness and majesty. It's a declaration that sets the tone for our prayer, centering our hearts on who God is. When we pray "your kingdom come, your will be done," we are surrendering our desires and aligning ourselves with God's perfect plan, inviting His reign into our lives and circumstances.

"Give us today our daily bread" is a humble acknowledgment of our dependence on God for our daily needs. It's a reminder that every provision comes from His hand. "Forgive us our debts, as we also have forgiven our debtors" teaches us about the importance of seeking forgiveness and extending it to others. It calls us to live in the freedom of God's grace and to pass that grace on to those around us.

"And lead us not into temptation, but deliver us from the evil one" is a plea for God's protection and guidance. It's a recognition of our need for His strength to overcome the challenges and trials of life.

Heavenly Father, thank You for teaching us how to pray through the Lord's Prayer. Help us to approach You with the reverence and intimacy that this prayer embodies. Guide us to align our lives with Your will, trust You for our needs, extend forgiveness, and seek Your protection. May this prayer transform our hearts and draw us closer to You. In Jesus' name, we pray. Amen.

DAY 169

Jesus' Miracles

"Jesus looked at them and said, 'With man this is impossible, but with God all things are possible.'" - Matthew 19:26 (NIV)

Throughout the Gospels, we see Jesus performing miracles that defy human understanding and reveal the limitless scope of God's love for His creation. From healing the sick and raising the dead to calming storms and multiplying loaves, each miracle serves as a signpost pointing to the reality of His kingdom breaking into the world.

These miracles are not merely displays of supernatural power; they are expressions of Jesus' deep empathy and desire to alleviate human suffering. In every miracle, we catch a glimpse of His heart for the broken, the marginalized, and the outcast. His miracles were not just acts of mercy; they were invitations to encounter His transformative love and power.

As followers of Christ, we are called to emulate His example by participating in His mission of restoration and reconciliation. While we may not perform the same miraculous feats as Jesus, we are empowered by His Spirit to continue His work of healing and hope in the world around us.

Heavenly Father, thank You for the example of Jesus and His miraculous works that reveal Your power and compassion. Empower us by Your Spirit to follow His example, bringing healing and hope to those in need. Use us as instruments of Your miraculous grace, that Your kingdom may come and Your will be done on earth as it is in heaven. In Jesus' name, we pray. Amen.

DAY 170

God's Covenant with Us

"But this is the covenant that I will make with the house of Israel after those days, says the LORD: I will put my law within them, and I will write it on their hearts; and I will be their God, and they shall be my people." - Jeremiah 31:33 (NRSV)

Throughout history, God has entered into covenants with humanity, promising His presence, protection, and provision. But the covenant described by Jeremiah is unique in its intimacy and depth, for it is not merely an agreement written on stone tablets but a transformation of the heart.

God's covenant with us is a testament to His unending desire for relationship with His beloved creation. It is a promise to dwell within us, to guide us, and to shape us into the image of Christ. Through His covenant, God invites us into a life of abundance and purpose, offering forgiveness for our sins and empowering us to live as His chosen people.

As recipients of God's covenant, we are called to respond with gratitude, obedience, and devotion. We are called to walk in faithfulness, allowing His word to dwell richly within us and to permeate every aspect of our lives.

Gracious God, thank You for the covenant You have made with us, sealing us as Your own and promising to be our God forever. Help us to walk in obedience and faithfulness, trusting in Your unfailing love and guidance. May Your covenant shape our lives and draw us ever closer to You. In Jesus' name, we pray. Amen.

DAY 171

Trusting in God's Timing

"But they who wait for the LORD shall renew their strength; they shall mount up with wings like eagles; they shall run and not be weary; they shall walk and not faint." - Isaiah 40:31 (ESV)

In a world that often demands instant results and immediate gratification, waiting can feel uncomfortable and challenging. However, when we wait upon the Lord, our strength is renewed, and we are uplifted on wings of faith.

Trusting in God's timing means surrendering our desires, plans, and timelines to His perfect will. It requires faith to believe that His timing is always best, even when it doesn't align with our own expectations. Just as a seed planted in the ground must wait for the right season to bloom, we too must patiently wait for God's timing to unfold in our lives.

Waiting on God is not passive; it is an active expression of our faith and dependence on Him. It is a time of preparation, growth, and refinement as we learn to lean on His promises and trust in His sovereignty. When we relinquish control and embrace His timing, we experience the peace that surpasses all understanding.

Heavenly Father, teach us to trust in Your timing, knowing that Your plans are perfect and Your ways are higher than ours. Give us patience to wait upon You and faith to believe that Your timing is always best. May we find strength and peace as we surrender our desires to Your will. In Jesus' name, we pray. Amen.

DAY 172

Spiritual Renewal

"Create in me a pure heart, O God, and renew a steadfast spirit within me." - Psalm 51:10 (NIV)

Just as a garden needs pruning and watering to flourish, so too our souls require renewal and refreshment to thrive in our walk with God.

Spiritual renewal is not a one-time event but a lifelong journey of growth and transformation. It involves surrendering our brokenness and sinfulness to God and allowing Him to work in us, molding us into vessels of His grace and love. It is a process of letting go of the old and embracing the new, of shedding the weight of the past and stepping into the freedom of God's redemption.

As we open our hearts to God's transforming power, He breathes new life into our weary souls. He restores our joy, strengthens our faith, and renews our passion for Him. In His presence, we find healing for our wounds, clarity in our confusion, and strength for our weakness. Through spiritual renewal, we are empowered to live lives that reflect the image of Christ and bear fruit that glorifies God.

Heavenly Father, we come before You with hearts open to Your transforming power. Create in us clean hearts and renew steadfast spirits within us, Lord. Help us to let go of the past and embrace the new life You offer us through Jesus Christ. May Your Spirit work in us, shaping us into vessels of Your grace and love. In Jesus' name, we pray. Amen.

DAY 173

The Bread of Life

"Then Jesus declared, 'I am the bread of life. Whoever comes to me will never go hungry, and whoever believes in me will never be thirsty.'" - John 6:35 (NIV)

Just as bread sustains our physical bodies, Jesus sustains our spiritual lives, providing nourishment, satisfaction, and fulfillment beyond anything this world can offer.

The imagery of bread carries rich symbolism throughout Scripture. In the Old Testament, manna provided by God sustained the Israelites in the wilderness, foreshadowing the true bread that would come down from heaven. Jesus, in calling Himself the bread of life, offers Himself as the ultimate source of sustenance, inviting all who hunger and thirst for righteousness to come and partake of Him freely.

As the bread of life, Jesus satisfies the deepest longings of our hearts. He offers forgiveness for our sins, healing for our brokenness, and purpose for our lives. Just as physical bread sustains our bodies, Jesus sustains our souls, filling us with His presence, His peace, and His joy.

Heavenly Father, thank You for the gift of Jesus, the bread of life who sustains us and satisfies our deepest hunger and thirst. Give us hearts that hunger and thirst for righteousness, and fill us with Your Holy Spirit. May we share the abundance of Your love and grace with those around us. In Jesus' name, we pray. Amen.

DAY 174

Living Water

"Jesus answered, 'Everyone who drinks this water will be thirsty again, but whoever drinks the water I give them will never thirst. Indeed, the water I give them will become in them a spring of water welling up to eternal life.'" - John 4:13-14 (NIV)

He speaks of living water, a metaphorical representation of the Holy Spirit and the eternal life found in Him. Just as physical water quenches our thirst temporarily, the living water offered by Jesus satisfies our deepest spiritual longings and sustains us for eternity.

Living water is not a finite resource that runs dry; it is an ever-flowing stream of grace, love, and truth that springs forth from the heart of God. It is the source of spiritual vitality and renewal, bringing life to our souls and refreshing us in times of drought and despair.

When we drink from the well of living water, we are filled with a sense of purpose, peace, and joy that surpasses all understanding. It is a transformational experience that quenches our spiritual thirst and leaves us craving more of God's presence in our lives.

Gracious God, thank You for the gift of living water that satisfies our deepest spiritual thirst. Fill us afresh with Your Holy Spirit and lead us to the streams of Your grace and love. Help us to drink deeply from Your wellspring of eternal life and to overflow with Your goodness to those around us. May Your living water continue to sustain us and refresh us as we journey with You. In Jesus' name, we pray. Amen.

DAY 175

God's Compassion

"But you, Lord, are a compassionate and gracious God, slow to anger, abounding in love and faithfulness." - Psalm 86:15 (NIV)

His compassion is not merely a fleeting emotion; it is a fundamental aspect of His character. God's compassion is boundless and unwavering, flowing from His infinite love and mercy toward His creation.

The compassion of God is seen throughout the pages of Scripture, from the tender care He showed to the Israelites in their times of need to the ultimate expression of compassion found in Jesus Christ. Jesus, the embodiment of God's compassion, healed the sick, fed the hungry, and comforted the brokenhearted, demonstrating God's love in tangible ways.

God's compassion extends to each one of us individually. He sees our pain, our struggles, and our fears, and He meets us with compassion and understanding. He does not turn His back on us in our moments of weakness; instead, He draws near to us with arms of love, offering comfort, healing, and hope.

Gracious God, thank You for Your boundless compassion that surrounds us like a warm embrace. Help us to experience Your compassion afresh today and to extend it to others in need. Fill our hearts with Your love and mercy, that we may be vessels of Your compassion in the world. May Your compassion be a beacon of hope to all who are hurting. In Jesus' name, we pray. Amen.

DAY 176

The Good Shepherd

"The Lord is my shepherd, I lack nothing. He makes me lie down in green pastures, he leads me beside quiet waters, he refreshes my soul. He guides me along the right paths for his name's sake." - Psalm 23:1-3 (NIV)

The imagery of the Good Shepherd speaks to the intimate relationship between God and His people, portraying His guidance, protection, and sustenance in every aspect of our lives.

Like sheep, we often find ourselves wandering aimlessly, lost in the wilderness of life's challenges and uncertainties. But our Good Shepherd knows us intimately, calling us by name and leading us with gentle hands and a compassionate heart. He guides us to places of rest and renewal, where our souls can find peace and restoration.

The Good Shepherd not only provides for our physical needs but also tends to the needs of our hearts. He knows the depths of our struggles, the burdens we carry, and the fears that plague us. Yet, He walks alongside us, offering comfort in times of sorrow, strength in times of weakness, and hope in times of despair.

Heavenly Father, thank You for being our Good Shepherd, guiding us with Your loving hand and leading us into places of peace and abundance. Give us the courage to extend Your love and care to those around us, that they too may experience the comfort and joy of knowing You as their Shepherd. In Jesus' name, we pray. Amen.

DAY 177

The Parables of Jesus

"He replied, 'The knowledge of the secrets of the kingdom of heaven has been given to you, but not to them. Whoever has will be given more, and they will have an abundance. Whoever does not have, even what they have will be taken from them.'" - Matthew 13:11-12 (NIV)

In Matthew 13:11-12, Jesus reveals the profound truth that His parables contain. They are not merely moral tales or simple anecdotes; they are windows into the mysteries of the kingdom of heaven.

Through these parables, Jesus conveys timeless truths about God's kingdom and the nature of discipleship. He uses familiar imagery from everyday life to convey deeper spiritual realities, inviting His listeners to ponder and reflect on the profound truths embedded within His stories.

Each parable is a masterpiece of divine wisdom, inviting us to delve deeper into the heart of God and His purposes for humanity. They challenge us to examine our own lives and attitudes, prompting us to align ourselves with the values and principles of the kingdom of heaven.

Heavenly Father, thank You for the gift of Jesus' parables, which illuminate the mysteries of Your kingdom. Open our hearts and minds to receive the truths You desire to reveal to us through these stories. May Your Spirit guide us as we journey deeper into the riches of Your truth. In Jesus' name, we pray. Amen.

DAY 178

Facing Trials with Joy

"Consider it pure joy, my brothers and sisters, whenever you face trials of many kinds, because you know that the testing of your faith produces perseverance." - James 1:2-3 (NIV)

It may seem counterintuitive to find joy in the midst of difficulties, but as believers, we are called to see beyond the temporary pain and to embrace the deeper purpose behind our trials.

Facing trials with joy does not mean denying or minimizing our struggles; rather, it means choosing to trust in God's sovereignty and goodness despite our circumstances. It means recognizing that God can use even the most challenging situations to refine our character, deepen our faith, and draw us closer to Him.

When we shift our perspective and view trials through the lens of faith, we can find joy in knowing that our struggles are not in vain. They serve a greater purpose in God's plan for our lives. Instead of allowing trials to defeat us, we can allow them to strengthen us, knowing that God is with us every step of the way.

Heavenly Father, thank You for the promise that You are with us in every trial we face. Give us the strength to persevere with joy, knowing that You are working all things together for our good. Help us to trust in Your wisdom and to find joy in Your presence, even when life feels overwhelming. May our faith be strengthened as we walk through trials, and may Your joy sustain us through every season. In Jesus' name, we pray. Amen.

DAY 179

The Gift of the Holy Spirit

"But the Advocate, the Holy Spirit, whom the Father will send in my name, will teach you all things and will remind you of everything I have said to you." - John 14:26 (NIV)

This gift is not merely a token of His affection or a symbol of His presence; it is the very essence of God Himself dwelling within us. The Holy Spirit is our Advocate, our Comforter, our Guide, and our Teacher. He empowers us, equips us, and transforms us from the inside out.

The gift of the Holy Spirit is not limited by time or space; it is available to all who believe in Jesus Christ as their Lord and Savior. Through the Holy Spirit, we are united with God in a profound and intimate relationship. He speaks to us in whispers of love, convicts us of sin, and empowers us to live holy and righteous lives.

As believers, we are called to walk in the power and presence of the Holy Spirit daily. He is our source of strength in times of weakness, our source of wisdom in times of confusion, and our source of comfort in times of sorrow. When we surrender our lives to His leading, He fills us with His love, joy, peace, patience, kindness, goodness, faithfulness, gentleness, and self-control.

Heavenly Father, we thank You for the precious gift of the Holy Spirit. Fill us anew with Your Spirit, and empower us to live lives that honor and glorify You. Teach us, guide us, and transform us by Your Spirit, that we may be vessels of Your love and grace in the world. In Jesus' name, we pray. Amen.

DAY 180

God's Sovereignty

"Remember the former things, those of long ago; I am God, and there is no other; I am God, and there is none like me. I make known the end from the beginning, from ancient times, what is still to come. I say, 'My purpose will stand, and I will do all that I please.'" - Isaiah 46:9-10 (NIV)

He is not bound by time or circumstance; He reigns over all creation with unmatched power and wisdom. God's sovereignty means that He is in control of all things, from the grandest cosmic events to the smallest details of our lives. Nothing happens outside of His divine plan and purpose.

Understanding God's sovereignty can be both comforting and challenging. On one hand, it assures us that we serve a God who is infinitely capable of orchestrating His will in our lives and in the world. We can trust that His plans are perfect and that He works all things together for our good, even in the midst of trials and uncertainties.

On the other hand, accepting God's sovereignty requires us to surrender our own desires and plans to His will. It means acknowledging that He knows what is best for us, even when His ways are beyond our understanding.

Heavenly Father, we praise You for Your sovereignty, which reigns over all creation. Help us to trust in Your wisdom and to surrender our will to Yours. Give us faith to believe that Your plans are perfect and Your purposes will prevail. In Jesus' name, we pray. Amen.

DAY 181

Finding Rest in God

"Come to me, all you who are weary and bur dened, and I will give you rest." - Matthew 11:28 (NIV)

In a world filled with chaos, stress, and busyness, the promise of finding rest in God is a beacon of hope and solace. But what does it mean to find rest in God?

Finding rest in God goes beyond physical relaxation or taking a break from our daily tasks. It is a soul-deep rest that comes from surrendering our burdens, worries, and anxieties to Him. It is trusting in His provision, His timing, and His perfect plan for our lives. When we come to God with open hearts, He envelops us in His peace, lifting the weight from our shoulders and soothing our troubled spirits.

Resting in God is not passive; it is an active choice to abide in His presence and align our will with His. It is finding refuge in His love and allowing Him to be our strength in times of weakness. It is a journey of faith, where we learn to release control and find security in His unfailing promises.

Heavenly Father, we thank You for the rest that comes from knowing You. In the midst of life's challenges and uncertainties, help us to find refuge in Your presence. Teach us to cast our cares upon You and to trust in Your provision. May Your peace fill our hearts and minds, guiding us through each day with faith and hope. In Jesus' name, we pray. Amen.

DAY 182

The Importance of Sabbath

"Remember the Sabbath day by keeping it holy." - Exodus 20:8
(NIV)

In our fast-paced world filled with endless responsibilities and distractions, the concept of Sabbath may seem outdated or impractical. However, the importance of Sabbath goes beyond merely resting from physical labor; it is a sacred time set apart for spiritual renewal, worship, and connection with God.

Sabbath is a divine invitation to pause, reflect, and realign our priorities with God's will. It is a deliberate choice to step away from the busyness of life and enter into God's rest, trusting Him to sustain us and provide for our needs. In observing the Sabbath, we acknowledge God's sovereignty over our time and reaffirm our dependence on Him as our source of strength and sustenance.

Sabbath also serves as a powerful antidote to the relentless pace of modern life. It offers us a chance to find rest for our souls, to recharge our spirits, and to experience the peace that comes from being in God's presence. By intentionally carving out time for Sabbath, we create space for God to speak to us, to refresh us, and to fill us with His peace and joy.

Heavenly Father, thank You for the gift of Sabbath, a holy time set apart for rest and renewal. Help us to honor this sacred day and to experience the fullness of Your presence as we rest in You. May our Sabbath observance bring glory to Your name and deepen our relationship with You. In Jesus' name, we pray. Amen.

DAY 183

Being a Light to the Nations

"Arise, shine, for your light has come, and the glory of the LORD rises upon you." - Isaiah 60:1 (NIV)

As followers of Christ, we are called to radiate His light to the nations, to be beacons of hope, love, and truth in a world desperate for the transformative power of God's presence.

Being a light to the nations is not just a metaphorical concept; it is a call to action rooted in the very nature of God. From the beginning, God's desire has been for His people to shine brightly, illuminating the darkness with His glory. As recipients of His grace and mercy, we are called to reflect His light to those around us, pointing others to the source of all light and life.

When we allow God's light to shine through us, we become agents of change and transformation in our communities and beyond. Our words and actions have the power to inspire, heal, and reconcile, bringing light into the darkest corners of the world. As we embrace our identity as lights to the nations, we participate in God's redemptive work, bringing hope and restoration to a broken world.

Heavenly Father, thank You for calling us to be lights to the nations, shining brightly with Your love and truth. Empower us by Your Spirit to radiate Your light in a world that desperately needs Your presence. Help us to live lives that reflect Your glory, bringing hope and healing wherever we go. May Your light shine brightly through us, drawing others into Your kingdom of light and life. In Jesus' name, we pray. Amen.

DAY 184

The Hope of Resurrection

"Jesus said to her, 'I am the resurrection and the life. The one who believes in me will live, even though they die; and whoever lives by believing in me will never die. Do you believe this?'" - John 11:25-26 (NIV)

These words spoken by Jesus to Martha before raising her brother Lazarus from the dead remind us that He is the source of eternal life. The hope of resurrection is not merely a distant promise but a present reality that transforms how we live and face death.

The hope of resurrection assures us that death does not have the final say. Even as we mourn the loss of loved ones, we cling to the belief that death is not the end but a transition into eternal life with God. This hope sustains us through seasons of grief and gives us comfort in the midst of sorrow.

But the hope of resurrection is not only for the future; it also has implications for how we live our lives today. Knowing that we have been promised resurrection empowers us to live with purpose and courage. It inspires us to embrace each day as a gift and to invest our time and energy in things that have eternal significance.

Heavenly Father, thank You for the hope of resurrection through Jesus Christ. In moments of doubt and despair, remind us of the promise of eternal life that we have in Him. Give us strength to live each day with confidence, knowing that our future is secure in Your hands. Help us to share this hope with others and to live as witnesses of Your grace and love. In Jesus' name, we pray. Amen.

DAY 185

The Promise of Heaven

"But our citizenship is in heaven. And we eagerly await a Savior from there, the Lord Jesus Christ, who, by the power that enables him to bring everything under his control, will transform our lowly bodies so that they will be like his glorious body." - Philippians 3:20-21 (NIV)

Our earthly lives are temporary, but our true citizenship lies in heaven, where we will dwell eternally with our Savior. The promise of heaven gives us hope in the midst of trials and challenges, knowing that this world is not our final destination.

Heaven is not merely a distant dream; it is a reality made possible through the sacrifice of Jesus Christ. Through His death and resurrection, Jesus conquered sin and death, securing for us an eternal inheritance in heaven. In heaven, we will experience the fullness of God's presence, free from pain, sorrow, and suffering.

The promise of heaven transforms our perspective on life and gives us strength to endure hardships with unwavering faith. It reminds us that our struggles on earth are temporary, but the glory that awaits us in heaven is eternal.

Heavenly Father, we thank You for the promise of heaven, where we will dwell with You for eternity. We eagerly await the return of our Savior, Jesus Christ, who will transform our bodies and welcome us into Your eternal kingdom. In His name, we pray. Amen.

DAY 186

God's Righteousness

"For in the gospel the righteousness of God is revealed—a righteousness that is by faith from first to last, just as it is written: 'The righteous will live by faith.'" - Romans 1:17 (NIV)

It is not a righteousness based on our own efforts or merits but one that is freely given to us through faith in Jesus Christ. God's righteousness is perfect, unblemished, and without fault, and it is through His righteousness that we are made right with Him.

Understanding God's righteousness is essential for every believer. It is a righteousness that surpasses human understanding and exceeds the standards of this world. It is a righteousness that is rooted in God's character of holiness, justice, and love. When we grasp the depth of His righteousness, we realize our need for His grace and mercy, and we are humbled by the magnitude of His love for us.

God's righteousness is not just a theological concept; it is a reality that transforms lives. It empowers us to live with integrity, honesty, and compassion, reflecting the character of our Heavenly Father. It gives us confidence and assurance in our relationship with God, knowing that His righteousness covers our sins and makes us acceptable in His sight.

Heavenly Father, thank You for the gift of Your righteousness revealed in the gospel. Help us to grasp the depth of Your righteousness and to live in a manner worthy of Your calling. Give us faith to trust in Your righteousness and courage to walk in obedience to Your Word. May Your righteousness shine through us, drawing others into relationship with You. In Jesus' name, we pray. Amen.

DAY 187

Building on the Rock

"Therefore everyone who hears these words of mine and puts them into practice is like a wise man who built his house on the rock." - Matthew 7:24 (NIV)

Matthew 7:24 presents us with a powerful metaphor of spiritual wisdom and resilience. Building our lives on the rock-solid foundation of God's Word is not just a wise choice; it's an essential one. Just as a house built on a firm foundation can withstand the fiercest storms, so too can a life grounded in the teachings of Jesus weather the trials and challenges of this world.

To build on the rock is to anchor our faith in the unchanging truths of Scripture. It means not just hearing God's word but putting it into practice, allowing it to shape our thoughts, words, and actions. When we align our lives with the principles of God's kingdom, we establish a foundation that cannot be shaken by the shifting sands of circumstance or doubt.

Building on the rock also requires intentionality and perseverance. It involves daily choices to trust in God's promises, to seek His will, and to walk in obedience. It means cultivating a deep relationship with Jesus, the ultimate cornerstone upon which our faith rests.

Heavenly Father, thank You for the firm foundation of Your Word upon which we can build our lives. Strengthen our faith, Lord, and guide us in the way of wisdom and truth. May our lives be a testament to Your faithfulness and grace. In Jesus' name, we pray. Amen.

DAY 188

Faith as Small as a Mustard Seed

"He replied, 'Because you have so little faith. Truly I tell you, if you have faith as small as a mustard seed, you can say to this mountain, 'Move from here to there,' and it will move. Nothing will be impossible for you.'" - Matthew 17:20 (NIV)

The mustard seed, known for its tiny size, becomes a powerful symbol of the potential within us when we place our trust in God. Faith, though seemingly small, has the ability to move mountains and overcome obstacles that seem insurmountable.

Faith as small as a mustard seed is not about the quantity of our faith but the quality of our trust in God. It's about believing in His promises, His goodness, and His ability to work miracles in our lives. When we have faith like this, we are able to step out in boldness, knowing that God is with us every step of the way.

God delights in using the seemingly insignificant to accomplish His purposes. He takes our small acts of faith and multiplies them, turning them into something extraordinary. Like the mustard seed that grows into a large tree, our faith has the potential to blossom and bear fruit beyond our wildest dreams.

Heavenly Father, thank You for the gift of faith, even as small as a mustard seed. Help us to trust in Your power and provision, knowing that nothing is impossible for You. Increase our faith, Lord, and give us the courage to step out in boldness, believing that You are able to move mountains in our lives. May our faith be a testimony to Your goodness and grace. In Jesus' name, we pray. Amen.

DAY 189

God's Abundant Grace

"But he said to me, 'My grace is sufficient for you, for my power is made perfect in weakness.' Therefore I will boast all the more gladly about my weaknesses, so that Christ's power may rest on me." - 2 Corinthians 12:9 (NIV)

God's grace isn't just a concept; it's a powerful reality that sustains us in our times of need, providing strength, comfort, and hope.

God's grace is boundless and overflowing, reaching into the depths of our souls with love and compassion. It is unearned and undeserved, freely given to all who call upon His name. No matter how far we may have strayed or how deeply we may have fallen, God's grace is always available to lift us up and set us on the path of righteousness.

When we encounter God's grace, it transforms our lives in profound ways. It brings healing to our brokenness, forgiveness to our sins, and redemption to our past mistakes. It empowers us to live with confidence and boldness, knowing that we are loved and accepted by our Heavenly Father.

Heavenly Father, thank You for Your abundant grace that sustains us in every season of life. Help us to fully embrace Your grace and to live in the freedom that it brings. May Your grace empower us to walk in obedience and love, reflecting Your mercy and compassion to the world around us. In Jesus' name, we pray. Amen.

DAY 190

Living a Life of Integrity

"The integrity of the upright guides them, but the unfaithful are destroyed by their duplicity." - Proverbs 11:3 (NIV)

Integrity is more than just doing what is right when others are watching; it is a steadfast commitment to moral and ethical principles, even in the face of temptation or adversity. It is the foundation upon which trust, respect, and honor are built.

Living a life of integrity means aligning our actions with our beliefs and values, even when it may be difficult or unpopular. It requires honesty, sincerity, and consistency in our words and deeds, reflecting the character of Christ in all aspects of our lives. When we walk in integrity, we honor God and demonstrate His righteousness to the world around us.

Integrity not only guides us in our decisions and interactions but also serves as a beacon of light in a world darkened by deception and deceit. It sets us apart as followers of Christ, drawing others to Him through our example of authenticity and truthfulness. As we strive to live with integrity, we not only honor God but also inspire others to pursue righteousness and goodness.

Heavenly Father, thank You for the gift of integrity and the example of Christ, who lived a life of perfect righteousness. Help us to walk in integrity, honoring You in all that we say and do. Give us strength to resist the temptation to compromise our values and to stand firm in our commitment to truth and goodness. May our lives be a reflection of Your glory and grace. In Jesus' name, we pray. Amen.

DAY 191

The Power of the Gospel

"For I am not ashamed of the gospel, because it is the power of God that brings salvation to everyone who believes: first to the Jew, then to the Gentile." - Romans 1:16 (NIV)

The gospel is more than just good news; it is the very power of God at work in the world, bringing salvation to everyone who believes. This divine message of grace, love, and redemption has the ability to change lives, heal broken hearts, and restore hope to the hopeless.

The power of the gospel lies in its simplicity and profound truth: that Jesus Christ, the Son of God, came to earth, lived a sinless life, died on the cross for our sins, and rose again, defeating death and offering eternal life to all who trust in Him. This message transcends time, culture, and circumstance, reaching into the depths of our souls and transforming us from the inside out.

As believers, we are called to share this powerful message with the world. It is a beacon of light in a dark world, a source of hope for the weary, and a testament to God's unfathomable love for humanity. The gospel empowers us to live lives of purpose and passion, driven by the knowledge that we are loved, forgiven, and redeemed.

Heavenly Father, thank You for the life-changing power of the gospel. Help us to never be ashamed of this message but to boldly share it with those around us. Fill us with Your Spirit, giving us the courage and wisdom to proclaim Your love and salvation to a world in need. May our lives be a living testimony of Your grace and power. In Jesus' name, we pray. Amen.

DAY 192

Seeking God's Kingdom First

"But seek first his kingdom and his righteousness, and all these things will be given to you as well." - Matthew 6:33 (NIV)

This command is both a challenge and an invitation. In a world that constantly demands our attention and pulls us in countless directions, Jesus gently reminds us to realign our focus and place our trust in Him.

Seeking God's kingdom first means making Him the center of our lives. It involves aligning our desires, decisions, and actions with His will. It is a daily commitment to pursue what matters most to God: love, justice, mercy, and humility. When we prioritize His kingdom, we begin to see the world through His eyes and our hearts beat in sync with His.

This verse also carries a profound promise. When we seek God's kingdom first, He assures us that all our needs will be met. This does not mean that we will have a life free of challenges or material abundance. Rather, it means that God, in His perfect wisdom, will provide for us in ways that lead to our ultimate good and His glory.

Heavenly Father, thank You for calling us to seek Your kingdom and righteousness first. Help us to prioritize You in all aspects of our lives and to trust in Your provision. Align our hearts with Yours, and let our lives reflect Your love, justice, and mercy. Give us the strength and wisdom to seek You first each day. In Jesus' name, we pray. Amen.

DAY 193

Spiritual Growth

"But seek first his kingdom and his righteousness, and all these things will be given to you as well." - Matthew 6:33 (NIV)

Yet, Jesus calls us to a higher pursuit in Matthew 6:33: to seek first the kingdom of God and His righteousness. This directive isn't merely about adding a spiritual dimension to our lives; it's about making our spiritual growth the central focus.

Spiritual growth involves cultivating a deeper relationship with God, aligning our hearts with His will, and allowing His Spirit to transform us from the inside out. It means making intentional choices that foster our faith, such as dedicating time for prayer, studying the Bible, and engaging in worship. These practices nurture our spiritual roots, enabling us to stand firm in faith and flourish in godly character.

When we prioritize spiritual growth, we experience a profound shift in perspective. Our worries and anxieties diminish as we trust in God's provision and guidance. Our desires align more closely with His purposes, and we find fulfillment in living out His calling for our lives.

Heavenly Father, we desire to seek You first in all things. Help us to prioritize our spiritual growth and to align our lives with Your will. Fill us with a hunger for Your word and a passion for Your presence. Transform us by Your Spirit, and guide us in living out Your purposes each day. May our lives reflect Your glory and draw others to Your kingdom. In Jesus' name, we pray. Amen.

DAY 194

Joy in Suffering

"Consider it pure joy, my brothers and sisters, whenever you face trials of many kinds, because you know that the testing of your faith produces perseverance." - James 1:2-3 (NIV)

The words of James 1:2-3 seem counterintuitive at first glance: finding joy in the midst of suffering. Yet, this profound truth challenges us to see our trials through the lens of faith. Suffering is an inevitable part of life, but within every hardship lies the potential for spiritual growth and deeper intimacy with God.

When we face trials, our immediate reaction may be to question or despair. However, James encourages us to "consider it pure joy" because these challenges are not meaningless. They serve a divine purpose, testing and strengthening our faith, much like refining gold in the fire. Each struggle becomes an opportunity to develop perseverance, deepen our trust in God, and draw closer to Him.

Finding joy in suffering doesn't mean denying our pain or pretending everything is okay. Instead, it's about recognizing that God is with us in our suffering, working all things for our good. It's about seeing the bigger picture, understanding that our trials can produce endurance, character, and hope (Romans 5:3-4).

Heavenly Father, thank You for being with us in our suffering and using our trials to refine and strengthen our faith. Help us to find joy in the midst of our struggles, knowing that You are at work within us and through us. May our lives be a testimony of Your grace and faithfulness. In Jesus' name, we pray. Amen.

DAY 195

Perseverance in Faith

"Let us not become weary in doing good, for at the proper time we will reap a harvest if we do not give up." - Galatians 6:9 (NIV)

Perseverance in faith is not about never experiencing doubt or struggle; it's about continuing to trust God in the midst of them. It's about pressing on, knowing that our efforts and faithfulness will yield a harvest in God's perfect timing.

Life can often feel like an uphill battle. There are moments when our strength wanes, and the path ahead seems unclear. It's in these times that perseverance in faith becomes crucial. Like a farmer who patiently waits for the harvest, we must continue to sow seeds of faith, kindness, and righteousness, trusting that God is at work even when we can't see immediate results.

Perseverance is deeply rooted in hope. Our hope is anchored in the promises of God, who assures us that our labor is not in vain. He sees every tear, hears every prayer, and honors every act of faithfulness. When we persevere, we demonstrate our trust in God's sovereignty and His ability to bring about good from every situation.

Heavenly Father, thank You for Your promise that we will reap a harvest if we do not give up. Strengthen our hearts and renew our spirits when we feel weary. Help us to persevere in faith, trusting in Your timing and Your plan. May we find hope in Your promises and courage to keep moving forward, knowing that You are with us every step of the way. In Jesus' name, we pray. Amen.

DAY 196

The Importance of Confession

"If we confess our sins, he is faithful and just and will forgive us our sins and purify us from all unrighteousness." - 1 John 1:9 (NIV)

Confession is more than an admission of wrongdoings; it is a vital spiritual practice that brings us closer to God, restoring our relationship with Him and renewing our hearts.

Confession requires humility and honesty. It involves recognizing our faults and shortcomings, bringing them into the light, and acknowledging our need for God's mercy and grace. This act of vulnerability opens the door for God's transformative power to work within us, freeing us from the burden of guilt and shame.

When we confess our sins, we experience God's forgiveness and cleansing, which leads to a deeper sense of peace and freedom. It allows us to let go of the past and move forward with a renewed spirit. Moreover, confession fosters a spirit of accountability and growth, helping us to become more aware of our actions and their impact on our relationship with God and others.

Heavenly Father, we come before You with humble hearts, acknowledging our sins and shortcomings. Thank You for Your promise to forgive and cleanse us when we confess. Help us to approach You with honesty and openness, trusting in Your mercy and grace. Renew our hearts and guide us on the path of righteousness. May we find freedom and peace in Your forgiveness. In Jesus' name, we pray. Amen.

DAY 197

Living a Transformed Life

"Do not conform to the pattern of this world, but be transformed by the renewing of your mind. Then you will be able to test and approve what God's will is—his good, pleasing and perfect will." - Romans 12:2 (NIV)

This transformation is not a mere outward change but a profound inward renewal that affects every aspect of our lives. It is about aligning our hearts, minds, and actions with the will of God.

Living a transformed life means letting go of old habits, thoughts, and behaviors that are contrary to God's desires for us. It involves embracing the new identity we have in Christ, allowing His love and truth to reshape us from the inside out. This process of transformation is ongoing, a daily surrender to the work of the Holy Spirit in our lives.

As we are transformed, we begin to see the world through the lens of God's love and purpose. Our values shift, our priorities realign, and our actions reflect the character of Christ. This transformation empowers us to discern and follow God's will, experiencing the fullness of life He promises.

Heavenly Father, we thank You for the power of transformation that comes through Your Holy Spirit. Renew our minds and change our hearts, so we may live lives that reflect Your love and truth. Help us to surrender daily to Your work within us and to seek Your will in all that we do. May our lives be a testimony to the transformative power of Your grace. In Jesus' name, we pray. Amen.

DAY 198

Jesus' Sacrifice

"But God demonstrates his own love for us in this: While we were still sinners, Christ died for us." - Romans 5:8 (NIV)

Romans 5:8 captures the essence of Jesus' sacrifice, a profound demonstration of God's immeasurable love for humanity. Jesus, the spotless Lamb of God, willingly endured the agony of the cross to redeem us from sin and reconcile us to the Father. This ultimate act of love and sacrifice changed the course of history, offering us forgiveness, redemption, and eternal life.

Jesus' sacrifice was not just a moment in time; it is an enduring testament to His love and commitment to us. He bore our sins, our shame, and our brokenness, taking upon Himself the punishment we deserved. Through His suffering, death, and resurrection, Jesus conquered sin and death, opening the way for us to experience abundant life and an intimate relationship with God.

As we contemplate the magnitude of Jesus' sacrifice, we are called to respond with gratitude and devotion. His love compels us to live in a manner worthy of His sacrifice, to embrace the grace He so freely gives, and to extend that same love and grace to others.

Heavenly Father, thank You for the incredible gift of Jesus' sacrifice. We are humbled and grateful for His love that knows no bounds. Help us to live in a way that honors His sacrifice, and fill our hearts with His love so that we may extend it to others. May our lives be a reflection of His grace and redemption, bringing glory to Your name. In Jesus' name, we pray. Amen.

DAY 199

God's Love for the Lost

"But God demonstrates his own love for us in this: While we were still sinners, Christ died for us." - Romans 5:8 (NIV)

His sacrifice on the cross is the ultimate demonstration of God's love, a profound and selfless act that changed the course of history and our eternal destinies.

Jesus' sacrifice was not an act of compulsion but a willing offering. He endured unimaginable pain and suffering, bearing the weight of our sins so that we might be reconciled with God. This act of love was not conditional upon our worthiness; it was given freely, with grace beyond measure. In His sacrifice, Jesus bridged the gap between humanity and God, offering us forgiveness, redemption, and the promise of eternal life.

Reflecting on Jesus' sacrifice compels us to respond with gratitude and humility. It reminds us of the depth of God's love and the lengths He went to rescue us from sin. It also calls us to live lives that honor His sacrifice, embracing the grace we have received and extending it to others.

Heavenly Father, thank You for the incredible sacrifice of Your Son, Jesus Christ. We are humbled and overwhelmed by the love that led Him to the cross for our sake. Help us to live in a way that honors His sacrifice, embracing Your grace and sharing Your love with those around us. Fill our hearts with gratitude and guide our actions to reflect the love we have received. In Jesus' name, we pray. Amen.

DAY 200

The Importance of Fellowship

"And let us consider how we may spur one another on toward love and good deeds, not giving up meeting together, as some are in the habit of doing, but encouraging one another—and all the more as you see the Day approaching." - Hebrews 10:24-25 (NIV)

As followers of Christ, we are called to come together in community, to support, encourage, and uplift one another on our spiritual journey. Fellowship is not merely a social gathering; it is a sacred opportunity to build each other up in faith and love.

In fellowship, we find strength and encouragement to persevere in our walk with God. We share in each other's joys and sorrows, lifting each other up in prayer and offering a listening ear. Fellowship reminds us that we are not alone in our faith journey; we are part of a larger family of believers who journey together toward the same goal.

Moreover, fellowship fosters spiritual growth as we learn from one another and hold each other accountable. It provides a safe space to ask questions, seek guidance, and share our struggles and victories. Through fellowship, we are sharpened and refined, becoming more Christlike in our attitudes and actions.

Gracious God, thank You for the gift of fellowship and the community of believers You have placed in our lives. Guide us to be supportive and encouraging to one another, spurring each other on toward love and good deeds. May our relationships with fellow believers reflect Your love and grace. In Jesus' name, we pray. Amen.

DAY 201

God's Provision

"And my God will meet all your needs according to the riches of his glory in Christ Jesus." - Philippians 4:19 (NIV)

It is a promise that speaks to the abundance of His grace and the depth of His care for us. In every season of life, God stands ready to meet our needs, not according to our own merits or efforts, but according to the boundless riches of His glory in Christ Jesus.

God's provision encompasses every aspect of our lives, from our physical needs to our emotional and spiritual well-being. He is our provider, sustainer, and source of strength. Just as He provided manna in the wilderness for the Israelites, He continues to supply us with everything we need for life and godliness.

Understanding God's provision goes beyond mere material blessings; it is about recognizing His presence and faithfulness in our lives. Even in times of scarcity or uncertainty, we can trust that God is working all things together for our good. His provision may not always come in the way we expect or desire, but it always comes at the perfect time and in the perfect way.

Gracious Father, we thank You for Your abundant provision in our lives. Help us to trust in Your faithfulness and to rest in the assurance that You will meet all our needs according to Your riches in Christ Jesus. Give us grateful hearts and open our eyes to opportunities to share Your provision with others. May Your name be praised forever. Amen.

DAY 202

Living with Purpose

"For I know the plans I have for you," declares the Lord, "plans to prosper you and not to harm you, plans to give you hope and a future." - Jeremiah 29:11 (NIV)

As Christians, we are called to live with purpose, to seek God's will for our lives, and to walk in obedience to His plans and promises.

Living with purpose means aligning our desires, goals, and actions with God's purposes for us. It involves seeking His guidance through prayer, studying His word, and listening to the promptings of the Holy Spirit. When we live with purpose, we find meaning and fulfillment in serving God and others, rather than pursuing selfish ambitions or fleeting pleasures.

Discovering our purpose is a journey that unfolds over time, requiring patience, faith, and trust in God's timing. It may involve stepping out of our comfort zones, facing challenges, and overcoming obstacles along the way. Yet, as we surrender to God's will, He leads us on a path of abundant life and eternal significance.

Heavenly Father, thank You for the promise of Your plans to prosper us and give us hope and a future. Help us to live with purpose, seeking Your will for our lives and walking in obedience to Your word. Guide us by Your Spirit, giving us wisdom and discernment to discern Your voice and follow Your lead. May our lives bring glory to Your name as we fulfill the purposes You have for us. In Jesus' name, we pray. Amen.

DAY 203

Spiritual Breakthrough

"For I am about to do something new. See, I have already begun! Do you not see it? I will make a pathway through the wilderness. I will create rivers in the dry wasteland." - Isaiah 43:19 (NLT)

A spiritual breakthrough is a moment of divine intervention, a season of breakthrough in which God brings about radical change, renewal, and restoration. It is a time when barriers are shattered, chains are broken, and new possibilities emerge.

Often, spiritual breakthroughs come during seasons of wilderness and drought, when we feel parched and weary in our faith journey. But it is precisely in these desert places that God chooses to reveal His power and grace. Like a river flowing through the dry wasteland, His Spirit brings life and vitality, rejuvenating our souls and leading us into deeper intimacy with Him.

A spiritual breakthrough may come in various forms: a renewed passion for prayer, a deeper understanding of Scripture, a healing of past wounds, or a fresh outpouring of God's presence. Regardless of the form it takes, a spiritual breakthrough is a testament to God's faithfulness and His desire to lead us into greater freedom and abundance in Him.

Heavenly Father, we thank You for Your promise to do something new in our lives. We invite Your Holy Spirit to move in power and bring about spiritual breakthroughs in our hearts and minds. May Your name be glorified as You make pathways through the wilderness and rivers in the dry wasteland of our lives. In Jesus' name, we pray. Amen.

DAY 204

The Call to Discipleship

"Then Jesus said to his disciples, 'Whoever wants to be my disciple must deny themselves and take up their cross and follow me.'" -
Matthew 16:24 (NIV)

To be a disciple of Christ is to embark on a transformative journey of faith, characterized by self-denial, sacrifice, and unwavering devotion. It is a call to wholeheartedly follow Jesus, surrendering our own desires and ambitions to align with His will.

The call to discipleship is not a casual invitation; it is a radical commitment to a life of obedience and service. It requires us to lay down our own agendas and take up the cross of Christ, embracing His mission of love, reconciliation, and redemption. It challenges us to live counter-culturally, prioritizing the kingdom of God above all else.

As disciples of Christ, we are called to emulate His example in every aspect of our lives. We are called to love as He loved, to serve as He served, and to proclaim His message of salvation to a broken and hurting world. Our discipleship is not defined by perfection but by a willingness to continually grow and be transformed by the power of His Spirit.

Lord Jesus, thank You for calling us to be Your disciples. Help us to embrace the call to self-denial and sacrifice, knowing that in losing our lives for Your sake, we find true life and purpose. Guide us by Your Spirit as we seek to walk in Your footsteps and make Your love known to the world. In Your name, we pray. Amen.

DAY 205

God's Sovereign Will

"And we know that in all things God works for the good of those who love him, who have been called according to his purpose." - Romans 8:28 (NIV)

It reassures us that God is at work in every circumstance, weaving together the threads of our lives into a tapestry of purpose and beauty. His sovereignty means that He is in complete control, orchestrating all things for our good and His glory.

Understanding God's sovereign will can be both comforting and challenging. It is comforting because it assures us that nothing happens outside of His knowledge and control. Every joy, every sorrow, every triumph, and every trial is known to Him, and He is working through them to shape us according to His purpose. This gives us hope and confidence, knowing that our lives are held in the hands of a loving and powerful God.

Yet, it can also be challenging to trust in God's sovereign will, especially when we face difficulties and uncertainties. In moments of pain or confusion, we might struggle to see how God is working for our good. However, faith calls us to trust in His wisdom and goodness, even when we do not understand His ways.

Sovereign Lord, thank You for Your perfect will and Your unfailing love. Help us to trust in Your plans, especially when we face challenges and uncertainties. Fill our hearts with peace and confidence in Your sovereign will. In Jesus' name, we pray. Amen.

DAY 206

The Beatitudes in Action

"Blessed are the peacemakers, for they will be called children of God." - Matthew 5:9 (NIV)

Each Beatitude offers a glimpse into the values of God's kingdom and challenges us to embody these principles in our daily lives. One such Beatitude, "Blessed are the peacemakers, for they will be called children of God," calls us to be agents of peace in a world often marked by division and conflict.

Being a peacemaker goes beyond merely avoiding conflict; it involves actively seeking to reconcile differences, heal wounds, and build bridges of understanding and compassion. It requires courage, humility, and a deep reliance on God's grace. As children of God, we are called to reflect His heart of peace and reconciliation in our interactions with others.

Imagine a world where we all took this Beatitude to heart—where forgiveness replaces bitterness, understanding overcomes prejudice, and love triumphs over hatred. By living out the Beatitudes, we become living testimonies of God's transformative power and His kingdom's values.

Heavenly Father, thank You for the teachings of Jesus that guide us in living out Your kingdom's values. Help us to be peacemakers in our homes, communities, and workplaces. Fill us with Your love and wisdom as we seek to reconcile and bring healing to those around us. May our actions reflect Your peace and bring glory to Your name. In Jesus' name, we pray. Amen.

DAY 207

Bearing Fruit in Every Season

"They are like trees planted along the riverbank, bearing fruit each season. Their leaves never wither, and they prosper in all they do."
- Psalm 1:3 (NLT)

This imagery speaks to the resilience and steadfastness that comes from being deeply connected to our Creator. Just as a tree draws sustenance from a nearby river, we draw spiritual nourishment from our relationship with God, enabling us to thrive and bear fruit regardless of our circumstances.

Bearing fruit in every season doesn't mean life is always easy or that we won't face challenges. It means that even in the midst of trials, our faith can remain strong, and our lives can reflect the character of Christ. The fruits of the Spirit—love, joy, peace, patience, kindness, goodness, faithfulness, gentleness, and self-control—can flourish in us if we stay connected to God, our source of life.

In seasons of abundance, our fruit can be a blessing to others, sharing God's love and provision. In seasons of drought, our roots remind us to rely on God's strength and trust in His timing.

Heavenly Father, thank You for being the source of our strength and nourishment. Help us to be like trees planted by the riverbank, bearing fruit in every season. Deepen our roots in Your word and presence, so that we may thrive and reflect Your love to those around us. Guide us to be a blessing to others, sharing the fruits of the Spirit in all circumstances. In Jesus' name, we pray. Amen

DAY 208

God's Steadfast Love

"The steadfast love of the LORD never ceases; his mercies never come to an end; they are new every morning; great is your faithfulness." - Lamentations 3:22-23 (ESV)

His steadfast love is a constant in a world of change and uncertainty. It is a love that never ceases, a love that remains faithful and true no matter the circumstances. This divine love is a source of comfort and strength, especially in our darkest moments.

God's steadfast love is not just an abstract concept; it is an active force in our lives. It is manifested in His daily mercies, which are renewed every morning. Each day we wake up, we are greeted by a fresh outpouring of His grace and compassion. This love is patient and kind, always ready to forgive and restore, no matter how many times we falter.

The assurance of God's steadfast love encourages us to live with hope and confidence. It reminds us that we are never alone, that we are cherished beyond measure by our Creator. His love is the foundation upon which we can build our lives, a rock that remains firm amidst life's storms.

Heavenly Father, thank You for Your steadfast love that never ceases and Your mercies that are new every morning. We are grateful for Your unwavering faithfulness and the assurance that Your love is always with us. Help us to live in the light of Your love, and to extend that same love to those around us. May our lives reflect Your grace and compassion in all that we do. In Jesus' name, we pray. Amen.

DAY 209

The Heart of Worship

"God is spirit, and his worshipers must worship in the Spirit and in truth." - John 4:24 (NIV)

John 4:24 calls us to worship Him in spirit and in truth, reminding us that true worship goes beyond rituals and songs. It is about connecting deeply with God, offering our whole selves in adoration and reverence. Worship is an intimate dialogue between our hearts and the heart of our Creator.

The heart of worship is a place of surrender, where we acknowledge God's sovereignty and grace. It is where we lay down our burdens, our joys, and our lives, recognizing that everything we are and have is because of Him. Worship is not confined to Sunday services or specific moments; it is a lifestyle, an ongoing expression of love and gratitude towards God.

When we worship, we align our hearts with God's will and open ourselves to His transformative power. It is in these moments of true worship that we experience His presence most profoundly, finding peace, strength, and renewed purpose. Worship reminds us of who God is—His greatness, His goodness, and His unending love for us.

Heavenly Father, we come before You with hearts full of gratitude and awe. Help us to worship You in spirit and in truth, offering our whole selves in adoration. Teach us to live lives that reflect Your glory, and let our worship be a true expression of our love for You. Fill us with Your presence and transform us through our worship. In Jesus' name, we pray. Amen.

DAY 210

The Value of Silence

"Be still, and know that I am God; I will be exalted among the nations, I will be exalted in the earth." - Psalm 46:10 (NIV)

Yet, Psalm 46:10 calls us to a sacred pause: "Be still, and know that I am God." This invitation to stillness is a powerful reminder that in the quiet moments, we can experience the profound presence of God.

Silence is not merely the absence of sound; it is the presence of stillness that allows us to hear the whisper of God's voice. It is in these moments of quiet that we can reflect, pray, and align our hearts with His will. Silence offers a respite from the chaos, a sanctuary where we can reconnect with the divine.

Jesus often sought solitude and silence, withdrawing to desolate places to pray and commune with His Father. His example teaches us the importance of carving out time from our busy lives to be alone with God. In the quiet, we can find clarity, peace, and strength. We are reminded of our dependence on Him and His sovereignty over all things.

Embracing silence requires intentionality. It means setting aside distractions and creating space for God to speak and move in our hearts.

Heavenly Father, teach us to value the gift of silence. Help us to carve out moments of stillness in our busy lives, where we can listen for Your voice and feel Your presence. May we find strength and renewal as we are still and know that You are God. In Jesus' name, we pray. Amen.

DAY 211

Spiritual Awakening

"Wake up, sleeper, rise from the dead, and Christ will shine on you." - Ephesians 5:14 (NIV)

Ephesians 5:14 calls out to our souls, urging us to awaken from spiritual slumber and embrace the transformative light of Christ. This verse captures the essence of spiritual awakening—a profound reawakening of our hearts and minds to the presence and purpose of God in our lives. It's a call to rise from complacency and live fully in the radiant light of Christ's love and truth.

Spiritual awakening often begins with a deep longing for more—a yearning for a closer, more intimate relationship with God. It is marked by a heightened awareness of His presence and a renewed passion for His word and His ways. This awakening leads to a transformation, shifting our focus from worldly distractions to heavenly pursuits. It breathes new life into our spiritual walk, filling us with purpose, joy, and a desire to serve.

To experience a spiritual awakening, we must be willing to open our hearts fully to God. This involves letting go of old habits and mindsets that keep us bound and embracing a new way of living rooted in faith and obedience.

Heavenly Father, awaken my spirit to Your presence and power. Illuminate my heart with the light of Christ, and guide me in Your truth. Break down any barriers that keep me from fully experiencing Your love and purpose. Fill me with a renewed passion for You, and help me to walk faithfully in Your ways. In Jesus' name, I pray. Amen.

DAY 212

God's Redemption Plan

"For he has rescued us from the dominion of darkness and brought us into the kingdom of the Son he loves, in whom we have redemption, the forgiveness of sins." - Colossians 1:13-14 (NIV)

Colossians 1:13-14 encapsulates the profound truth of God's redemption plan. From the beginning of time, God orchestrated a plan to rescue humanity from the clutches of sin and darkness, bringing us into the light of His kingdom through Jesus Christ. This divine plan of redemption is the heartbeat of the Gospel, a story of love, grace, and restoration.

God's redemption plan began long before we were born. It is woven throughout the narrative of Scripture, from the promise of a Savior in Genesis to the fulfillment of that promise in the life, death, and resurrection of Jesus. At the heart of this plan is God's unwavering love for His creation. He saw us in our brokenness and made a way for us to be whole again.

Through Jesus, we have been redeemed—set free from the bondage of sin and granted forgiveness and new life. This redemption is not something we earn; it is a gift of grace. Jesus' sacrifice on the cross paid the price for our sins, and His resurrection ensures our victory over death.

Gracious God, thank You for Your incredible plan of redemption. We are humbled by the depth of Your love and the sacrifice of Jesus Christ. Give us boldness to share our testimony and to spread the hope of Your salvation. In Jesus' name, we pray. Amen.

DAY 213

The New Covenant

"This is the covenant I will make with the people of Israel after that time, declares the Lord. I will put my law in their minds and write it on their hearts. I will be their God, and they will be my people."
- Jeremiah 31:33 (NIV)

Unlike the old covenant, which was based on the law written on tablets of stone, the New Covenant is inscribed on our hearts. It signifies a deep, intimate relationship with God, where His will and love are woven into the very fabric of our being.

The New Covenant is fulfilled in Jesus Christ, whose life, death, and resurrection ushered in a new era of grace and truth. Through His sacrifice, we are not only forgiven but also given new hearts, renewed by the Holy Spirit. This covenant assures us of God's unwavering commitment to us, His people, and our place in His family. We are no longer bound by the law but are led by the Spirit, living lives that reflect the heart of God.

This transformative relationship calls us to live differently. It invites us to embrace a life marked by love, grace, and obedience to God's will. The law written on our hearts means that our actions and decisions are guided by an internal compass aligned with God's desires.

Gracious God, thank You for the gift of the New Covenant, written on our hearts through Jesus Christ. Transform our hearts and minds to align with Your will, and empower us to be faithful witnesses of Your grace and truth. In Jesus' name, we pray. Amen.

DAY 214

Jesus' Teaching on Prayer

"But when you pray, go into your room, close the door and pray to your Father, who is unseen. Then your Father, who sees what is done in secret, will reward you." - Matthew 6:6 (NIV)

He teaches us that prayer is not about public display but about a personal and intimate connection with God. When we retreat into our quiet spaces and pour out our hearts to our Heavenly Father, we engage in a transformative dialogue that transcends the noise of the world.

Jesus' teaching on prayer invites us into a deeper relationship with God. Prayer is not merely a ritual or obligation; it is a lifeline that connects us to the Creator of the universe. Through prayer, we express our deepest longings, seek guidance, find comfort, and offer our praises. It is in these quiet moments that we experience the profound love and presence of God, who listens and responds to our hearts.

Jesus exemplified a life of prayer. He often withdrew to solitary places to commune with His Father, demonstrating the importance of prayer in His own life. His example teaches us that prayer is essential for spiritual strength and clarity.

Heavenly Father, thank You for the gift of prayer, a precious opportunity to connect with You. Help us to seek You earnestly in the quiet moments, opening our hearts fully to Your presence. Teach us to pray with sincerity and faith, trusting that You hear and respond to our prayers. Strengthen our relationship with You through our times of prayer. In Jesus' name, we pray. Amen.

DAY 215

Living a Life of Service

"For even the Son of Man did not come to be served, but to serve, and to give his life as a ransom for many." - Mark 10:45 (NIV)

He, the Son of God, humbled Himself to serve humanity, demonstrating the epitome of selflessness by sacrificing His life for our salvation. His life was a testament to the transformative power of service, and He calls us to do likewise.

Living a life of service means adopting a mindset of humility and compassion, mirroring the love of Christ in all that we do. It means seeking opportunities to meet the needs of others, whether physical, emotional, or spiritual, without seeking recognition or reward. It means putting others before ourselves, just as Jesus did when He washed the feet of His disciples.

Service is not just a one-time act of charity; it is a way of life, a daily commitment to love and serve those around us. It is found in the small, ordinary moments as well as the grand gestures. It is in the smile we offer to a stranger, the listening ear we lend to a friend, and the helping hand we extend to those in need.

Heavenly Father, thank You for the example of Jesus, who came not to be served but to serve. Help us to follow His example and to live lives of humility and compassion, seeking opportunities to love and serve those around us. Give us eyes to see the needs of others and hearts willing to respond with love. May our lives be a reflection of Your grace and mercy. In Jesus' name, we pray. Amen.

DAY 216

The Role of the Trinity

"For there are three that bear record in heaven: the Father, the Word, and the Holy Ghost: and these three are one." - 1 John 5:7 (KJV)

The Trinity is not merely a theological concept; it is the dynamic relationship of three distinct persons within the Godhead, united in perfect love and harmony. Understanding the role of the Trinity is like unraveling the layers of a beautiful tapestry, each thread intricately woven together to form a masterpiece.

The Father, as the Creator and Sustainer of all things, is the source of life and love. He is the architect of the universe, the master craftsman who spoke the world into existence with His word. The Son, Jesus Christ, is the embodiment of God's love and redemption. Through His sacrificial death and resurrection, He reconciled humanity to the Father, offering salvation and eternal life to all who believe. The Holy Spirit, the divine Comforter and Advocate, dwells within believers, empowering them to live lives of faith and obedience.

The Trinity exemplifies perfect unity in diversity, each person fulfilling a unique role yet working together in perfect harmony. It is a relationship of mutual love and submission, each person glorifying the others. As believers, we are invited into this divine fellowship, adopted as children of God and filled with the Holy Spirit. Our lives are meant to reflect the love and unity of the Trinity, drawing others into relationship with the triune God.

Holy Trinity, we stand in awe of Your perfect unity and love. Help us to deepen our understanding of Your triune nature and to experience the fullness of Your presence in our lives. May we reflect Your love and unity to a world in need of Your grace. In the name of the Father, the Son, and the Holy Spirit, we pray. Amen.

DAY 217

Overcoming Spiritual Obstacles

"For though we live in the world, we do not wage war as the world does. The weapons we fight with are not the weapons of the world. On the contrary, they have divine power to demolish strongholds."
- 2 Corinthians 10:3-4 (NIV)

We face spiritual obstacles that can hinder our relationship with God and impede our growth in faith. These obstacles may come in various forms—doubt, fear, temptation, or spiritual apathy—but they all seek to separate us from the abundant life that God desires for us.

Overcoming spiritual obstacles requires a concerted effort rooted in prayer, faith, and the power of God's Word. We must recognize that we are engaged in a spiritual battle and equip ourselves accordingly. Instead of relying on our own strength or worldly strategies, we must rely on the divine power of God to overcome.

One key action plan for overcoming spiritual obstacles is to immerse ourselves in prayer and Scripture. Prayer is our direct line of communication with God, and through it, we can seek His guidance, strength, and protection.

Heavenly Father, we thank You for the power and authority You have given us to overcome spiritual obstacles. Help us to recognize the battles we face and equip us with Your divine weapons to demolish every stronghold. Guide us in prayer and Scripture study, that we may be strengthened and encouraged to press on in our journey with You. In Jesus' name, we pray. Amen.

DAY 218

God's Unfailing Love

"The LORD is compassionate and gracious, slow to anger, abounding in love." - Psalm 103:8 (NIV)

His love is not fleeting or conditional; it is steadfast and unwavering, enduring through every season of our lives. In a world filled with uncertainty and change, God's love remains constant, a beacon of hope and assurance that we can always rely on.

God's love is boundless and infinite, extending beyond our comprehension. It is a love that knows no bounds, reaching down to the depths of our brokenness and lifting us up with tender care. It is a love that is patient and kind, forgiving our shortcomings and embracing us with open arms.

No matter where we find ourselves, God's love is there, surrounding us like a warm embrace. In moments of joy, His love celebrates with us. In moments of sorrow, His love comforts us. In moments of doubt, His love reassures us. There is nothing in all creation that can separate us from the love of God.

Heavenly Father, thank You for Your unfailing love that surrounds us every moment of every day. Help us to fully grasp the depth and breadth of Your love for us, that we may live each day in the assurance of Your grace. Empower us to share Your love with others, extending kindness, compassion, and forgiveness to those in need. May Your love shine brightly through us, drawing others into Your embrace. In Jesus' name, we pray. Amen.

DAY 219

The Joy of Giving

"Each of you should give what you have decided in your heart to give, not reluctantly or under compulsion, for God loves a cheerful giver." - 2 Corinthians 9:7 (NIV)

Giving is not merely an obligation or duty but a privilege and an opportunity to experience the abundant blessings of God. When we give with a cheerful heart, we align ourselves with God's generous nature and participate in His kingdom work on earth.

The joy of giving is not limited to material possessions; it extends to giving of our time, talents, and love. It is a reflection of the selfless love of Jesus Christ, who gave His life so that we might have eternal life. As we follow His example, we discover that true joy is found not in accumulating wealth or possessions but in sharing what we have with others, especially those in need.

When we give with a cheerful heart, we experience a deep sense of fulfillment and purpose. Our hearts overflow with gratitude as we witness the impact of our generosity in the lives of others. Giving becomes an act of worship, a tangible expression of our love for God and our commitment to His kingdom.

Heavenly Father, thank You for the privilege of giving. Teach us to give with cheerful hearts, knowing that every act of generosity is a reflection of Your love and provision. May our giving be a source of joy and blessing to others, and may it bring glory to Your name. Open our eyes to the needs around us and fill us with Your compassion. In Jesus' name, we pray. Amen.

DAY 220

Embracing God's Truth

"Then you will know the truth, and the truth will set you free." -
John 8:32 (NIV)

The truth spoken of here is not merely factual knowledge but a deep understanding of God's Word and His will for our lives. When we embrace God's truth, we are liberated from the bondage of lies, confusion, and darkness. We are set free to walk in the light of His love and purpose.

Embracing God's truth begins with a willingness to seek it earnestly, to study His Word with open hearts and minds. As we immerse ourselves in Scripture, we encounter the truth of who God is, His character, His promises, and His commands. We also come to understand the truth of who we are in Christ, our identity as beloved children of God, redeemed and empowered by His grace.

But embracing God's truth is more than just intellectual assent; it requires a surrender of our will and a commitment to live in alignment with His Word. It means allowing His truth to penetrate every aspect of our lives, shaping our thoughts, attitudes, and actions.

Gracious God, thank You for the gift of Your truth, which sets us free from the bondage of lies and deception. Open our eyes to see Your truth more clearly and our hearts to embrace it more fully. Help us to walk in Your truth each day, living lives that honor and glorify You. May Your truth guide us, shape us, and transform us into vessels of Your love and grace. In Jesus' name, we pray.
Amen.

DAY 221

The Power of Testimony

"They triumphed over him by the blood of the Lamb and by the word of their testimony; they did not love their lives so much as to shrink from death." - Revelation 12:11 (NIV)

Testimony is more than just sharing our personal stories; it is declaring the faithfulness and transformative work of God in our lives. Our testimonies serve as powerful weapons against the enemy, reminding us and others of the victory we have in Christ.

When we share our testimonies, we offer glimpses of God's grace and redemption, inspiring hope and faith in those who hear. Our stories become testimonies of God's faithfulness, His healing power, and His ability to bring beauty out of brokenness. They serve as reminders that no situation is beyond His reach and no heart is beyond His love.

Testimony is not limited to grand gestures or miraculous events. It can be found in the everyday moments of life, in the quiet whispers of God's presence and provision. Whether it's overcoming struggles, experiencing answered prayers, or encountering God's peace in the midst of chaos, every testimony carries the potential to impact lives and draw others closer to God.

Heavenly Father, thank You for the power of testimony that reminds us of Your faithfulness and love. Help us to boldly share our stories of Your goodness and grace, knowing that You can use even the smallest testimony to bring hope and healing to others. Give us courage and wisdom to be witnesses of Your transforming power in our lives. In Jesus' name, we pray. Amen.

DAY 222

The Importance of Sabbath Rest

"Remember the Sabbath day by keeping it holy." - Exodus 20:8
(NIV)

In our fast-paced and busy lives, it can be easy to overlook the significance of this divine gift. Yet, the Sabbath is a precious opportunity to pause, to connect with God, and to replenish our souls.

Sabbath rest is not merely a suggestion; it is a commandment given by God Himself. In observing the Sabbath, we honor God's rhythm of creation, acknowledging His sovereignty over our time and our lives. It is a day to cease from our labors, to release the burdens of the week, and to find refreshment in His presence.

In a world that glorifies busyness and productivity, the Sabbath serves as a countercultural reminder of our need for rest and restoration. It is a time to prioritize our relationship with God and with others, nurturing our spiritual and emotional well-being. When we honor the Sabbath, we declare our trust in God's provision and our dependence on His grace.

Heavenly Father, thank You for the gift of Sabbath rest. Help us to honor this day and to keep it holy, as You have commanded. Teach us to find true rest in Your presence and to trust in Your provision for our lives. May the Sabbath be a time of spiritual renewal and refreshment, as we draw near to You and find rest for our souls. In Jesus' name, we pray. Amen.

DAY 223

The Glory of God

"The heavens declare the glory of God; the skies proclaim the work of his hands." - Psalm 19:1 (NIV)

From the majestic mountains to the vast expanse of the oceans, from the delicate petals of a flower to the fiery hues of a sunset, every aspect of the natural world testifies to the greatness and beauty of our Creator. The glory of God is not confined to the pages of Scripture or the walls of a church; it is woven into the very fabric of creation, waiting to be discovered and marveled at.

When we pause to behold the wonders of God's handiwork, our hearts are stirred with awe and reverence. We catch glimpses of His majesty and power, His creativity and wisdom, His faithfulness and love. The glory of God surrounds us, inviting us to join in the symphony of praise that rises from all creation.

Yet, the glory of God is not limited to the natural world. It is also revealed in the person of Jesus Christ, who came to earth to reveal the fullness of God's glory. In His life, death, and resurrection, we see the ultimate expression of God's love and redemption, bringing glory to His name for all eternity.

Heavenly Father, we thank You for the beauty and majesty of Your creation, which declares Your glory to all the earth. Open our eyes to see Your handiwork and our hearts to respond in worship and praise. May our lives be a reflection of Your glory, shining brightly for all to see. In Jesus' name, we pray. Amen.

DAY 224

Walking in Forgiveness

"Be kind and compassionate to one another, forgiving each other, just as in Christ God forgave you." - Ephesians 4:32 (NIV)

As recipients of God's boundless forgiveness through Christ, we are called to extend that same forgiveness to others. Forgiveness is not merely an act of pardoning someone for their wrongdoing; it is a transformative journey of healing and restoration, both for the offender and the offended.

Walking in forgiveness begins with a recognition of our own need for forgiveness. Just as God has forgiven us through Christ's sacrifice, we are compelled to extend that forgiveness to those who have wronged us. It is a conscious decision to release the burden of bitterness and resentment, choosing instead to embrace the freedom that comes from letting go and extending grace.

Forgiveness does not mean forgetting or excusing the offense; it means releasing the grip of anger and choosing to love and show compassion instead. It is a deliberate act of obedience to Christ's command to love one another as He has loved us.

Heavenly Father, thank You for the forgiveness we have received through Jesus Christ. Help us to walk in forgiveness, extending grace and compassion to those who have wronged us. May Your love and forgiveness flow through us, bringing healing and restoration to broken relationships. In Jesus' name, we pray. Amen.

DAY 225

The Role of the Bible

"All Scripture is God-breathed and is useful for teaching,
rebuking, correcting and training in righteousness, so that the
servant of God may be thoroughly equipped for every good work."
- 2 Timothy 3:16-17 (NIV)

The Scriptures are not merely human words but the very breath of God, inspired and authoritative for teaching, rebuking, correcting, and training in righteousness. The Bible is more than just a book; it is a living, dynamic guide that shapes our beliefs, convicts our hearts, and equips us for every good work.

Through the pages of Scripture, we encounter the living Word of God, Jesus Christ Himself. The Bible reveals God's character, His promises, and His plan of redemption for humanity. It speaks truth into every aspect of our lives, providing wisdom and guidance for navigating the challenges of this world. When we immerse ourselves in the Word, we are transformed from the inside out, renewed in mind and spirit.

As Christians, our relationship with the Bible is essential for spiritual growth and maturity. It is through the study and meditation of Scripture that we deepen our understanding of God's will and His purposes for our lives.

Heavenly Father, thank You for the gift of Your Word, which is a
lamp to our feet and a light to our path. May Your Word dwell
richly in us, guiding and shaping us into the image of Your Son,
Jesus Christ. In His name, we pray. Amen.

DAY 226

God's Protective Hand

"He will cover you with his feathers, and under his wings you will find refuge; his faithfulness will be your shield and rampart." - Psalm 91:4 (NIV)

The imagery of a bird sheltering its young under its wings speaks of the intimate and nurturing relationship we have with our Heavenly Father. Just as a mother bird shields her chicks from harm, so God covers us with His protective hand, providing refuge and security in the midst of life's storms.

God's protective hand is not a distant or passive force; it is a tangible expression of His love and faithfulness toward us. It is a shield that guards us from the attacks of the enemy and a fortress that surrounds us with His presence. Even in the face of adversity and danger, we can take comfort in knowing that we are held securely in the palm of His hand.

As believers, we are called to trust in God's protective care and to rest confidently in His promises. This does not mean that we will be exempt from trials or hardships, but it means that we can face them with courage and peace, knowing that God is with us every step of the way.

Heavenly Father, thank You for Your unfailing love and protective care. We are grateful for the assurance that we find refuge under Your wings and that Your faithfulness is our shield and rampart. May Your presence be our constant source of strength and peace. In Jesus' name, we pray. Amen.

DAY 227

Finding Joy in Trials

"Consider it pure joy, my brothers and sisters, whenever you face trials of many kinds, because you know that the testing of your faith produces perseverance." - James 1:2-3 (NIV)

At first glance, this may seem counterintuitive. How can we possibly rejoice when we are facing difficulties, hardships, and pain? Yet, James invites us to shift our perspective and see trials not as obstacles to joy but as opportunities for growth and transformation.

Trials are an inevitable part of life this side of heaven. They come in various forms—physical, emotional, relational, and spiritual—and can often leave us feeling overwhelmed, discouraged, and weary. However, as followers of Christ, we are called to respond differently. Instead of allowing trials to crush our spirits, we are encouraged to embrace them with joy, knowing that God is at work even in the midst of our suffering.

Finding joy in trials does not mean denying or minimizing our pain. It means choosing to trust in God's sovereignty and goodness, even when circumstances seem bleak. It means clinging to the hope that God can redeem even the most difficult situations for His glory and our ultimate good.

Heavenly Father, thank You for the promise that You are with us in every trial we face. Help us to find joy in the midst of difficulties, knowing that You are working all things together for our good and Your glory. May Your joy be our strength as we walk through the valleys of life. In Jesus' name, we pray. Amen.

DAY 228

God's Everlasting Covenant

"I establish my covenant with you: Never again will all life be destroyed by the waters of a flood; never again will there be a flood to destroy the earth." - Genesis 9:11 (NIV)

This covenant, rooted in God's love and mercy, assures us of His enduring commitment to His people throughout all generations. It is a covenant marked by grace, forgiveness, and the unbreakable bond between Creator and creation.

God's everlasting covenant extends beyond the pages of Scripture; it encompasses the entirety of human history and eternity itself. From the moment He made His covenant with Noah, God has been faithfully fulfilling His promises, guiding and sustaining His people through every trial and triumph. His covenant stands as a testament to His character—unchanging, steadfast, and true.

As recipients of God's covenant, we are invited into a relationship of trust and obedience. Just as God remained faithful to His promises, so too are we called to honor our commitment to Him. Our response to His covenant is one of gratitude and devotion, as we strive to live in alignment with His will and purposes for our lives.

Heavenly Father, we thank You for Your everlasting covenant, which stands as a testament to Your faithfulness and love. Give us the strength to live in faithful obedience to Your covenant, knowing that You are always with us, guiding and sustaining us through every season of life. In Jesus' name, we pray. Amen.

DAY 229

God's Amazing Grace

"For it is by grace you have been saved, through faith—and this is not from yourselves, it is the gift of God—not by works, so that no one can boast." - Ephesians 2:8-9 (NIV)

Grace is the unmerited favor of God extended to us, despite our unworthiness. It is the extravagant love of our Heavenly Father poured out upon us, lavishing us with forgiveness, redemption, and eternal life through Jesus Christ.

God's grace is truly astounding because it reaches us in our brokenness and sinfulness, offering us a second chance and a new beginning. It is the ultimate demonstration of His love and mercy, surpassing all human understanding. In His grace, God not only forgives our sins but also empowers us to live transformed lives, filled with purpose and hope.

When we grasp the depth of God's grace, it humbles us and fills us with gratitude. We realize that we are saved not because of anything we have done but because of God's great love for us. His grace is a constant reminder of His faithfulness and steadfastness, even when we falter and fail.

Heavenly Father, thank You for Your amazing grace that has saved us and transformed our lives. Help us to fully comprehend the depth of Your love and the magnitude of Your mercy. Fill us with gratitude and awe for Your unfailing love. In Jesus' name, we pray. Amen.

DAY 230

The Role of Faithfulness

"His master replied, 'Well done, good and faithful servant! You have been faithful with a few things; I will put you in charge of many things. Come and share your master's happiness!'" - Matthew 25:23 (NIV)

In this parable of the talents, Jesus teaches us the importance of being faithful stewards of the gifts and resources entrusted to us by God. Faithfulness is not just about reliability or consistency; it is a deep commitment to honor God with our lives and to fulfill His purposes with diligence and integrity.

Faithfulness is a characteristic that reflects the very nature of God Himself. He is faithful in all His ways, steadfast in His love and promises toward His people. As followers of Christ, we are called to emulate His faithfulness in our relationships, responsibilities, and commitments. Whether in our work, our families, our communities, or our service to God, faithfulness is the hallmark of a life lived in obedience and devotion to Him.

When we are faithful with the little things, God entrusts us with greater responsibilities and opportunities for His kingdom. Our faithfulness is not measured by the size of our accomplishments but by the sincerity of our hearts and the obedience of our actions.

Heavenly Father, thank You for Your faithfulness that endures forever. Help us to be faithful stewards of the gifts and resources You have entrusted to us. May our faithfulness bring glory to Your name and advance Your kingdom here on earth. In Jesus' name, we pray. Amen.

DAY 231

The Call to Discipleship

"Then Jesus said to his disciples, 'Whoever wants to be my disciple must deny themselves and take up their cross and follow me.'" - Matthew 16:24 (NIV)

To be His disciple is not merely to be a follower in name only but to fully commit one's life to Him. It is a call to radical obedience, self-denial, and wholehearted devotion to the cause of Christ.

Discipleship involves more than just believing in Jesus; it requires surrendering our will, our desires, and our ambitions at the foot of the cross. It means embracing the way of the cross, willingly carrying the burdens and challenges that come with following Christ. It is a journey of transformation, as we allow His love and truth to shape every aspect of our lives.

As disciples of Jesus, we are called to walk in His footsteps, to love as He loved, to serve as He served, and to proclaim His message of hope and salvation to the world. It is a high calling, marked by sacrifice and perseverance, but it is also a journey filled with purpose, joy, and the promise of eternal reward.

Heavenly Father, thank You for calling us to be Your disciples, to follow You and to proclaim Your kingdom here on earth. May our lives be a reflection of Your love and grace, drawing others into relationship with You. Guide us on this journey of discipleship, and empower us to live for Your glory alone. In Jesus' name, we pray. Amen.

DAY 232

Living a Life of Faith

"Now faith is confidence in what we hope for and assurance about what we do not see." - Hebrews 11:1 (NIV)

Faith is not merely a passive belief; it is an active, vibrant confidence in the promises of God, even when they are not yet realized. It is the assurance that God is faithful and that His plans for us are good, even in the midst of uncertainty and doubt.

Living a life of faith requires us to trust in God's character and His promises, even when circumstances seem bleak. It means surrendering our own desires and agendas to His perfect will, knowing that He sees the bigger picture and works all things together for our good. Faith enables us to step out into the unknown, guided by the assurance that God is with us every step of the way.

As we walk in faith, we are called to live with courage and perseverance, trusting that God will provide for our needs and guide our paths. It is a journey of surrender and obedience, where we learn to rely on His strength rather than our own.

Heavenly Father, thank You for the gift of faith that enables us to trust in Your goodness and Your promises. Help us to live with boldness and confidence, knowing that You are with us always. Strengthen our faith, Lord, and help us to surrender every area of our lives to Your perfect will. May our lives be a testament to Your faithfulness and grace. In Jesus' name, we pray. Amen.

DAY 233

God's Everlasting Love

"The LORD appeared to us in the past, saying: 'I have loved you with an everlasting love; I have drawn you with unfailing kindness.'" - Jeremiah 31:3 (NIV)

From the beginning of time, God has poured out His love upon His children, drawing us close to Himself with unfailing kindness and compassion.

God's love is unlike any other love we may experience in this world. It is a love that surpasses human understanding, reaching beyond our faults and failures to embrace us in our brokenness. His love is not dependent on our performance or worthiness; it is rooted in His nature as a loving and merciful Father.

The depth of God's love is revealed most fully in the sacrifice of Jesus Christ. Through His death on the cross, Jesus demonstrated the incomprehensible extent of God's love for us. He willingly laid down His life to reconcile us to God, offering forgiveness, redemption, and the promise of eternal life.

As recipients of God's everlasting love, we are called to respond in gratitude and devotion. We are invited into a relationship with the One who loves us beyond measure, to abide in His love and to share it with others.

Heavenly Father, thank You for loving us with an everlasting love that knows no bounds. Help us to grasp the depth of Your love for us and to live in the fullness of Your grace and mercy. May Your love be the guiding force in our lives, leading us closer to You each day. In Jesus' name, we pray. Amen.

DAY 234

The Power of God's Word

"For the word of God is alive and active. Sharper than any double-edged sword, it penetrates even to dividing soul and spirit, joints and marrow; it judges the thoughts and attitudes of the heart." -
Hebrews 4:12 (NIV)

It is not merely a collection of ancient texts but a living, breathing testament to the character and will of God. The Word of God is alive and active, capable of penetrating the deepest recesses of our being, discerning our thoughts and motivations, and bringing about lasting change.

When we immerse ourselves in the Scriptures, we encounter the very voice of God speaking to us. His Word has the power to convict us of sin, comfort us in times of sorrow, and guide us in paths of righteousness. It is a source of strength for the weary, hope for the discouraged, and wisdom for the seeking.

The Word of God is like a sharp sword, cutting through the lies and deception of the enemy and exposing the truth. It is a weapon of spiritual warfare, equipping us to stand firm against the schemes of the devil and to overcome every obstacle in our path.

Heavenly Father, thank You for the power and authority of Your Word. Help us to approach Scripture with reverence and humility, recognizing it as the ultimate source of truth and wisdom. Give us the strength and discipline to hide Your Word in our hearts, that we may walk in obedience and experience the fullness of Your blessings. In Jesus' name, we pray. Amen.

DAY 235

God's Eternal Kingdom

"But store up for yourselves treasures in heaven, where moths and vermin do not destroy, and where thieves do not break in and steal." - Matthew 6:20 (NIV)

the fleeting treasures of this world, the treasures of heaven are imperishable and secure, unaffected by the passing of time or the trials of life. God's eternal kingdom is a promise of hope and fulfillment, a future inheritance reserved for those who place their trust in Him.

The concept of God's eternal kingdom invites us to shift our perspective from the temporal to the eternal. It challenges us to set our hearts on things above, where Christ is seated at the right hand of God. In a world consumed by materialism and instant gratification, the assurance of God's eternal kingdom offers a counter-cultural vision of true abundance and lasting significance.

God's eternal kingdom is not merely a future reality but a present reality that shapes our lives here and now. It is a kingdom characterized by righteousness, peace, and joy in the Holy Spirit.

Heavenly Father, thank You for the promise of Your eternal kingdom, where righteousness reigns and peace abounds. Help us to fix our eyes on the things that are unseen and to live with an eternal perspective. Empower us to be faithful stewards of the blessings You have entrusted to us, knowing that our true inheritance awaits us in eternity. In Jesus' name, we pray. Amen.

DAY 236

Spiritual Revival

"If my people, who are called by my name, will humble themselves and pray and seek my face and turn from their wicked ways, then I will hear from heaven, and I will forgive their sin and will heal their land." - 2 Chronicles 7:14 (NIV)

Spiritual revival is not merely an emotional experience or a temporary excitement; it is a deep and profound awakening of our souls to the presence and power of God.

In times of spiritual dryness or complacency, we may find ourselves longing for a renewed passion for God and His kingdom. Spiritual revival is the answer to that longing—a fresh outpouring of the Holy Spirit that revitalizes our faith, renews our commitment to Christ, and restores our zeal for His purposes.

True revival begins with humility, as we acknowledge our need for God and repent of our sins. It is fueled by prayer, as we earnestly seek God's face and His will for our lives. Revival requires a turning away from sinful habits and attitudes, as we align our lives with God's righteousness and holiness.

As we humble ourselves, pray, seek God's face, and turn from our wicked ways, we open the door for God to move in power and bring about transformation in our lives and in the world around us.

Heavenly Father, we humbly come before You, recognizing our need for spiritual revival in our lives and in our world. Pour out Your Spirit upon us, Lord, and ignite a fire of revival in our hearts and in our communities. In Jesus' name, we pray. Amen.

DAY 237

Love Over Pain

"And now these three remain: faith, hope and love. But the greatest of these is love." - 1 Corinthians 13:13 (NIV)

Love is not merely an emotion; it is a choice, a commitment to prioritize the well-being and happiness of others above our own. Love transcends circumstances and conquers even the deepest wounds and hurts.

In a world marred by brokenness and pain, love stands as a beacon of hope and healing. It is the antidote to bitterness, resentment, and despair. When we choose to love others, even in the midst of our own pain, we participate in God's redemptive work, bringing light into darkness and restoration into brokenness.

The love of Christ exemplifies this principle most profoundly. Jesus endured unimaginable suffering on the cross, bearing the weight of our sins and experiencing the depths of human pain. Yet, even in His agony, He chose to love, offering forgiveness and redemption to all who would receive it. His love overcame the pain of the cross and brought salvation to the world.

Heavenly Father, thank You for the gift of Your unconditional love, which triumphs over pain and suffering. Help us to love others as You have loved us, even when it requires sacrifice and vulnerability. Give us hearts filled with compassion and grace, that we may extend Your love to those who need it most. May Your love be the guiding force in our lives, leading us to heal brokenness and bring hope to the hurting. In Jesus' name, we pray. Amen.

DAY 238

Walking in Righteousness

"But seek first his kingdom and his righteousness, and all these things will be given to you as well." - Matthew 6:33 (NIV)

It urges us to prioritize God's kingdom and His righteousness above all else, trusting that He will provide for our needs as we seek to live in alignment with His will. Walking in righteousness is not just about following a set of rules or performing religious rituals; it is about surrendering our lives to God and allowing His righteousness to permeate every aspect of our being.

To walk in righteousness is to pursue a life of integrity, obedience, and holiness. It means choosing to align our thoughts, words, and actions with God's truth and His standards of righteousness. It requires humility to acknowledge our dependence on God and a willingness to submit to His guidance and correction.

Walking in righteousness is also a journey of transformation. As we yield to the Holy Spirit's work in our lives, He empowers us to overcome sin, grow in character, and reflect the image of Christ to the world. It is a daily decision to die to self and allow Christ to live in and through us, shining His light in the darkness and drawing others to Him.

Heavenly Father, thank You for calling us to walk in righteousness and for providing us with everything we need to live according to Your will. Give us the strength and wisdom to walk in integrity and obedience, reflecting Your righteousness to the world around us. May our lives be a testimony to Your grace and goodness, drawing others into relationship with You. In Jesus' name, we pray. Amen.

DAY 239

God's Promises

"For no matter how many promises God has made, they are 'Yes' in Christ. And so through him the 'Amen' is spoken by us to the glory of God." - 2 Corinthians 1:20 (NIV)

In Christ, every promise finds its fulfillment, every word spoken by God finds its "Yes." His promises are not empty declarations but are backed by the full weight of His character and power. They are anchors for our souls, guiding us through the storms of life and leading us into the abundance of His blessings.

God's promises are as numerous as they are precious. From the promise of salvation and eternal life to the promise of His presence and provision, His word is filled with assurances of His love and faithfulness toward His children. Each promise is a testament to His unchanging nature and His desire to bless and prosper us according to His perfect plan.

As Christians, we have the privilege of claiming God's promises as our own. We are called to walk in faith, trusting that He who promised is faithful to fulfill His word. Even in the face of doubt or uncertainty, we can hold fast to His promises, knowing that His word never returns void but accomplishes what He desires.

Gracious God, we thank You for Your countless promises that sustain us and give us hope. Help us to anchor our faith in Your word, trusting in Your faithfulness to fulfill all that You have spoken. May Your promises be a source of strength and encouragement to us and to all who hear Your word. In Jesus' name, we pray. Amen.

DAY 240

The Call to Evangelize

"But you will receive power when the Holy Spirit comes on you; and you will be my witnesses in Jerusalem, and in all Judea and Samaria, and to the ends of the earth." - Acts 1:8 (NIV)

This call to evangelize is not reserved for a select few but is extended to every believer, empowered by the Holy Spirit to boldly proclaim the gospel.

To evangelize is to embody the love and mission of Jesus Christ. It is to carry His light into the darkness, bringing hope to the lost and broken. The call to evangelize is rooted in the Great Commission, where Jesus commands His followers to go and make disciples of all nations, baptizing them in the name of the Father, Son, and Holy Spirit.

As Christians, we are entrusted with the privilege and responsibility of sharing the good news of salvation with others. Our lives are living testimonies of God's grace and mercy, and our words have the power to bring life and transformation to those who are lost and searching for truth.

Heavenly Father, thank You for entrusting us with the privilege of sharing the gospel with others. Empower us with Your Holy Spirit to be bold and courageous witnesses for Christ, proclaiming His love and salvation to all who will listen. Open doors of opportunity and prepare hearts to receive Your truth. May Your kingdom come and Your will be done as we faithfully respond to Your call to evangelize. In Jesus' name, we pray. Amen.

DAY 241

The Role of the Holy Spirit

"But the Advocate, the Holy Spirit, whom the Father will send in my name, will teach you all things and will remind you of everything I have said to you." - John 14:26 (NIV)

This verse encapsulates the vital role of the Holy Spirit in the life of every believer. The Holy Spirit is not merely a distant force but a personal presence, sent by the Father to dwell within us, empowering us to live out our faith and to walk in obedience to God's will.

The Holy Spirit is our constant companion, comforting us in times of trouble, convicting us of sin, and leading us into truth. He illuminates the Scriptures, helping us to understand and apply God's Word to our lives. He equips us with spiritual gifts for the building up of the body of Christ and empowers us to bear fruit that glorifies God.

As Christians, we are called to live in dependence on the Holy Spirit, surrendering ourselves to His guidance and direction. We cannot navigate the journey of faith on our own strength; we need the empowering presence of the Holy Spirit to lead us and empower us for every step of the way.

Heavenly Father, we thank You for the gift of the Holy Spirit, who dwells within us as our Advocate and Guide. Fill us afresh with Your Spirit today, that we may bear fruit that glorifies You and reflects Your love to the world. In Jesus' name, we pray. Amen.

DAY 242

God's Healing Power
"Heal me, LORD, and I will be healed; save me and I will be
saved, for you are the one I praise." - Jeremiah 17:14 (NIV)

Throughout Scripture, we see God's compassionate and miraculous healing power at work, bringing restoration to broken bodies, minds, and spirits. God's healing power is not limited by time or circumstance; it is as real and relevant today as it was in biblical times.

God's healing power encompasses every aspect of our being – physical, emotional, and spiritual. He is the Great Physician who can mend our brokenness, soothe our pain, and bring wholeness to our lives. Whether we are battling illness, grief, addiction, or emotional wounds, God's healing power is available to us, offering hope and comfort in our times of need.

As we journey through life, we may encounter seasons of suffering and pain. In those moments, it can be tempting to rely on our own strength or seek worldly solutions. But God invites us to turn to Him in faith, trusting in His unfailing love and healing touch. He is able to bring beauty from ashes and turn our mourning into dancing.

Heavenly Father, we thank You for Your boundless love and mercy, and for Your healing power that knows no bounds. We come before You today, lifting up our brokenness and pain, and asking for Your healing touch. Use us as instruments of Your healing love, that Your name may be glorified and Your kingdom advanced. In Jesus' name, we pray. Amen.

DAY 243

Spiritual Warfare

"For our struggle is not against flesh and blood, but against the rulers, against the authorities, against the powers of this dark world and against the spiritual forces of evil in the heavenly realms." - Ephesians 6:12 (NIV)

While we may face challenges in the physical realm, the ultimate struggle is spiritual. Behind the scenes, unseen to the human eye, spiritual forces of darkness seek to oppose and undermine the work of God in our lives and in the world.

Spiritual warfare is not a concept to be taken lightly; it is a reality that every believer must confront. The enemy seeks to deceive, distract, and destroy, but we are not defenseless. Ephesians 6:10-18 reminds us to put on the full armor of God, equipping ourselves with truth, righteousness, faith, salvation, and the Word of God.

In the midst of spiritual battles, we are called to stand firm in our faith, trusting in the power of God to overcome every obstacle. We are not fighting alone; the Holy Spirit empowers us to resist the enemy's schemes and to walk in victory.

Heavenly Father, we thank You for the victory we have in Christ Jesus. Give us eyes to see beyond the physical realm and discern the spiritual battles we face. Clothe us with Your armor and empower us with Your Spirit to stand firm against the schemes of the enemy. May Your light dispel every darkness and Your truth reign supreme in our lives. In Jesus' name, we pray. Amen.

DAY 244

Living in Freedom

"It is for freedom that Christ has set us free. Stand firm, then, and do not let yourselves be burdened again by a yoke of slavery." - Galatians 5:1 (NIV)

As followers of Jesus, we are called to live in the fullness of this freedom, embracing the abundant life He offers us. Yet, living in freedom is not merely the absence of external constraints; it is a state of the heart and mind, rooted in our identity as beloved children of God.

Living in freedom means casting off the chains of guilt, shame, and fear that once held us captive. It means walking in the light of God's truth and grace, confident in His unconditional love and forgiveness. It means letting go of the past and pressing forward with hope and purpose, knowing that our future is secure in Christ.

But living in freedom also requires intentionality and perseverance. It's all too easy to slip back into old patterns of thinking and behavior, allowing ourselves to be burdened once again by the weight of our insecurities and struggles. Yet, as Galatians 5:1 reminds us, we are called to stand firm in our freedom, refusing to be enslaved by anything that would rob us of the abundant life Christ has won for us.

Heavenly Father, we thank You for the freedom we have in Christ, purchased for us through His sacrifice on the cross. Help us to fully embrace this freedom and to live in the victory You have won for us. May Your Spirit empower us to walk in freedom each day, bringing glory to Your name. In Jesus' name, we pray. Amen.

DAY 245

The Peace of God

"Peace I leave with you; my peace I give you. I do not give to you as the world gives. Do not let your hearts be troubled and do not be afraid." - John 14:27 (NIV)

It is a peace that calms our troubled hearts, soothes our anxious minds, and fills us with a sense of serenity and security, even in the midst of life's storms.

The peace of God is not dependent on external circumstances; it flows from a deep and abiding trust in God's sovereignty and goodness. It is rooted in the assurance of His presence with us, His power to overcome any obstacle, and His promise to work all things together for our good. This peace enables us to face trials and tribulations with unwavering faith, knowing that we are held securely in the palm of His hand.

As Christians, we are called to actively cultivate and embrace the peace of God in our lives. This requires surrendering our worries, fears, and anxieties to Him, trusting that He is able to handle them far better than we ever could. It involves choosing to dwell on His promises rather than dwelling on our problems, and fixing our eyes on Jesus, the author and perfecter of our faith.

Heavenly Father, thank You for the gift of Your peace, which surpasses all understanding. Help us to trust in Your sovereignty and goodness, even in the midst of life's challenges. Fill us with Your peace that calms our fears and anchors our souls in Your unfailing love. In Jesus' name, we pray. Amen.

DAY 246

The Role of Grace

"For it is by grace you have been saved, through faith—and this is not from yourselves, it is the gift of God—not by works, so that no one can boast." - Ephesians 2:8-9 (NIV)

Grace is the unmerited favor of God, freely given to us despite our unworthiness. It is the cornerstone of our relationship with God, the foundation upon which our faith rests. Without grace, we are lost; but through grace, we are found, redeemed, and made new.

Grace is a concept that transcends human understanding. It is the divine mercy that pardons our sins and reconciles us to God. It is the undeserved kindness that lavishes blessings upon us and empowers us to live lives of purpose and meaning. Grace is the heartbeat of the gospel, the good news that proclaims salvation to all who believe.

Understanding the role of grace in our lives is both humbling and liberating. It reminds us that we cannot earn our salvation through good works or religious rituals. Instead, salvation is a gift freely given by God, received through faith in Jesus Christ.

Heavenly Father, we thank You for Your amazing grace that has saved us and set us free. Help us to grasp the depth of Your love and mercy, and to live in a way that reflects Your grace to others. Fill us with gratitude for the gift of salvation, and empower us to extend grace and forgiveness to those who need it. May Your grace abound in our lives, drawing others into Your loving embrace. In Jesus' name, we pray. Amen.

DAY 247

Trusting in God's Plan

"For I know the plans I have for you," declares the LORD, "plans to prosper you and not to harm you, plans to give you hope and a future." - Jeremiah 29:11 (NIV)

In a world filled with uncertainty and upheaval, we can find solace in the knowledge that God has a purposeful plan for each of us. His plans are not haphazard or arbitrary; they are meticulously crafted with our best interests at heart.

Trusting in God's plan requires surrendering our own desires and agendas to His divine wisdom. It means relinquishing control and embracing the unknown with faith and confidence in His goodness. While we may not always understand His ways or the paths He leads us down, we can trust that He is working all things together for our ultimate good and His glory.

When we entrust our lives to God's plan, we open ourselves up to a journey of faith and adventure. We step into the unknown with anticipation, knowing that His plans are far greater than anything we could imagine for ourselves. Even in the midst of trials and hardships, we can rest assured that God is with us, guiding us every step of the way.

Heavenly Father, thank You for Your perfect plan for our lives. Help us to trust in Your wisdom and goodness, even when we cannot see the way ahead. Give us the courage to surrender our will to Yours and to follow wherever You lead us. May Your plan unfold in our lives, bringing glory to Your name and fulfillment to our hearts. In Jesus' name, we pray. Amen.

DAY 248

The Value of Humility

*"Humble yourselves before the Lord, and he will lift you up." -
James 4:10 (NIV)*

Humility is not weakness or self-deprecation; it is a posture of the heart that acknowledges our dependence on God and our willingness to submit to His will. It is the recognition of our own limitations and imperfections, coupled with a deep trust in God's wisdom and sovereignty.

Humility is exemplified in the life of Jesus Christ, who, though being God Himself, humbled Himself to the point of death on a cross for our sake. His life of humility serves as the ultimate model for us to follow, demonstrating that true greatness is found in serving others and obeying God's commands.

The value of humility lies in its transformative power. When we humble ourselves before the Lord, we open ourselves to His grace and guidance. We become vessels through which His love and mercy can flow freely, impacting the lives of those around us. Humility paves the way for reconciliation, unity, and growth in our relationships with God and others.

Gracious Father, teach us the value of humility in our lives. Help us to follow the example of Your Son, Jesus Christ, who humbled Himself for our sake. Give us the strength to surrender our pride and self-reliance, trusting in Your wisdom and guidance. May our lives be a reflection of Your humility and love, bringing glory to Your name. In Jesus' name, we pray. Amen.

DAY 249

Spiritual Discipline

"Do not conform to the pattern of this world, but be transformed by the renewing of your mind. Then you will be able to test and approve what God's will is—his good, pleasing and perfect will." - Romans 12:2 (NIV)

In a world filled with distractions and temptations, spiritual discipline is our pathway to intimacy with God and alignment with His will. It involves intentionally cultivating habits and practices that deepen our relationship with God, strengthen our faith, and shape us into the likeness of Christ.

Spiritual discipline encompasses a wide range of practices, including prayer, meditation, fasting, worship, Bible study, and service. These disciplines are not ends in themselves but are means of grace through which we encounter God's presence and experience His transforming power. By engaging in spiritual disciplines regularly, we create space in our lives for God to work in and through us, molding us into vessels for His glory.

While spiritual discipline requires commitment and effort, it is not about striving in our own strength. Rather, it is about surrendering to the work of the Holy Spirit within us, allowing Him to shape our desires, attitudes, and actions according to God's will.

Heavenly Father, thank You for the gift of spiritual discipline, which leads us closer to You and transforms us from the inside out. Fill us with Your Spirit, empowering us to live lives that honor and glorify You. Jesus' name, we pray. Amen.

DAY 250

God's Protective Hand

"The Lord is my rock, my fortress and my deliverer; my God is my rock, in whom I take refuge, my shield and the horn of my salvation, my stronghold." - Psalm 18:2 (NIV)

Like a sturdy rock or an impenetrable fortress, God surrounds us with His strength and security, offering refuge and deliverance in times of trouble. His protective hand is a constant presence, shielding us from harm and guiding us through the storms of life.

Throughout Scripture, we see countless examples of God's protective hand at work. From the Israelites crossing the Red Sea to Daniel in the lion's den, God has always been faithful to His promises of protection for those who trust in Him. His love is a shelter in the midst of chaos, a refuge in times of uncertainty, and a source of strength when we feel weak.

As followers of Christ, we can take comfort in knowing that God's protective hand is always with us. He is not a distant or indifferent deity but a loving Father who watches over His children with care and compassion. Even when we face trials or challenges, we can trust that God is working all things together for our good, according to His perfect plan.

Heavenly Father, thank You for Your unwavering protection and care. Help us to trust in Your promises and to find refuge in Your presence. We rest in the assurance of Your protective hand, knowing that nothing can separate us from Your love. In Jesus' name, we pray. Amen.

DAY 251

The Call to Forgive

"Be kind and compassionate to one another, forgiving each other, just as in Christ God forgave you." - Ephesians 4:32 (NIV)

As recipients of God's boundless grace and forgiveness, we are instructed to extend the same mercy and compassion to others. Forgiveness is not just a suggestion; it is a commandment rooted in the love and forgiveness we have received from God through Jesus Christ.

Forgiveness is a foundational principle of the Christian faith, yet it is often one of the most challenging to practice. When we have been wronged or hurt by others, our natural inclination may be to hold onto resentment or seek revenge. But God calls us to a higher standard, inviting us to release the burden of unforgiveness and embrace the freedom that comes through forgiveness.

Forgiveness does not mean condoning or excusing the actions of others; rather, it is a choice to let go of bitterness and resentment, entrusting justice to God. It is a process of healing and restoration that begins with a willing heart and a desire to obey God's command to love one another as He has loved us.

Gracious Father, thank You for the forgiveness You have shown us through Jesus Christ. Give us the strength and grace to extend mercy and compassion to those who have wronged us, knowing that You are the ultimate source of justice and healing. In Jesus' name, we pray. Amen.

DAY 252

Living with Purpose

"For I know the plans I have for you," declares the Lord, "plans to prosper you and not to harm you, plans to give you hope and a future." - Jeremiah 29:11 (NIV)

Living with purpose is not merely existing; it is embracing the unique calling and destiny that God has ordained for us. It's about recognizing that we are not accidents of fate but intentional creations of a loving Creator, each with a role to play in His grand design.

Living with purpose means seeking to align our lives with God's will, surrendering our desires to His perfect plan. It involves discovering our gifts, passions, and talents and using them to serve others and glorify God. When we live with purpose, every moment becomes an opportunity to make a difference, to impact lives, and to advance God's kingdom on earth.

Yet, finding and living out our purpose is not always easy. We may face doubts, fears, and uncertainties along the way. But we can take comfort in the knowledge that God is with us, guiding our steps and empowering us to fulfill His purpose for our lives.

Heavenly Father, thank You for the promise of a hope-filled future and for the purpose You have for each of our lives. Help us to discern Your will and to live with passion and intentionality. May our lives be a reflection of Your love and grace, bringing glory to Your name. In Jesus' name, we pray. Amen.

DAY 253

The Power of Hope

"May the God of hope fill you with all joy and peace as you trust in him, so that you may overflow with hope by the power of the Holy Spirit." - Romans 15:13 (NIV)

Romans 15:13 reminds us that our God is the God of hope, and it is through Him that we find the strength to endure, the courage to persevere, and the joy to overcome.

In a world filled with uncertainty and despair, hope shines as a beacon of light, illuminating the darkest of nights. It is the unwavering confidence that God is at work, even in the midst of our trials and tribulations. Hope empowers us to face the challenges of life with resilience and determination, knowing that our future is secure in the hands of our Heavenly Father.

But hope is not passive; it requires action. It calls us to trust in God's promises and to actively pursue His will for our lives. It compels us to lift our eyes beyond our present circumstances and to fix our gaze on the eternal glory that awaits us. When we anchor our hope in God, we are filled with joy and peace that surpasses all understanding, and we become vessels through which His hope overflows to those around us.

Heavenly Father, thank You for being the source of our hope and strength. Fill us with Your joy and peace as we trust in You, so that we may overflow with hope by the power of Your Holy Spirit.. May Your hope shine brightly through us, drawing others into Your eternal embrace. In Jesus' name, we pray. Amen.

DAY 254

God's Unfailing Love

"But God demonstrates his own love for us in this: While we were still sinners, Christ died for us." - Romans 5:8 (NIV)

His love is not conditional or based on our worthiness; it is unconditional, unwavering, and unending. It is a love that surpasses all understanding, a love that took the form of Jesus Christ sacrificing Himself on the cross for our sins.

God's unfailing love is a constant presence in our lives, even when we feel unworthy or undeserving. It is a love that pursues us relentlessly, seeking to draw us near and to reconcile us to Himself. No matter how far we may wander or how many mistakes we may make, God's love remains steadfast, offering forgiveness, redemption, and restoration.

As we meditate on the unfailing love of God, let us be reminded of the incredible privilege we have as His children. We are loved with a love that knows no bounds, a love that was willing to endure the agony of the cross for our sake. May this truth fill us with gratitude, humility, and awe, inspiring us to live lives that honor and glorify the One who loves us so deeply.

Heavenly Father, thank You for the incomprehensible gift of Your unfailing love. Help us to grasp the depth and breadth of Your love for us, and to live in response to that love each day. May Your love be our guiding light, leading us closer to You and to lives of purpose and joy. In Jesus' name, we pray. Amen.

DAY 255

God's Provision

"And my God will supply every need of yours according to his riches in glory in Christ Jesus." - Philippians 4:19 (ESV)

As believers, we can take comfort in knowing that our Heavenly Father not only knows our needs but is also fully capable of meeting them. God's provision extends beyond mere material sustenance; it encompasses every aspect of our lives, including our emotional, spiritual, and relational needs.

God's provision is a testament to His faithfulness and love for us. Just as He provided manna in the wilderness for the Israelites and multiplied the loaves and fishes to feed the multitude, He continues to provide for His people today. His provision is not limited by our circumstances or resources but is rooted in His boundless grace and generosity.

But God's provision does not always come in the way we expect or desire. Sometimes, it may come in the form of unexpected blessings, opportunities, or even challenges that ultimately lead us closer to Him. Regardless of how it manifests, we can trust that God's provision is always timely, sufficient, and perfectly tailored to our needs.

Heavenly Father, thank You for Your abundant provision in our lives. Help us to trust in Your unfailing love and to rely on Your faithfulness in all circumstances. May we be grateful stewards of Your blessings and instruments of Your provision to others. In Jesus' name, we pray. Amen.

DAY 256

The Joy of Worship

"Shout for joy to the Lord, all the earth. Worship the Lord with gladness; come before him with joyful songs." - Psalm 100:1-2 (NIV)

Worship is more than just a duty; it is a delight, an expression of our love and adoration for the Almighty God who created us and sustains us each day.

The joy of worship stems from recognizing the greatness of God and His unconditional love for us. It's about lifting our voices in praise and thanksgiving, acknowledging His sovereignty and faithfulness. In worship, we find a sacred space where we can pour out our hearts, our fears, our hopes, and our dreams before the One who listens and cares deeply for us.

Worship is not confined to a church building or a specific time of day; it is a lifestyle—a continual offering of ourselves to God in every moment. Whether through song, prayer, scripture reading, or acts of service, we can worship God with gladness, knowing that He delights in our worship and draws near to us as we draw near to Him.

Gracious God, we thank You for the privilege of worshiping You. Fill our hearts with joy as we come before You with gladness and praise. May our worship be pleasing to You and draw us closer to Your presence. In Jesus' name, we pray. Amen.

DAY 257

Spiritual Maturity

"As iron sharpens iron, so one person sharpens another." -
Proverbs 27:17 (NIV)

It is not merely about accumulating knowledge or religious practices but about deepening our relationship with God and allowing His Spirit to mold us into vessels of His love and grace.

To achieve spiritual maturity, we must be willing to engage in intentional spiritual disciplines such as prayer, study of Scripture, worship, and fellowship with other believers. These practices cultivate a heart that is sensitive to God's voice and a mind that is aligned with His truth. Just as iron sharpens iron, we sharpen and encourage one another in our faith journey, walking alongside fellow believers who challenge, inspire, and support us.

Spiritual maturity also involves the development of virtues such as love, patience, humility, and forgiveness. As we grow in these qualities, we reflect the image of Christ more fully to the world around us. Our lives become a living testimony to the transformative power of God's grace, drawing others into relationship with Him.

Gracious God, thank You for the journey of spiritual growth and maturity that You have called us to. Help us to be intentional in our pursuit of You, seeking to know You more deeply and to become more like Your Son, Jesus Christ. May our lives bear witness to Your transforming power, bringing glory to Your name. In Jesus' name, we pray. Amen.

DAY 258

The Importance of Scripture

"All Scripture is God-breathed and is useful for teaching, rebuking, correcting and training in righteousness, so that the servant of God may be thoroughly equipped for every good work."
- 2 Timothy 3:16-17 (NIV)

In 2 Timothy 3:16-17, we are reminded of the profound importance of Scripture in the life of every believer. It is through the pages of the Bible that we encounter the living God, learn His ways, and are equipped to live lives that honor Him.

The importance of Scripture cannot be overstated. It serves as our ultimate authority, providing timeless truths and principles to guide us in every aspect of life. Through its pages, we gain wisdom for decision-making, comfort in times of trouble, and encouragement to persevere in faith. The Bible reveals to us the character of God, His promises, and His plan of redemption through Jesus Christ.

As Christians, it is crucial that we prioritize regular study and meditation on Scripture. We are called to immerse ourselves in God's Word, allowing it to permeate our hearts and minds, shaping our thoughts, attitudes, and actions. Through the power of the Holy Spirit, the Word of God transforms us from the inside out, renewing our minds and conforming us to the image of Christ.

Heavenly Father, thank You for the precious gift of Your Word. Help us to treasure Scripture and to recognize its significance in our lives. May it be a lamp to our feet and a light to our path, guiding us closer to You each day. In Jesus' name, we pray. Amen.

DAY 259

The Role of Prayer

"Pray continually." - 1 Thessalonians 5:17 (NIV)

In 1 Thessalonians 5:17, we are urged to "pray continually," highlighting the importance of a consistent and fervent prayer life. But what exactly is the role of prayer in our lives?

Prayer is our lifeline to God, our direct line of communication with the One who knows us intimately and cares for us deeply. It is in prayer that we pour out our joys, sorrows, hopes, and fears before the throne of grace. Through prayer, we express our gratitude for God's blessings, seek His guidance in times of uncertainty, and intercede on behalf of others.

Moreover, prayer is not a one-sided conversation; it is a sacred dialogue in which we listen as much as we speak. It is in the quiet moments of prayer that we can hear the still, small voice of God speaking to our hearts, offering comfort, wisdom, and reassurance.

Gracious God, thank You for the gift of prayer, a precious privilege that allows us to draw near to You. Help us to cultivate a fervent prayer life, one that is characterized by intimacy, sincerity, and faith. Teach us to pray according to Your will and to trust in Your unfailing love and wisdom. May our prayers be a sweet fragrance to Your ears and a source of strength and comfort in our lives. In Jesus' name, we pray. Amen.

DAY 260

God's Mercy

"The steadfast love of the Lord never ceases; his mercies never come to an end; they are new every morning; great is your faithfulness." - Lamentations 3:22-23 (ESV)

His love is unwavering, His compassion endless. Despite our failings and shortcomings, His mercy remains constant, like a beacon of hope in the darkest of nights. God's mercy is not a one-time gift; it is renewed each day, a fresh outpouring of His grace and forgiveness.

As Christians, we are called to reflect the mercy of our Heavenly Father in our own lives. Just as we have received mercy, so too are we to extend it to others. It is through acts of compassion, forgiveness, and love that we become vessels of God's mercy in the world. When we show mercy to those who have wronged us, when we offer kindness to the hurting and grace to the undeserving, we mirror the heart of our Savior.

God's mercy is not only a gift to be received but also a responsibility to be shared. We are called to be agents of reconciliation and healing, bridging the gap between brokenness and restoration.

Gracious God, thank You for Your endless mercy that knows no bounds. Help us to be vessels of Your love and compassion in a world that so desperately needs it. Give us the strength to extend mercy to others as You have extended it to us. May Your mercy flow through us, bringing healing and hope to those around us. In Jesus' name, we pray. Amen.

DAY 261

The Hope of Heaven

"But our citizenship is in heaven. And we eagerly await a Savior from there, the Lord Jesus Christ." - Philippians 3:20 (NIV)

The hope of heaven is not just a distant promise; it is a reality that shapes our perspective and sustains us in the midst of life's trials and uncertainties. It is the assurance that beyond the struggles of this present age, there awaits a glorious eternity in the presence of our Savior.

The hope of heaven is like a beacon of light shining in the darkness, guiding us through the storms of life. It reminds us that this world is not our final destination and that our sufferings here are temporary compared to the eternal joy that awaits us. In the face of pain, loss, and adversity, the hope of heaven gives us strength to persevere, knowing that our ultimate reward is secure in Christ.

As we eagerly anticipate the fulfillment of God's promise, let us live with a sense of purpose and expectancy. Let us fix our eyes not on the troubles of this world but on the hope of heaven, knowing that one day we will be united with our Savior for all eternity.

Heavenly Father, thank You for the hope of heaven that sustains us in the midst of life's challenges. Help us to fix our eyes on the eternal promises of Your Word and to live with confident expectation of the glorious future You have prepared for us. May our lives be a testimony to Your grace and goodness, as we eagerly await the return of our Savior, Jesus Christ. Amen.

DAY 262

Living in God's Grace

"But he said to me, 'My grace is sufficient for you, for my power is made perfect in weakness.' Therefore I will boast all the more gladly about my weaknesses, so that Christ's power may rest on me." - 2 Corinthians 12:9 (NIV)

In 2 Corinthians 12:9, we are reminded that God's grace is more than enough to sustain us in every circumstance. It is in our weaknesses and struggles that His power shines brightest, lifting us up and carrying us through.

Living in God's grace means surrendering our burdens, our failures, and our shortcomings at the foot of the cross, and allowing His grace to wash over us like a healing balm. It means accepting that we are not worthy on our own merit, but through the sacrifice of Jesus Christ, we are made righteous in God's eyes.

When we live in God's grace, we are set free from the chains of guilt and shame. We no longer have to strive for perfection or earn His love, for it is freely given to us. Instead, we can rest in the assurance that God's grace covers us completely, filling every crevice of our brokenness with His unending love.

Heavenly Father, thank You for Your boundless grace that sustains us in every season of life. Help us to fully embrace Your grace, knowing that it is more than sufficient for all our needs. May Your grace overflow from our lives, touching those around us with Your love and mercy. In Jesus' name, we pray. Amen.

DAY 263

The Power of Faith

"Now faith is confidence in what we hope for and assurance about what we do not see." - Hebrews 11:1 (NIV)

It's not merely believing in what is visible or tangible but trusting in the promises of God even when they seem distant or intangible. The power of faith lies in its ability to move mountains, to overcome obstacles, and to transform lives.

Faith is the bedrock of our relationship with God. It's the unwavering confidence that He is who He says He is and that He will do what He promises to do. When we have faith, we can face the uncertainties of life with courage and hope, knowing that God is in control and that His plans for us are good.

Throughout the Bible, we see countless examples of individuals whose lives were transformed by their faith. From Abraham, who believed God's promise of descendants as numerous as the stars, to David, who faced the giant Goliath with unwavering trust in God's strength, faith has always been the catalyst for miraculous breakthroughs and extraordinary feats.

Heavenly Father, thank You for the gift of faith that enables us to trust in Your promises and to walk in confidence even when we cannot see the outcome. Strengthen our faith, Lord, and help us to surrender our doubts and fears to You. May we step out in faith, knowing that You are always faithful to fulfill Your promises. In Jesus' name, we pray. Amen.

DAY 264

Overcoming Fear

"For God has not given us a spirit of fear, but of power and of love and of a sound mind." - 2 Timothy 1:7 (NKJV)

It whispers lies of doubt and insecurity, robbing us of the peace and confidence that God desires for us. But as followers of Christ, we are called to overcome fear with faith, trusting in the promises of God's Word.

In 2 Timothy 1:7, we are reminded that fear does not come from God. Instead, He has given us the power of His Spirit, the love of Christ, and a sound mind to conquer our fears. This verse is a beacon of hope, a reminder that we are not alone in our struggles, and that God equips us with everything we need to overcome.

Overcoming fear begins with acknowledging its presence in our lives and choosing to confront it with faith. It means shifting our focus from our circumstances to the promises of God. It means choosing to trust His goodness and sovereignty, even when our circumstances seem overwhelming.

Heavenly Father, thank You for Your promise to never leave us nor forsake us. Give us the courage to step out in faith and trust Your plan, even when we cannot see the way forward. May Your perfect love cast out all fear in our lives, and may we live boldly for Your glory. In Jesus' name, we pray. Amen.

DAY 265

The Joy of Fellowship

"How good and pleasant it is when God's people live together in unity!" - Psalm 133:1 (NIV)

There is a unique and profound beauty in the unity of God's people, a joy that transcends individual happiness and resonates deep within our souls. Fellowship is more than just gathering together; it is a sacred bond forged by our shared faith and love for God.

In fellowship, we find strength, encouragement, and support. It is in the company of fellow believers that we experience the tangible presence of God, as He promises to be with us when two or three are gathered in His name (Matthew 18:20). Through fellowship, we share in each other's joys and sorrows, lifting one another up in prayer and standing shoulder to shoulder through life's trials.

The joy of fellowship is not limited to the walls of a church but extends to every aspect of our lives. It is found in the laughter of friends gathered around a table, in the warmth of a hug from a brother or sister in Christ, and in the shared experiences of serving others in Jesus' name.

Heavenly Father, thank You for the gift of fellowship and the joy it brings to our lives. Help us to cherish and nurture the bonds of unity among Your people, that we may be a light shining in the darkness and a beacon of hope to the world. Guide us as we seek to love one another as You have loved us, and may our fellowship be a reflection of Your glory. In Jesus' name, we pray. Amen.

DAY 267

The Love of God

"For God so loved the world that he gave his one and only Son, that whoever believes in him shall not perish but have eternal life."
- John 3:16 (NIV)

It speaks of a love that is unconditional, sacrificial, and boundless. The love of God is not confined by human limitations; it surpasses all understanding and extends to every corner of creation. It is a love that knows no bounds, reaching out to embrace the broken, the lost, and the hurting.

The love of God is not merely a theological concept; it is a tangible reality that has the power to transform lives. It is the source of our hope, our strength, and our redemption. When we grasp the depth of God's love for us, we are filled with awe and gratitude. We realize that we are cherished beyond measure, chosen and adopted into His family as beloved children.

God's love is not passive but active. It compels us to love others as He has loved us, to extend grace, forgiveness, and compassion to those around us. It calls us to be vessels of His love in a world that is often filled with hatred and division.

Heavenly Father, thank You for the incomprehensible love that You have lavished upon us through Your Son, Jesus Christ. Help us to grasp the depth and breadth of Your love and to live in the reality of Your grace each day. May Your love shine brightly through us, drawing others into Your embrace. In Jesus' name, we pray. Amen.

DAY 268

Trusting in God

"Trust in the Lord with all your heart and lean not on your own understanding; in all your ways submit to him, and he will make your paths straight." - Proverbs 3:5-6 (NIV)

Trusting in God is not always easy, especially in a world filled with uncertainty and challenges. Yet, Proverbs 3:5-6 reminds us of the steadfast promise that when we place our trust in the Lord wholeheartedly, He will guide us and make our paths straight. Trusting in God means surrendering our fears, doubts, and worries to Him, believing that He is faithful and true to His promises.

Trusting in God doesn't mean we won't face difficulties or trials. Instead, it means having the confidence that God is with us every step of the way, working all things together for our good. Even in the darkest of times, we can find strength and peace in knowing that God is in control and that His plans for us are always for our welfare.

Heavenly Father, we thank You for Your unwavering faithfulness and love. Help us to trust You more fully, knowing that You are always with us and that Your plans for us are good. Strengthen our faith and grant us the courage to surrender our fears and doubts to You. Guide us along the path of trust, that we may walk in Your peace and experience Your abundant blessings. In Jesus' name, we pray. Amen.

DAY 269

God's Sovereignty

"Yours, Lord, is the greatness and the power and the glory and the majesty and the splendor, for everything in heaven and earth is yours. Yours, Lord, is the kingdom; you are exalted as head over all." - 1 Chronicles 29:11 (NIV)

His greatness knows no bounds, and His power extends over all creation. God's sovereignty means that He is the ultimate ruler and authority over the universe. Nothing happens outside of His control, and His plans will always prevail.

Understanding and embracing God's sovereignty can bring immense comfort and peace to our lives. In a world filled with uncertainty and chaos, we can take refuge in the unchanging nature of our God. Even when circumstances seem overwhelming, we can trust that God is still on the throne, working all things together for our good and His glory.

God's sovereignty also invites us into a deeper relationship with Him. When we acknowledge His lordship over our lives, we surrender our own desires and agendas, allowing Him to direct our paths. This surrender is not a sign of weakness but of trust and obedience.

Heavenly Father, thank You for Your sovereignty and for the assurance it brings to our lives. Help us to trust in Your perfect plan and to surrender our will to Yours. May Your sovereignty be a source of comfort and peace, guiding us through every season of life. In Jesus' name, we pray. Amen.

DAY 270

The Importance of Repentance

"Repent, then, and turn to God, so that your sins may be wiped out, that times of refreshing may come from the Lord." - Acts 3:19 (NIV)

Repentance is not merely feeling sorry for our mistakes; it is a transformative act of turning away from sin and returning to God. It's acknowledging our faults, seeking forgiveness, and committing to a life of obedience and righteousness. Repentance is not a burden but a pathway to freedom and restoration.

Understanding the importance of repentance begins with recognizing our own brokenness and need for redemption. We are all sinners, prone to wander from God's ways and indulge in selfish desires. Yet, in His mercy and grace, God offers us the opportunity to repent and experience His forgiveness. Through repentance, we are cleansed of our sins, reconciled to God, and welcomed into His loving embrace.

Repentance is not a one-time event but a lifelong journey of surrender and growth. It requires humility to admit our wrongs, courage to confront our shortcomings, and perseverance to walk in righteousness.

Gracious God, thank You for Your unfailing love and mercy toward us. Grant us the strength and courage to confront our sins and to walk in righteousness. May Your Spirit guide us in the path of repentance and lead us into times of refreshing and renewal. In Jesus' name, we pray. Amen.

DAY 271

The Role of Fasting

"But when you fast, put oil on your head and wash your face, so that it will not be obvious to others that you are fasting, but only to your Father, who is unseen; and your Father, who sees what is done in secret, will reward you." - Matthew 6:17-18 (NIV)

Yet, it holds a significant place in the life of a Christian, offering a pathway to deeper intimacy with God and greater spiritual breakthroughs. In Matthew 6:17-18, Jesus Himself instructs us on the proper attitude and approach to fasting. It's not about drawing attention to ourselves but about drawing closer to God in humility and sincerity.

Fasting involves abstaining from food or other pleasures for a period of time to focus on prayer, repentance, and seeking God's will. It is a powerful way to quiet the noise of the world and attune our hearts to the voice of God. Through fasting, we deny our physical appetites to nourish our spiritual hunger, allowing us to experience God's presence in a more profound way.

Fasting also serves as a reminder of our dependence on God and our need for His grace. It humbles us before Him, breaking the chains of pride and self-sufficiency.

Heavenly Father, thank You for the gift of fasting as a means to draw closer to You. Teach us to fast with the right heart attitude, seeking Your will above all else. Help us to rely on Your strength as we deny ourselves and seek Your presence. May our fasting be pleasing to You and lead us to deeper intimacy with You. In Jesus' name, we pray. Amen.

DAY 272

Living a Holy Life

"But just as he who called you is holy, so be holy in all you do; for it is written: 'Be holy, because I am holy.'" - 1 Peter 1:15-16 (NIV)

To be holy is to be set apart, to strive for purity and righteousness in every aspect of our being. It's not merely about following a list of rules or adhering to religious rituals; it's about embodying the character of Christ in our thoughts, words, and actions.

Living a holy life is a journey of transformation, a continuous process of surrendering our will to God's and allowing His Spirit to work in us, molding us into His likeness. It requires intentional effort and a deep desire to honor God in all that we do. As we draw closer to God and His Word, our hearts are purified, and our lives reflect His glory more brightly.

However, living a holy life doesn't mean perfection. We will stumble and fall along the way, but the key is to keep pressing forward, relying on God's grace to pick us up and strengthen us to continue the journey. It's about striving for progress, not perfection, and trusting in God's faithfulness to complete the work He has begun in us.

Holy God, we thank You for calling us to live lives that reflect Your holiness. Help us to walk in purity and righteousness, guided by Your Spirit and empowered by Your grace. May our lives be a living testimony to Your goodness and mercy, drawing others closer to You. In Jesus' name, we pray. Amen.

DAY 273

The Joy of the Lord

"Nehemiah said, 'Go and enjoy choice food and sweet drinks, and send some to those who have nothing prepared. This day is holy to our Lord. Do not grieve, for the joy of the Lord is your strength.'" - Nehemiah 8:10 (NIV)

This joy is not fleeting or dependent on circumstances; it is an enduring, soul-deep gladness that springs from our relationship with God.

The joy of the Lord is not just a feeling; it is a powerful force that sustains us through life's trials and triumphs. It is a buoyant hope that lifts our spirits even in the darkest of times. When we tap into the joy of the Lord, we find renewed energy, courage, and resilience to face whatever challenges come our way.

Living in the joy of the Lord means choosing to rejoice in God's goodness and faithfulness, regardless of our circumstances. It's about shifting our focus from our problems to the promises of God, from our worries to His sovereignty. When we abide in His joy, we experience a deep sense of peace and contentment that transcends understanding.

Heavenly Father, thank You for the gift of Your joy, which strengthens and sustains us through every season of life. Help us to abide in Your joy, finding our hope and strength in Your presence. Fill us with Your Holy Spirit, that our lives may overflow with joy and gladness, reflecting Your love to the world around us. In Jesus' name, we pray. Amen.

DAY 274

God's Compassion

"But you, O Lord, are a compassionate and gracious God, slow to anger, abounding in love and faithfulness." - Psalm 86:15 (NIV)

His compassion is not merely a fleeting emotion but an intrinsic part of His character. It is a deep, abiding love that knows no bounds, a love that reaches out to the broken, the lost, and the hurting with tender mercy and unfailing kindness.

God's compassion is evident throughout Scripture, from His tender care for the Israelites in their wilderness wanderings to Jesus' ministry of healing and restoration. Time and time again, we see His heart moved with compassion for the sick, the marginalized, and the sinners. He doesn't turn away from our pain or dismiss our struggles; instead, He draws near, offering comfort, forgiveness, and hope.

As recipients of God's compassion, we are called to reflect His love and mercy to others. We are called to be channels of His grace, extending compassion to those in need, just as He has shown compassion to us. Whether it's lending a listening ear to a friend in distress, offering a helping hand to someone in need, or speaking words of encouragement to the discouraged, we have the privilege of embodying God's compassion in our daily lives.

Gracious Father, thank You for Your boundless compassion that knows no end. Help us to be vessels of Your love and mercy, extending compassion to those who need it most., and restoration to a broken world. In Jesus' name, we pray. Amen.

DAY 275

The Power of the Gospel

"For I am not ashamed of the gospel, because it is the power of God that brings salvation to everyone who believes: first to the Jew, then to the Gentile." - Romans 1:16 (NIV)

The gospel is not just a message; it is the very essence of God's love and redemption for humanity. It is the good news that brings hope to the hopeless, healing to the broken, and salvation to all who believe. The gospel is the heartbeat of Christianity, pulsating with the divine power to change lives and eternities.

At the core of the gospel is the truth that God, in His infinite love and mercy, sent His Son, Jesus Christ, to reconcile us to Himself. Through His death and resurrection, Jesus conquered sin and death, offering forgiveness and new life to all who repent and believe in Him. This message has the power to pierce through darkness, to shatter chains of bondage, and to set captives free.

As believers, we are entrusted with the privilege and responsibility of sharing this life-transforming message with others. Our lives should be a living testimony to the power of the gospel, reflecting the love, grace, and mercy of Christ in all that we do.

Heavenly Father, thank You for the power of the gospel that brings salvation to all who believe. Empower us to boldly proclaim Your truth and to share Your love with those around us. Open hearts and minds to receive the message of hope and redemption found in Jesus Christ. May Your gospel continue to transform lives and bring glory to Your name. In Jesus' name, we pray. Amen.

DAY 276

Living by Faith

"Now faith is confidence in what we hope for and assurance about what we do not see." - Hebrews 11:1 (NIV)

It is a powerful reminder that faith is not just a belief in something unseen; it is an unwavering trust in the promises of God, even when circumstances seem bleak and uncertain. Living by faith means stepping out into the unknown with confidence, knowing that God is faithful to fulfill His promises and to guide us every step of the way.

Faith is not passive; it is an active and intentional choice to trust in God's goodness and sovereignty, even in the face of adversity. It is the fuel that propels us forward when fear and doubt threaten to paralyze us. Living by faith requires us to surrender our own plans and desires to God's perfect will, trusting that His ways are higher and His purposes are greater than our own.

In a world that often values tangible evidence and logical reasoning, living by faith may seem counterintuitive. Yet, it is in those moments of uncertainty that our faith is tested and strengthened. It is when we choose to trust God wholeheartedly, even when we cannot see the outcome, that our faith grows deeper roots and bears fruit in our lives.

Heavenly Father, thank You for the gift of faith and for Your faithfulness in our lives. Help us to trust You more deeply and to live with unwavering confidence in Your promises. May our lives be a testament to Your goodness and grace, bringing glory to Your name. In Jesus' name, we pray. Amen.

DAY 277

The Call to Holiness

"But just as he who called you is holy, so be holy in all you do; for it is written: 'Be holy, because I am holy.'" - 1 Peter 1:15-16 (NIV)

As children of God, we are called to reflect His holiness in every aspect of our lives. Holiness is not about perfection but about a heart set apart for God, dedicated to His purposes and aligned with His character.

Living a holy life means striving for purity, righteousness, and obedience to God's Word. It's about living in a way that honors God and brings glory to His name. In a world filled with temptation and sin, the call to holiness sets us apart as lights in the darkness, shining the love and truth of Christ to those around us.

However, living a holy life is not always easy. We may stumble and fall along the way, but God's grace is always available to lift us up and empower us to press on toward the goal of holiness. It is through His strength that we can overcome sin and grow in sanctification day by day.

Heavenly Father, thank You for calling us to holiness and for empowering us to live lives that honor You. Give us the strength to resist temptation and to pursue righteousness in all we do. Help us to walk in obedience to Your Word, knowing that You are with us every step of the way. May our lives be a reflection of Your holiness and grace, drawing others closer to You. In Jesus' name, we pray. Amen.

DAY 278

God's Faithfulness

"The Lord is faithful to all his promises and loving toward all he has made." - Psalm 145:13b (NIV)

Psalm 145:13 reminds us that God's faithfulness knows no bounds; it extends to all His promises and encompasses every aspect of our lives. His faithfulness is not contingent upon our circumstances or deservingness but flows from His unchanging character of love and mercy.

God's faithfulness is evident throughout history, from the creation of the world to the redemption of mankind through Jesus Christ. Time and again, He has proven Himself faithful to His word, fulfilling His promises with perfect precision and timing. He is the same yesterday, today, and forever, steadfast in His love and commitment to His people.

As we reflect on God's faithfulness, we are inspired to trust Him more deeply and to lean on His promises with unwavering confidence. No matter what challenges we may face or how dark the circumstances may seem, we can rest assured that God is faithful to fulfill His purposes in our lives. His faithfulness provides a firm foundation on which we can build our lives, anchoring us in hope and peace.

Gracious Father, we thank You for Your unwavering faithfulness and love toward us. Help us to trust in Your promises and to rest confidently in Your steadfast character. May we live each day with the assurance that You are faithful to fulfill Your purposes in us. In Jesus' name, we pray. Amen.

DAY 279

Spiritual Renewal

"Create in me a pure heart, O God, and renew a steadfast spirit within me." - Psalm 51:10 (NIV)

Spiritual renewal is not merely about superficial changes or temporary fixes; it is about experiencing a profound inward transformation that revitalizes our relationship with God and restores our hearts to their original purity.

In our journey of faith, we may encounter seasons of spiritual dryness, apathy, or even disobedience. Yet, just as the psalmist David cried out to God for renewal, so too can we approach Him with honesty and humility, trusting in His mercy and grace to breathe new life into our souls.

Spiritual renewal involves surrendering our brokenness, sins, and burdens to God and allowing His love to wash over us, cleansing us from within. It is about rekindling the fire of passion for God, reawakening our spirits to His presence, and realigning our hearts with His will.

Heavenly Father, we come before You with humble hearts, acknowledging our need for Your renewing power in our lives. Create in us clean hearts, O God, and renew a steadfast spirit within us. Wash away our sins and fill us afresh with Your Holy Spirit. Help us to walk in obedience and intimacy with You, experiencing the fullness of Your love and grace. May our lives be a testimony to Your transforming power. In Jesus' name, we pray. Amen.

DAY 280

The Importance of Obedience

"If you love me, keep my commands." - John 14:15 (NIV)

Obedience is not merely a set of rules to follow but a heartfelt response to the love of God. It is a demonstration of our love for Him, a tangible expression of our faith and trust in His wisdom and goodness.

The importance of obedience lies in its role in deepening our relationship with God. When we obey His commands, we align our will with His, surrendering our desires and preferences to His divine plan. Obedience is the pathway to intimacy with God, as we learn to trust His guidance and follow His lead in every aspect of our lives.

Moreover, obedience is a reflection of our faith in God's promises. Throughout the Bible, we see the faithfulness of God to those who obey Him wholeheartedly. When we walk in obedience, we position ourselves to receive the blessings, protection, and provision that God has promised to His children.

Heavenly Father, thank You for Your Word that guides us and Your Spirit that empowers us to live lives of obedience. Give us a heart that delights in Your commands and a willingness to obey You in all things. Help us to trust in Your wisdom and goodness, knowing that Your ways are higher than ours. May our obedience be a testimony to Your faithfulness and love. In Jesus' name, we pray. Amen.

DAY 281

Trusting God's Timing

"But they that wait upon the Lord shall renew their strength; they shall mount up with wings as eagles; they shall run, and not be weary; and they shall walk, and not faint." - Isaiah 40:31 (KJV)

In a world that often demands instant gratification, waiting upon the Lord requires patience, faith, and a deep understanding of His sovereignty. It means surrendering our desires, plans, and timelines to His perfect will, knowing that His timing is always impeccable.

Trusting God's timing doesn't mean sitting idly by or passively waiting for things to happen. It involves actively seeking His guidance, obeying His word, and aligning our hearts with His purposes. It's about recognizing that God sees the bigger picture and knows what is best for us, even when we can't see it ourselves.

In the waiting, we learn valuable lessons of faith, perseverance, and dependence on God. We discover that His ways are higher than ours and that His timing is always right. As we trust Him in the waiting, we find renewed strength, soaring on wings of faith and experiencing His sustaining grace.

Heavenly Father, thank You for Your perfect timing in our lives. Help us to trust You wholeheartedly, even when we don't understand Your ways. Give us patience and faith as we wait upon You. Renew our strength, Lord, and help us to soar on wings of faith, knowing that Your plans for us are good. May Your will be done in our lives, in Your perfect timing. In Jesus' name, we pray. Amen.

DAY 282

God's Enduring Love

"The Lord your God is in your midst, a mighty one who will save;
he will rejoice over you with gladness; he will quiet you by his
love; he will exult over you with loud singing." - Zephaniah 3:17
(ESV)

It speaks of a love that is not passive or indifferent but active and passionate—a love that rejoices, comforts, and celebrates over His beloved children. God's love is not bound by time or circumstance; it is eternal, unchanging, and unconditional.

Throughout Scripture, we see evidence of God's enduring love manifested in His relentless pursuit of humanity, His faithfulness in times of trial, and His compassion toward the brokenhearted. From the dawn of creation to the cross of Calvary and beyond, God's love has been the driving force behind His interactions with His creation.

God's enduring love is a source of hope and comfort in the midst of life's storms. It is a steady anchor that holds us firm in times of uncertainty and a healing balm that soothes our wounds. No matter how far we may stray or how many times we may stumble, God's love remains constant, beckoning us back into His embrace.

Heavenly Father, thank You for Your enduring love that knows no bounds. Thank You for loving us with a love that is steadfast and unchanging, a love that surpasses all understanding. Empower us to love others as You have loved us, sharing Your love with a world in need. In Jesus' name, we pray. Amen.

DAY 283

The Hope of Christ

"May the God of hope fill you with all joy and peace as you trust in him, so that you may overflow with hope by the power of the Holy Spirit." - Romans 15:13 (NIV)

Romans 15:13 reminds us that our God is not only the source of hope but also the One who fills us with joy and peace as we place our trust in Him. The hope of Christ is not a fleeting wish or a temporary fix; it is a steadfast anchor for our souls, grounding us in the unchanging promises of God.

When we embrace the hope of Christ, we are infused with a sense of purpose and assurance that transcends our circumstances. It is a hope that empowers us to face life's challenges with courage and resilience, knowing that we are never alone. Even in our darkest moments, we can find comfort in the knowledge that God is with us, guiding us through the storms and leading us into His perfect peace.

Heavenly Father, we thank You for being the God of hope who fills us with joy and peace as we trust in You. Help us to anchor our hearts in the hope of Christ, knowing that You are always with us and that Your promises never fail. Fill us afresh with Your Holy Spirit, that we may overflow with hope and be beacons of light in a world in need of Your love. In Jesus' name, we pray. Amen.

DAY 284

The Importance of Repentance

"Repent, then, and turn to God, so that your sins may be wiped out,
that times of refreshing may come from the Lord." - Acts 3:19
(NIV)

Repentance is not merely a one-time event but a continual posture of the heart—a turning away from sin and a turning toward God. It is an acknowledgment of our need for His forgiveness and a genuine desire to align our lives with His will.

Repentance is vital because it opens the door to restoration and renewal in our relationship with God. When we humbly confess our sins and seek His forgiveness, He promises to wipe away our transgressions and grant us times of refreshing and spiritual rejuvenation.

However, repentance is more than just words; it requires action. It involves a sincere commitment to change, to forsake our sinful ways, and to pursue righteousness. It's a journey of transformation guided by the Holy Spirit, leading us to live lives that honor and glorify God.

Heavenly Father, we acknowledge our need for Your forgiveness
and grace. Help us to humbly repent of our sins and turn to You
with contrite hearts. Grant us the strength and wisdom to live lives
that are pleasing to You, filled with righteousness and obedience.
May we experience the fullness of Your love and mercy each day.
In Jesus' name, we pray. Amen.

DAY 285

The Joy of Salvation

"Restore to me the joy of your salvation and grant me a willing spirit, to sustain me." - Psalm 51:12 (NIV)

The joy of salvation is not just a fleeting emotion; it is a deep, abiding sense of gratitude, peace, and fulfillment that springs from knowing we are forgiven, redeemed, and loved by our Heavenly Father.

When we encounter the saving grace of Jesus Christ, it transforms our lives in ways that we could never imagine. It lifts the heavy burden of sin from our shoulders and replaces it with the lightness of freedom and grace. The joy of salvation fills the deepest recesses of our hearts, casting out fear, doubt, and despair, and replacing them with hope, confidence, and assurance in God's promises.

As Christians, we are called to continually dwell in the joy of our salvation, allowing it to permeate every aspect of our lives. It is a joy that sustains us through life's trials and tribulations, reminding us that our ultimate victory is found in Christ alone.

Heavenly Father, we thank You for the immeasurable gift of salvation that You have freely given us through Your Son, Jesus Christ. Restore to us the joy of Your salvation, Lord, and fill our hearts with Your peace and presence. Help us to live each day with grateful hearts, overflowing with the joy of knowing You and being known by You. May our lives be a testament to Your saving grace, drawing others into the abundant life found in Christ. In His precious name, we pray. Amen.

DAY 286

Living in Grace

"For it is by grace you have been saved, through faith—and this is not from yourselves, it is the gift of God." - Ephesians 2:8 (NIV)

Living in grace is about understanding and embracing this unmerited favor lavished upon us by our Heavenly Father. It is recognizing that we are deeply loved and fully accepted by God, not because of anything we have done, but because of who He is and what He has done for us through Jesus Christ.

Grace is the foundation of our relationship with God and the lens through which we view ourselves and others. It is a constant reminder that we are forgiven, redeemed, and empowered to live lives of freedom and purpose. Living in grace means extending that same forgiveness and love to others, just as God has freely given to us.

In a world often driven by performance and perfectionism, living in grace offers a profound sense of peace and rest for our souls. It frees us from the burden of trying to measure up and instead invites us to rest in the assurance of God's unfailing love and faithfulness.

Heavenly Father, we thank You for the immeasurable gift of Your grace poured out for us through Jesus Christ. Help us to fully embrace and live in the freedom of Your grace each day. May Your grace transform our hearts and overflow into our relationships with others, that we may be vessels of Your love and mercy in the world. In Jesus' name, we pray. Amen.

DAY 287

God's Eternal Kingdom

"But store up for yourselves treasures in heaven, where moths and vermin do not destroy, and where thieves do not break in and steal." - Matthew 6:20 (NIV)

While earthly treasures may fade and be lost, the treasures we store up in heaven are secure and everlasting. God's eternal kingdom is not merely a future destination; it is a present reality that shapes our lives and gives us hope for the future.

The concept of God's eternal kingdom speaks to the ultimate fulfillment of His redemptive plan for humanity. It is a kingdom of righteousness, peace, and joy, where God reigns supreme and His will is fully realized. In this kingdom, there is no more pain, sorrow, or death, but only the glorious presence of God and His beloved children.

Living with an awareness of God's eternal kingdom transforms our perspective on life. It shifts our focus from the temporary pleasures and pursuits of this world to the eternal values of God's kingdom. We are called to invest our time, talents, and resources in things that have eternal significance, such as sharing the Gospel, serving others, and living lives of holiness and obedience to God.

Heavenly Father, we thank You for the promise of Your eternal kingdom, where we will dwell with You forever in perfect peace and joy. Help us to live with an eternal perspective, storing up treasures in heaven rather than on earth. May our lives be a reflection of Your kingdom values, bringing glory to Your name. In Jesus' name, we pray. Amen.

DAY 288

Trusting in God

"Trust in the Lord with all your heart and lean not on your own understanding; in all your ways submit to him, and he will make your paths straight." - Proverbs 3:5-6 (NIV)

Trusting in God is not always easy, especially in the face of uncertainty, challenges, and trials. Yet, it is in those moments of doubt and fear that our trust in God is truly tested and strengthened.

Trusting in God means surrendering our limited understanding and placing our confidence in His infinite wisdom and goodness. It is about releasing our grip on control and allowing God to guide our steps, even when the path ahead seems unclear. When we trust in God, we acknowledge His sovereignty over every aspect of our lives, trusting that He has a perfect plan and purpose for us.

Trusting in God is not passive; it requires action. It means actively seeking His will through prayer, studying His Word, and listening to His voice. It means stepping out in faith, even when the circumstances around us may seem daunting. It means holding onto His promises with unwavering faith, knowing that He is faithful to fulfill them.

Heavenly Father, we thank You for Your faithfulness and goodness. Help us to trust in You with all our hearts, leaning not on our own understanding but acknowledging You in all our ways. Strengthen our faith, Lord, and help us to surrender our fears and doubts to You. Guide our steps and make our paths straight according to Your perfect will. In Jesus' name, we pray. Amen.

DAY 289

The Power of Faith

"Now faith is confidence in what we hope for and assurance about what we do not see." - Hebrews 11:1 (NIV)

Faith is not merely a passive belief; it is an active trust that propels us forward, even in the face of adversity. It is the cornerstone of our relationship with God, the foundation upon which we build our lives.

The power of faith lies in its ability to transcend the limitations of human understanding and to unlock the miraculous in our lives. It is through faith that we experience the presence of God, receive His blessings, and witness His wonders. Faith enables us to see beyond the natural realm and to embrace the supernatural possibilities that God has in store for us.

But faith is not without its challenges. We may be tempted to doubt, to question, and to waver in our trust in God's promises. Yet, even in our moments of weakness, God remains faithful. He invites us to come to Him with mustard seed faith, believing that He is able to do exceedingly abundantly above all that we ask or think.

Heavenly Father, thank You for the gift of faith that enables us to trust in Your promises and Your goodness, even when we cannot see the outcome. Strengthen us to step out in faith, knowing that You are with us every step of the way. May our lives be a testimony to the power of faith to move mountains and to bring glory to Your name. In Jesus' name, we pray. Amen.

DAY 290

The Role of the Holy Spirit

*"But you will receive power when the Holy Spirit comes on you;
and you will be my witnesses in Jerusalem, and in all Judea and
Samaria, and to the ends of the earth." - Acts 1:8 (NIV)*

The Holy Spirit is not merely a theological concept but a divine presence and power that empowers us to fulfill God's purpose for our lives. He is our Comforter, Advocate, and Guide, dwelling within us and equipping us to live as bold witnesses for Christ.

The Holy Spirit is the divine agent of transformation, working within us to convict us of sin, lead us into truth, and conform us to the image of Christ. He empowers us with spiritual gifts and abilities to serve God and build up the body of Christ. Through the Holy Spirit, we are empowered to overcome obstacles, walk in obedience, and bear fruit that glorifies God.

Holy Spirit, we thank You for Your presence and power in our lives. Fill us afresh with Your Spirit, empowering us to live as bold witnesses for Christ. Lead us, guide us, and empower us to walk in obedience and fulfill Your purposes for our lives. May our lives be a testimony to Your transforming work within us. In Jesus' name, we pray. Amen.

DAY 291

Spiritual Victory

"But thanks be to God! He gives us the victory through our Lord Jesus Christ." - 1 Corinthians 15:57 (NIV)

As Christians, we are not called to live defeated lives, shackled by sin, fear, or despair. Instead, we are called to walk in the freedom and victory that Christ has secured for us through His death and resurrection.

Spiritual victory is not just a distant hope or a future promise; it is a present reality that we can experience every day. It is the assurance that no matter what challenges or obstacles we face, we can overcome them by the power of God working within us. It is the confidence that even in our weakest moments, God's strength is made perfect, and His grace is always sufficient.

But spiritual victory is not passive; it requires active participation on our part. It involves putting on the full armor of God, standing firm in faith, and fighting the good fight with courage and perseverance. It means surrendering our will to God's will, trusting in His promises, and allowing His Spirit to lead us into triumph.

Gracious Father, we thank You for the victory that we have through Jesus Christ our Lord. Help us to walk in the power of Your Spirit, overcoming every obstacle and defeating every foe. Strengthen us in faith, fill us with courage, and lead us into the abundant life You have promised. May Your victory shine through us, bringing glory to Your name. In Jesus' name, we pray. Amen.

DAY 292

God's Promises

"For no matter how many promises God has made, they are 'Yes' in Christ. And so through him, the 'Amen' is spoken by us to the glory of God." - 2 Corinthians 1:20 (NIV)

God's promises are not empty words; they are the bedrock of our faith, the foundation upon which we build our lives. They serve as beacons of hope in times of darkness, guiding us through life's trials and uncertainties.

God's promises are like precious treasures waiting to be discovered and embraced. They offer comfort in moments of despair, strength in times of weakness, and peace in the midst of chaos. From Genesis to Revelation, the Bible is filled with countless promises that speak to every aspect of our lives, from salvation and forgiveness to provision and protection.

As believers, we are called to not only believe in God's promises but to claim them as our own. Through Christ, we have been given the privilege to say "Amen" to God's promises, affirming our trust in His faithfulness and sovereignty. When we stand on the solid ground of God's promises, we can face any circumstance with unwavering confidence, knowing that He who promised is faithful.

Heavenly Father, we thank You for Your faithful promises that sustain us and give us hope. Help us to trust in Your word and to hold fast to Your promises, knowing that You are always true to Your word. May Your promises be a source of encouragement and strength as we journey through life with You. In Jesus' name, we pray. Amen.

DAY 293

The Love of Christ

"For I am convinced that neither death nor life, neither angels nor demons, neither the present nor the future, nor any powers, neither height nor depth, nor anything else in all creation, will be able to separate us from the love of God that is in Christ Jesus our Lord."
- Romans 8:38-39 (NIV)

It is a love that transcends all barriers and conquers all fears. The love of Christ is not mere sentimentality or fleeting emotion; it is a sacrificial, unconditional love that was demonstrated on the cross for all humanity.

The love of Christ is a love that knows no limits. It is a love that pursued us even in our rebellion, that endured the agony of the cross to offer us forgiveness and redemption. It is a love that reaches into the darkest corners of our hearts, offering healing, restoration, and hope.

As recipients of this unfathomable love, we are called to respond in kind. We are called to love God with all our hearts, minds, and souls, and to love our neighbors as ourselves. Our lives are to be a reflection of the love of Christ, shining brightly in a world filled with darkness and despair.

Heavenly Father, we thank You for the incomparable love demonstrated to us through Your Son, Jesus Christ. Help us to grasp the depth and breadth of this love, that it may transform our hearts and lives. May Your love shine through us, drawing others into Your embrace. In Jesus' name, we pray. Amen.

DAY 294

The Joy of Worship

"Shout for joy to the Lord, all the earth. Worship the Lord with gladness; come before him with joyful songs." - Psalm 100:1-2 (NIV)

It calls us to lift our voices in exultation, to approach the throne of God with hearts overflowing with gladness and gratitude. Worship is not just a routine or obligation; it is a joyous celebration of our relationship with the Almighty, a precious opportunity to commune with Him in spirit and truth.

The joy of worship stems from recognizing and responding to God's goodness, faithfulness, and majesty. It is a response to His unfailing love and mercy poured out upon us each day. When we enter into worship with hearts open and spirits attuned to His presence, we experience a deep sense of joy and peace that transcends circumstances.

In worship, we lay aside our worries, doubts, and fears, and we focus our attention solely on God. We sing praises to His name, we lift our hands in surrender, and we offer our lives as living sacrifices, holy and pleasing to Him.

Heavenly Father, we thank You for the privilege of worshiping You, our loving and faithful Creator. Fill our hearts with joy as we come before Your throne with songs of praise and thanksgiving. May our lives be a constant offering of worship to You, our King and Redeemer. In Jesus' name, we pray. Amen.

DAY 295

God's Sovereignty

"Remember the former things, those of long ago; I am God, and there is no other; I am God, and there is none like me. I make known the end from the beginning, from ancient times, what is still to come. I say, 'My purpose will stand, and I will do all that I please.'" - Isaiah 46:9-10 (NIV)

He is not bound by time or circumstance; rather, He reigns supreme over all creation. God's sovereignty encompasses His power to rule over every aspect of existence, from the grandeur of the cosmos to the intricacies of our daily lives. It is a comforting truth that assures us of His unchanging nature and His absolute control over the course of history.

Understanding God's sovereignty can be both awe-inspiring and humbling. It means acknowledging that He is the ultimate authority, and His purposes will prevail, regardless of the challenges we face or the plans we make. It invites us to trust in His wisdom and goodness, even when we cannot comprehend His ways.

In light of God's sovereignty, we are called to surrender our lives completely to Him, knowing that He works all things together for our good and His glory.

Gracious God, we praise You for Your sovereign rule over all creation. Help us to trust in Your perfect wisdom and to surrender our lives completely to Your will. Guide us in obedience and faithfulness, as we seek to honor You in all that we do. In Jesus' name, we pray. Amen.

DAY 296

The Role of Scripture

"All Scripture is God-breathed and is useful for teaching, rebuking, correcting and training in righteousness, so that the servant of God may be thoroughly equipped for every good work."
- 2 Timothy 3:16-17 (NIV)

In 2 Timothy 3:16-17, we are reminded that all Scripture is inspired by God Himself, given to us for our instruction, correction, and growth in righteousness. The Bible is not just a book of stories or moral lessons; it is the very voice of God speaking to us, guiding us, and shaping us into the people He has called us to be.

The role of Scripture in the life of a Christian is indispensable. It serves as our compass in a world filled with confusion and uncertainty, providing us with timeless truths and principles to navigate life's challenges. Through Scripture, we gain insight into God's character, His promises, and His will for our lives. It illuminates the path of righteousness, leading us closer to God and empowering us to live lives that honor Him.

Heavenly Father, we thank You for the gift of Your Word, which is a lamp unto our feet and a light unto our path. Help us to approach Scripture with reverence and humility, recognizing its authority in our lives. Open our hearts and minds to receive Your truth and wisdom, and empower us to live according to Your will. May Your Word dwell richly in us, transforming us from the inside out. In Jesus' name, we pray. Amen.

DAY 297

Living a Godly Life

"For the grace of God has appeared that offers salvation to all people. It teaches us to say 'No' to ungodliness and worldly passions, and to live self-controlled, upright and godly lives in this present age." - Titus 2:11-12 (NIV)

Living a godly life is not about adhering to a set of rules or striving for perfection on our own strength. It is about embracing the gift of salvation offered to us through Jesus Christ and allowing His grace to mold and shape us into His image.

To live a godly life means to reflect the character of God in all areas of our existence. It involves surrendering our will to His, allowing His Word to guide our thoughts, words, and actions. It means loving others sacrificially, forgiving as we have been forgiven, and extending grace to those around us.

Living a godly life also requires discernment and discipline. We must be intentional about guarding our hearts and minds against the influences of the world, resisting temptation, and choosing righteousness over sin. It's a daily commitment to walk in obedience to God's commands, trusting in His strength to help us overcome every obstacle.

Heavenly Father, thank You for Your grace that empowers us to live godly lives in a world filled with challenges and temptations. Help us to walk in the light of Your truth, reflecting Your love and character to those around us. May our lives be a testimony to Your transforming power and grace. In Jesus' name, we pray. Amen.

DAY 298

God's Faithfulness

"The steadfast love of the Lord never ceases; his mercies never come to an end; they are new every morning; great is your faithfulness." - Lamentations 3:22-23 (ESV)

Despite the trials and tribulations that surround us, His love remains unwavering, His mercies endless. God's faithfulness is not contingent upon our circumstances; it is an unchanging reality that sustains us through every season of life.

God's faithfulness is a beacon of hope in the darkness, a reminder that we are never alone, even in our deepest valleys. It is a promise that He will never abandon us, never forsake us. His faithfulness endures through every storm, every trial, every doubt. When we are weak, He is strong. When we falter, He remains steadfast.

Reflect on the countless times God has shown His faithfulness in your life. Remember the answered prayers, the unexpected blessings, the moments of grace and provision. Even in the midst of uncertainty, hold fast to the assurance that His faithfulness remains unchanged.

Gracious Father, we thank You for Your unwavering faithfulness that sustains us through every trial and triumph. Help us to trust in Your goodness and mercy, knowing that Your love never fails. May Your faithfulness be a beacon of hope in our hearts, guiding us always closer to You. In Jesus' name, we pray. Amen.

DAY 299

The Importance of Prayer

"Rejoice always, pray continually, give thanks in all circumstances; for this is God's will for you in Christ Jesus." - 1 Thessalonians 5:16-18 (NIV)

Prayer is not merely a religious duty or a ritualistic practice; it is a powerful means of communication with our Heavenly Father. It is through prayer that we cultivate intimacy with God, align our hearts with His will, and experience His presence in our lives.

Prayer is our lifeline to God, a direct line of access to the throne room of heaven. It is where we pour out our hearts, share our joys and sorrows, and seek guidance, strength, and comfort from the One who knows us intimately and loves us unconditionally. Through prayer, we acknowledge our dependence on God and entrust our lives into His loving hands.

Furthermore, prayer is not confined to specific times or places; it is a continuous conversation with God that permeates every aspect of our lives. Whether we're facing challenges, celebrating victories, or simply going about our daily routines, prayer is our constant companion, guiding and sustaining us through every season.

Heavenly Father, we thank You for the gift of prayer and the privilege of coming before Your throne with confidence. Help us to cultivate a fervent prayer life, rejoicing always, praying continually, and giving thanks in all circumstances. May our prayers be a sweet fragrance unto You, and may they draw us ever closer to Your heart. In Jesus' name, we pray. Amen.

DAY 300

The Power of the Gospel

"For I am not ashamed of the gospel, because it is the power of God that brings salvation to everyone who believes: first to the Jew, then to the Gentile." - Romans 1:16 (NIV)

It is not merely a message; it is the very embodiment of God's power to transform lives, reconcile sinners to Himself, and bring salvation to all who believe. The gospel is the heartbeat of Christianity, the foundation upon which our faith stands, and the hope that sustains us through every trial and triumph.

At the core of the gospel is the story of God's unconditional love and sacrificial grace. It is the story of Jesus Christ, who left the glory of heaven to walk among us, to suffer and die on a cross, and to rise again triumphantly, conquering sin and death once and for all. Through His death and resurrection, Jesus offers forgiveness, redemption, and eternal life to all who repent and believe in Him.

The power of the gospel transcends cultural barriers, societal divides, and personal struggles. It is the power to bring hope to the hopeless, joy to the sorrowful, and freedom to the captive. No other message in human history has the power to transform hearts and change lives like the gospel of Jesus Christ.

Heavenly Father, thank You for the incredible power of the gospel to bring salvation to all who believe. Help us to never be ashamed of this message but to boldly proclaim it to the ends of the earth. May Your gospel continue to transform lives and bring glory to Your name. In Jesus' name, we pray. Amen.

DAY 301

Spiritual Gifts

"Now to each one the manifestation of the Spirit is given for the common good." - 1 Corinthians 12:7 (NIV)

These gifts are not meant to elevate us but to serve others and to build up the church. They are expressions of God's grace and power working through us, each gift uniquely tailored to our calling and purpose.

Spiritual gifts are diverse, ranging from wisdom and knowledge to healing, prophecy, and acts of service. Each gift, whether it seems grand or humble, plays a crucial role in God's kingdom. When we embrace and utilize our spiritual gifts, we become active participants in God's work, shining His light and spreading His love to those around us.

Discovering and developing our spiritual gifts is a journey of faith and obedience. It begins with a desire to serve and a willingness to be used by God. As we seek His guidance through prayer and Scripture, He reveals the gifts He has bestowed upon us.

Heavenly Father, thank You for the precious gifts You have given each of us through Your Spirit. Help us to recognize and embrace these gifts, using them for Your glory and the good of others. Fill us with courage and humility as we step out in faith to serve. May our lives be a testament to Your love and power, inspiring those around us to seek and use their own gifts. In Jesus' name, we pray. Amen.

DAY 302

The Call to Serve

"For even the Son of Man did not come to be served, but to serve, and to give His life as a ransom for many." - Mark 10:45 (NIV)

This profound example set by Jesus calls each of us to embrace a life of service. The call to serve is not merely an option but a central aspect of our Christian faith. It is through serving others that we truly reflect the love and humility of our Savior.

In a world that often celebrates power, status, and self-interest, Jesus' life teaches us the beauty of selfless love. He washed the feet of His disciples, healed the sick, fed the hungry, and ultimately sacrificed His life for our salvation. His actions demonstrate that true greatness is found in serving others with compassion and humility.

Embracing the call to serve means looking beyond our own needs and desires to the needs of those around us. It is about being the hands and feet of Jesus in a broken world, offering hope, kindness, and support wherever it is needed. When we serve, we become channels of God's love, bringing light to dark places and healing to broken hearts.

Heavenly Father, thank You for the perfect example of service You have given us in Jesus. Help us to embrace the call to serve others with love and humility. Open our eyes to the needs around us and give us the courage to step forward in faith. May our acts of service bring glory to Your name and reflect Your incredible love to the world. In Jesus' name, we pray. Amen.

DAY 303

God's Protection

"The Lord is my rock, my fortress, and my deliverer; my God is my rock, in whom I take refuge, my shield and the horn of my salvation, my stronghold." - Psalm 18:2 (NIV)

In times of uncertainty and fear, this verse reassures us that we are never alone; we have a mighty fortress in God. He is our rock, our unshakable foundation, and our deliverer who saves us from danger. When life feels overwhelming, and we find ourselves facing battles we cannot fight on our own, we can take refuge in the shadow of His wings, knowing He is our shield and stronghold.

God's protection is not just about physical safety; it encompasses our emotional, spiritual, and mental well-being. He guards our hearts and minds, offering peace that transcends understanding even in the midst of chaos. His protection is a testament to His love and faithfulness, reminding us that no matter the circumstances, we are held securely in His hands.

It's easy to forget God's protective presence when we're surrounded by challenges. Doubts may creep in, and fear may cloud our vision. But in those moments, we need to remember His promises and hold on to the truth that God is always with us, fighting for us and shielding us from harm.

Heavenly Father, thank You for being our rock, fortress, and deliverer. We are grateful for Your constant protection and for the assurance that we are never alone. Strengthen our faith so that we may stand firm in the knowledge that You are always with us. In Jesus' name, we pray. Amen.

DAY 304

Living with Purpose

"For we are God's handiwork, created in Christ Jesus to do good works, which God prepared in advance for us to do." - Ephesians 2:10 (NIV)

Living with purpose is about recognizing that we are not here by chance, but by divine design. Each of us is a masterpiece created in Christ Jesus, uniquely fashioned to carry out the good works God has prepared for us.

Living with purpose means embracing the calling God has placed on our lives. It's about understanding that our skills, talents, and passions are gifts from God meant to be used for His glory and the benefit of others. When we live purposefully, we align our actions and decisions with God's will, finding fulfillment in knowing we are part of His grand plan.

Purpose gives our lives direction and meaning. It transforms mundane tasks into acts of worship and service. Whether it's in our careers, relationships, or daily interactions, living with purpose brings a sense of joy and satisfaction that comes from knowing we are contributing to something greater than ourselves.

However, discovering our purpose can sometimes feel daunting. We might struggle with doubt or uncertainty about what God has planned for us.

Heavenly Father, thank You for creating us with purpose and for the unique calling You have placed on our lives. May our lives bring glory to Your name and fulfill the good works You have prepared for us. In Jesus' name, we pray. Amen.

DAY 305

The Joy of Fellowship

"How good and pleasant it is when God's people live together in unity!" - Psalm 133:1 (NIV)

It is a delight and blessing to be united with fellow believers, sharing life, faith, and love. Fellowship is more than just a social gathering; it is a profound experience of community where we support, encourage, and uplift one another in our spiritual journeys.

The joy of fellowship is rooted in our shared relationship with Christ. As members of His body, we are connected in a deep and meaningful way. This connection transcends differences in background, culture, and personality, creating a bond that is both sacred and life-giving. In fellowship, we find a safe haven where we can be authentic, share our burdens, and celebrate our victories.

Through fellowship, we experience the tangible presence of God's love. It is through our interactions with one another that we often feel His comfort, guidance, and joy. The early church in Acts 2:42-47 exemplified this beautifully as they devoted themselves to teaching, breaking bread, and prayer, resulting in a community filled with awe and gladness.

Heavenly Father, we thank You for the gift of fellowship. Help us to cherish and nurture the relationships we have with our brothers and sisters in Christ. Fill our hearts with love and unity, and let our interactions reflect Your grace and compassion. May our fellowship be a beacon of joy and hope to the world. In Jesus' name, we pray. Amen.

DAY 306

The Hope of the Righteous

"The hope of the righteous brings joy, but the expectation of the wicked will perish." - Proverbs 10:28 (ESV)

This hope is not a fleeting wish or a mere desire for good things to come; it is a confident assurance rooted in the faithfulness of God. For those who walk in righteousness, hope is an anchor for the soul, steadfast and sure, grounded in the promises of a loving and sovereign God.

The world often offers false hopes—promises of success, pleasure, and security that ultimately fade away. But the hope of the righteous is eternal and unshakable. It is the hope of salvation through Jesus Christ, the hope of eternal life, and the hope of God's continual presence and guidance in our lives. This hope sustains us through trials, comforts us in sorrow, and fills us with joy that transcends our circumstances.

Living with this hope transforms our outlook on life. It fills our hearts with joy, even in the midst of difficulties, because we know that our future is secure in God's hands. It encourages us to persevere, to keep our eyes fixed on Jesus, and to trust that God is working all things together for our good.

Heavenly Father, thank You for the hope that we have in You. This hope brings joy to our hearts and sustains us through all of life's challenges. Fill us with Your peace and use us to bring hope to those around us. In Jesus' name, we pray. Amen.

DAY 307

The Birth of Christ

"But the angel said to them, 'Do not be afraid. I bring you good news that will cause great joy for all the people. Today in the town of David a Savior has been born to you; he is the Messiah, the Lord.'" - Luke 2:10-11 (NIV)

In Luke 2:10-11, the angel's proclamation to the shepherds heralds the arrival of a Savior, bringing joy, hope, and redemption to a weary world. This divine event, wrapped in humility and simplicity, reveals God's profound love for us and His desire to draw us close.

Imagine the scene: a humble stable in Bethlehem, where the King of Kings entered the world not in grandeur but in modesty. The infinite God took on human flesh, becoming Emmanuel—God with us. This miraculous birth fulfilled ancient prophecies and illuminated the darkness with the light of salvation. It reminds us that God often works through the unexpected, the overlooked, and the ordinary to accomplish His extraordinary purposes.

As we reflect on the birth of Christ, we are invited to respond with awe and gratitude. This event is not just a historical fact but a personal gift to each of us. Jesus' birth signifies God's unending love, His willingness to meet us where we are, and His commitment to our redemption.

Heavenly Father, thank You for the incredible gift of Your Son, Jesus Christ. As we celebrate His birth, fill our hearts with wonder and gratitude. Empower us to share this good news with others and to live in a way that reflects the joy and hope of our Savior. In Jesus' name, we pray. Amen.

DAY 308

God's Unfailing Love

"The steadfast love of the Lord never ceases; His mercies never come to an end; they are new every morning; great is Your faithfulness." - Lamentations 3:22-23 (ESV)

God's unfailing love and unending mercies. The steadfast love of the Lord is a constant in our ever-changing world, a source of strength and comfort that never fades. No matter the circumstances we face, His love remains unwavering, a rock upon which we can securely stand.

God's love is not conditional or dependent on our actions. It is a love that embraces us in our brokenness, forgives us in our failures, and sustains us in our trials. This divine love was most profoundly demonstrated through Jesus Christ, who laid down His life for us. Through His sacrifice, we are invited into a relationship with God, where His love continually renews and restores us.

Experiencing God's unfailing love transforms our lives. It fills us with hope, even in the darkest moments, and empowers us to love others with the same grace and compassion we have received.

Heavenly Father, thank You for Your unfailing love and endless mercies. Help us to remember that Your love is constant, even when life is challenging. Fill our hearts with gratitude and empower us to share Your love with those around us. May our lives be a testament to Your great faithfulness. In Jesus' name, we pray. Amen.

DAY 309

The Role of Grace

"But he said to me, 'My grace is sufficient for you, for my power is made perfect in weakness.'" - 2 Corinthians 12:9a (NIV)

This verse, spoken by the Lord to the Apostle Paul, reassures us that grace is not only sufficient but also perfects us in our weakness. Grace is the unmerited favor of God, a divine gift that empowers us, sustains us, and brings us into a deeper relationship with Him.

The role of grace in our lives is multifaceted and essential. It is through grace that we are saved, as Ephesians 2:8 tells us: "For it is by grace you have been saved, through faith—and this is not from yourselves, it is the gift of God." Grace justifies us, making us righteous before God despite our sins. It sanctifies us, helping us to grow in holiness and conform to the image of Christ. Grace also sustains us in times of trial and weakness, offering us strength and comfort when we need it most.

Embracing grace means accepting that we are not perfect and that we cannot earn God's favor through our own efforts. It requires us to trust in God's mercy and to rely on His strength. This trust frees us from the burden of trying to achieve righteousness on our own and allows us to rest in the assurance of His love and forgiveness.

Heavenly Father, thank You for Your amazing grace that is sufficient for all our needs. Help us to embrace our weaknesses and to rely on Your strength. Teach us to live each day in the light of Your grace, trusting in Your power to perfect us. May Your grace flow through us, touching the lives of those around us and bringing glory to Your name. In Jesus' name, we pray. Amen.

DAY 310

Spiritual Renewal

"Create in me a pure heart, O God, and renew a steadfast spirit within me." - Psalm 51:10 (NIV)

This heartfelt plea from David, written in a moment of profound repentance, resonates with anyone seeking a fresh start and a renewed connection with God. Spiritual renewal is about more than just turning over a new leaf; it's about a transformative encounter with God's grace that revives our soul and reignites our passion for Him.

Life can be overwhelming, and our spiritual vitality can wane under the weight of daily struggles, sin, and complacency. But God, in His infinite mercy, offers us renewal. He invites us to bring our weary hearts to Him, to allow His love to cleanse and restore us. Spiritual renewal involves a sincere turning back to God, a rediscovery of His presence and power in our lives.

Imagine your heart as a garden. Over time, weeds of worry, bitterness, and sin can take root, choking out the beauty that God intends to flourish there. Spiritual renewal is God's work of pulling out those weeds and planting new seeds of hope, faith, and love.

Heavenly Father, we come to You with humble hearts, longing for Your renewing touch. Create in us pure hearts, O God, and renew steadfast spirits within us. Remove anything that hinders our relationship with You and fill us afresh with Your Holy Spirit. Help us to walk closely with You, experiencing the joy and peace that comes from a renewed spirit. In Jesus' name, we pray. Amen.

DAY 311

Trusting God's Timing

"But do not forget this one thing, dear friends: With the Lord a day is like a thousand years, and a thousand years are like a day." - 2 Peter 3:8 (NIV)

While we may be consumed by impatience and urgency, God operates outside of time, orchestrating His plans with perfect precision and divine wisdom. Trusting God's timing requires us to surrender our desire for immediate results and to place our faith in His sovereign control over all things.

Trusting God's timing is not passive resignation; it is an active expression of faith. It means believing that God's delays are not denials and that His timing is always for our ultimate good and His glory. It involves releasing our need for control and embracing a posture of surrender, knowing that God's ways are higher than our ways and His thoughts are higher than our thoughts.

When we trust God's timing, we find peace amidst the uncertainties of life. We no longer fret and worry about the future but instead rest in the assurance that God is working all things together for our good. We can confidently face each day, knowing that God's plans for us are far greater than anything we could imagine.

Heavenly Father, help us to trust in Your perfect timing, even when we cannot see the way forward. Give us patience to wait on You and faith to believe that Your plans for us are good and purposeful. May Your will be done in our lives, according to Your perfect timing. In Jesus' name, we pray. Amen.

DAY 312

The Power of Hope

"May the God of hope fill you with all joy and peace as you trust in him, so that you may overflow with hope by the power of the Holy Spirit." - Romans 15:13 (NIV)

Hope is not merely wishful thinking or optimistic sentimentality; it is a confident expectation rooted in the promises of God. It is the anchor for our souls in the midst of life's storms, the light that pierces through the darkness of despair, and the source of strength that sustains us through trials and tribulations.

Hope is what sustains us when all seems lost, when circumstances threaten to overwhelm us, and when the future appears uncertain. It is the assurance that God is faithful, that His plans for us are good, and that He is working all things together for our ultimate good. As Christians, our hope is not grounded in fleeting worldly things but in the eternal promises of God, which are unchanging and unfailing.

In a world marked by brokenness, pain, and suffering, the power of hope is a beacon of light that guides us toward the promise of redemption and restoration. It is what enables us to persevere in faith, to hold fast to God's promises, and to live with confidence and courage in the midst of adversity.

Heavenly Father, thank You for being the God of hope who fills us with joy and peace as we trust in You. Help us to anchor our hearts and minds in Your promises, that we may overflow with hope by the power of Your Holy Spirit. May our lives be a testimony to the transformative power of hope found in You. In Jesus' name, we pray. Amen.

DAY 313

God's Enduring Love

"The Lord your God is in your midst, a mighty one who will save; he will rejoice over you with gladness; he will quiet you by his love; he will exult over you with loud singing." - Zephaniah 3:17 (ESV)

It speaks of a God who not only saves and rejoices over us but also quiets our fears and anxieties with His boundless love. God's love is not fleeting or conditional; it is steadfast and unwavering, a constant source of comfort and strength in the midst of life's trials and uncertainties.

God's enduring love is a foundational truth that anchors our faith. It is a love that transcends our shortcomings and failures, reaching out to us in our brokenness and lifting us up with His grace and mercy. It is a love that never gives up on us, even when we stray or stumble along the way.

As we meditate on the depth of God's love, we are called to respond with gratitude and devotion. We are invited to rest in the assurance of His love, allowing it to fill our hearts with peace and joy. And we are challenged to reflect God's love to others, sharing His grace and compassion with those around us.

Gracious God, thank You for Your enduring love that never fails. In moments of doubt and fear, help us to remember Your promise to rejoice over us with gladness and to quiet us by Your love. May Your love be our guiding light and our source of strength each day. In Jesus' name, we pray. Amen.

DAY 314

The Wisdom of Proverbs

"The fear of the Lord is the beginning of knowledge, but fools despise wisdom and instruction." - Proverbs 1:7 (NIV)

The book begins with a powerful declaration: "The fear of the Lord is the beginning of knowledge." This verse encapsulates the foundational principle upon which all wisdom is built – reverence and awe for God. True wisdom begins with acknowledging God's sovereignty, submitting to His will, and seeking His guidance in all things.

In Proverbs, we find timeless truths that address a wide range of topics, including relationships, finances, speech, character, and decision-making. Each proverb is like a precious gem, offering insights that are both profound and practical. As we meditate on these words of wisdom, we are not only enlightened but also transformed, for they have the power to shape our thoughts, attitudes, and actions.

The wisdom of Proverbs is not meant to be merely intellectual knowledge but a lived experience. It calls us to embody wisdom in our daily lives, to walk in integrity, humility, and righteousness. It challenges us to be discerning in our choices, to seek counsel from the wise, and to heed correction with humility.

Heavenly Father, we thank You for the gift of Your Word, which is a lamp to our feet and a light to our path. Grant us wisdom, O Lord, to understand Your truth and to walk in Your ways. May Your wisdom guide us in all that we do, bringing honor and glory to Your name. In Jesus' name, we pray. Amen.

DAY 315

Trust in God's Promises

"For no matter how many promises God has made, they are 'Yes' in Christ. And so through him the 'Amen' is spoken by us to the glory of God." - 2 Corinthians 1:20 (NIV)

Every word spoken by our Heavenly Father is filled with power and purpose, and they are all fulfilled in Christ Jesus. Trusting in God's promises is not merely an exercise of faith; it is an anchoring of our souls to the unshakeable foundation of His character and love.

In a world filled with uncertainty and turmoil, God's promises stand as unwavering pillars of hope. They remind us that we serve a God who is faithful and true, who never wavers in His commitment to His children. From the promise of salvation and eternal life to the assurance of His presence and provision in our daily lives, God's promises are a source of comfort, strength, and peace.

Trusting in God's promises requires us to let go of our doubts and fears and to fix our eyes firmly on Him. It means surrendering our plans and desires to His will, knowing that His plans for us are good and perfect.

Heavenly Father, we thank You for Your precious promises that sustain us through every season of life. Help us to trust in Your unfailing love and faithfulness, even when circumstances seem uncertain. Give us the courage to hold fast to Your promises and to live with confident expectation of Your goodness. May our lives bring glory to Your name as we walk in faith and obedience. In Jesus' name, we pray. Amen.

DAY 316

The Gift of Grace

"For it is by grace you have been saved, through faith—and this is not from yourselves, it is the gift of God." - Ephesians 2:8 (NIV)

Grace is the unmerited favor of God, a gift we could never earn or deserve. It is through grace that we are saved, embraced by God's boundless love, and invited into a relationship with Him. This grace is not a result of our works but is a free and precious gift from our Heavenly Father.

The gift of grace is the cornerstone of our faith, a testament to God's incredible love and mercy. It assures us that no matter how far we have strayed, no matter how many times we have failed, God's grace is sufficient to cover all our sins. It is a source of endless hope and a reminder of God's unwavering commitment to us. When we truly grasp the depth of this grace, our hearts are filled with gratitude and our lives are transformed.

Living in the light of grace means extending it to ourselves and others. It calls us to forgive as we have been forgiven, to love as we have been loved, and to show mercy as we have received mercy. Grace invites us to live with a spirit of humility, knowing that every good thing we have comes from God's hand.

Heavenly Father, thank You for the incredible gift of grace. Help us to comprehend the depth of Your love and mercy towards us. Fill our hearts with gratitude and transform our lives by Your grace. Teach us to extend grace to others, showing forgiveness, love, and mercy in all we do. May our lives be a reflection of Your amazing grace. In Jesus' name, we pray. Amen.

DAY 317

God's Righteous Judgment

"The Lord is a righteous judge, a God who displays his wrath every day." - Psalm 7:11 (NIV)

While the concept of God's judgment can be daunting, it is also a profound testament to His righteousness and love. God's judgment is not arbitrary or capricious; it is a reflection of His perfect justice and unwavering commitment to truth and righteousness.

God's righteous judgment assures us that evil will not go unpunished and that justice will ultimately prevail. It is a promise that every wrong will be righted and every sin will be accounted for. This is both comforting and challenging. It comforts us because we know that God sees the injustices we face and will make all things right. It challenges us because it calls us to live in accordance with His standards, knowing that our actions matter and that we are accountable to Him.

Understanding God's righteous judgment also deepens our appreciation for His mercy. Despite our sins, God offers us grace through Jesus Christ. Jesus bore the weight of our sins on the cross, satisfying the demands of justice so that we might receive forgiveness and eternal life.

Righteous Judge, we come before You acknowledging our need for Your mercy and grace. Help us to live in a way that reflects Your righteousness and justice. Give us the courage to confront our sins and to stand up against injustice. Thank You for the forgiveness and redemption we have through Jesus Christ. In Jesus' name, we pray. Amen.

DAY 318

Embracing God's Peace

"Peace I leave with you; my peace I give you. I do not give to you as the world gives. Do not let your hearts be troubled and do not be afraid." - John 14:27 (NIV)

Unlike the fleeting and often fragile peace the world offers, Christ's peace is enduring, unshakable, and rooted in the depths of God's love. It is a peace that transcends circumstances, soothing our troubled hearts and calming our fears. In a world filled with chaos, uncertainty, and stress, embracing God's peace becomes a powerful anchor for our souls.

Embracing God's peace means surrendering our anxieties and burdens to Him, trusting that He is in control and that His plans for us are good. It involves shifting our focus from the tumult around us to the steadfast presence of God within us. This peace is not the absence of conflict or challenges, but the presence of God in the midst of them, providing comfort and strength.

To live in God's peace, we must cultivate a deep and abiding relationship with Him through prayer, meditation on His Word, and reliance on the Holy Spirit. As we draw near to God, His peace begins to permeate every aspect of our lives, transforming our worries into worship and our fears into faith.

Heavenly Father, thank You for the gift of Your peace that surpasses all understanding. Help us to embrace this peace, letting it guard our hearts and minds in Christ Jesus. Fill us with Your peace and let it flow through us, bringing comfort to others. In Jesus' name, we pray. Amen.

DAY 319

Living Out the Gospel

"In the same way, let your light shine before others, that they may see your good deeds and glorify your Father in heaven." - Matthew 5:16 (NIV)

Matthew 5:16 calls us to live out the gospel in our daily lives, letting the light of Christ shine through us so that others may see our good deeds and glorify our Father in heaven. Living out the gospel means embodying the teachings and love of Jesus in everything we do. It is not just about words or beliefs, but about actions that reflect the heart of Christ.

The gospel transforms us from the inside out, filling us with love, compassion, and a desire to serve others. When we live out the gospel, we become living testimonies of God's grace and mercy. Our lives, though imperfect, can be powerful witnesses to the hope and redemption found in Jesus.

Living out the gospel challenges us to love our neighbors, forgive those who wrong us, and extend grace even in difficult situations. It means seeking justice, showing kindness, and walking humbly with God. It involves being the hands and feet of Jesus, reaching out to the lost, the hurting, and the marginalized.

Heavenly Father, thank You for the transforming power of the gospel. Help us to live out Your love in our daily lives, letting our light shine before others. May our lives glorify You and draw others to the hope and salvation found in Jesus. In His precious name, we pray. Amen.

DAY 320

The Power of the Blood of Jesus

"But if we walk in the light, as he is in the light, we have fellowship with one another, and the blood of Jesus, his Son, purifies us from all sin." - 1 John 1:7 (NIV)

1 John 1:7 reminds us that through His blood, we are purified from all sin. This cleansing power is not merely symbolic; it represents the ultimate sacrifice and the boundless love of our Savior. Jesus' blood shed on the cross is the means by which we are reconciled to God, forgiven of our sins, and granted eternal life.

The blood of Jesus signifies redemption and freedom. It breaks the chains of sin and shame that bind us, offering us a new beginning and a fresh start. No longer are we defined by our past mistakes or failures; through His blood, we are made new, whole, and holy. It is the blood that seals the new covenant between God and humanity, a covenant of grace, mercy, and everlasting love.

Reflecting on the power of Jesus' blood can bring deep emotional and spiritual healing. It reassures us of God's immense love and the lengths He went to save us. In moments of doubt, guilt, or fear, remembering the sacrifice of Jesus and the cleansing power of His blood can restore our faith and renew our hope.

Heavenly Father, thank You for the precious blood of Jesus that purifies us from all sin. We stand in awe of Your love and sacrifice. Help us to live in the light of this truth, embracing the freedom and redemption that His blood provides. Cleanse our hearts and renew our spirits, Lord. May we always remember and proclaim the power of Jesus' blood. In His holy name, we pray. Amen.

DAY 321

God's Majestic Creation

"The heavens declare the glory of God; the skies proclaim the work of his hands." - Psalm 19:1 (NIV)

Every sunrise that paints the sky with hues of gold and crimson, every mountain standing tall in silent testimony, and every star that twinkles in the night speaks of the Creator's unparalleled artistry and power. God's creation is a symphony of His glory, a living testament to His infinite wisdom and love.

In the vast expanse of the universe, we find a reflection of God's grandeur. The intricate design of a single flower, the rhythmic ebb and flow of the oceans, and the delicate balance of ecosystems all point to a Creator who is both meticulous and mighty. His handiwork is evident in the smallest details and the grandest vistas, reminding us of His presence and His care.

As we contemplate the wonders of nature, our hearts are drawn into worship. We are reminded that the same God who set the stars in place knows us intimately and cares for us deeply. This realization should fill us with awe and reverence, inspiring us to live in harmony with His creation and to honor Him in all we do.

Heavenly Father, we stand in awe of Your majestic creation. The beauty and complexity of the world around us declare Your glory and power. Thank You for the gift of nature that reveals Your character and care. Help us to be faithful stewards of Your creation, to cherish and protect it as a reflection of our love for You. Fill our hearts with wonder and gratitude, and draw us closer to You through the beauty we see. In Jesus' name, we pray. Amen.

DAY 322

The Importance of Faith

"Now faith is confidence in what we hope for and assurance about what we do not see." - Hebrews 11:1 (NIV)

Faith is more than belief; it is the confident assurance in God's promises, even when we cannot see the outcome. It is the bedrock upon which we build our lives, guiding us through trials, uncertainties, and the unseen future with unwavering trust in God's sovereignty and goodness.

The importance of faith cannot be overstated. It is through faith that we please God, as Hebrews 11:6 reminds us: "And without faith it is impossible to please God." Faith is the lifeline that connects us to God's power and love, enabling us to overcome challenges and grow in our spiritual walk. It is by faith that we receive salvation, experience God's miracles, and witness His hand in our daily lives.

Faith also fuels our hope and perseverance. When life's storms rage, faith anchors us in God's promises, reminding us that He is in control and that His plans for us are good. It empowers us to move forward, even when the path ahead is unclear, and to trust that God is working all things for our good.

Heavenly Father, we come before You with grateful hearts, thanking You for the gift of faith. Help us to grow in our confidence and assurance in Your promises. Strengthen our faith, especially in times of doubt and difficulty. May we always trust in Your goodness and sovereignty, knowing that You are with us and working all things for our good. Increase our faith, Lord, and use us to encourage and uplift others. In Jesus' name, we pray. Amen.

DAY 323

Spiritual Restoration

"He restores my soul; He leads me in the paths of righteousness for His name's sake." - Psalm 23:3 (NKJV)

In a world filled with constant demands, disappointments, and distractions, our souls can become weary and burdened. Yet, our loving Shepherd, God, is ever-present, ready to restore our weary spirits and lead us back to the paths of righteousness.

Spiritual restoration is a profound renewal of our inner being. It is God's way of refreshing our hearts, renewing our minds, and rejuvenating our spirits. This process often involves stepping away from the chaos of life and seeking God's presence through prayer, scripture, and quiet reflection. It is in these moments of stillness that we experience the gentle touch of God's healing and restorative power.

God desires for us to live in the fullness of His peace and joy. When we are spiritually restored, we are better equipped to face life's challenges with grace and resilience. We find strength in our weaknesses, hope in our despair, and joy in our sorrows. Spiritual restoration also deepens our relationship with God, allowing us to walk more closely with Him and to align our lives with His will.

Heavenly Father, thank You for being our Shepherd who restores our souls. We come before You, weary and in need of Your renewing touch. Fill us with Your peace and refresh our spirits. Lead us in Your paths of righteousness and help us to trust in Your loving care. May our lives reflect the beauty of Your restoration and bring glory to Your name. In Jesus' name, we pray. Amen.

DAY 324

The Call to Evangelism

"Therefore go and make disciples of all nations, baptizing them in the name of the Father and of the Son and of the Holy Spirit." - Matthew 28:19 (NIV)

This call to evangelism is not just for a select few but for every believer. It is an invitation to share the life-changing message of the gospel with a world that desperately needs hope, love, and redemption.

Evangelism is more than just a duty; it is an act of love. It is about sharing the greatest gift we have received—God's grace and salvation through Jesus Christ. When we understand the depth of what Christ has done for us, our hearts overflow with a desire to tell others about Him. We are compelled by the love of Christ to reach out to those who are lost, hurting, and in need of the Savior.

However, the call to evangelism can sometimes feel intimidating. We may fear rejection, feel inadequate, or be unsure of how to start. But we are not alone in this mission. Jesus promises to be with us always, empowering us through the Holy Spirit. Our role is to be faithful and obedient, trusting that God will use our efforts to touch hearts and change lives.

Heavenly Father, thank You for the incredible gift of salvation through Your Son, Jesus Christ. Fill us with a passion for sharing Your gospel with those around us. Give us boldness and wisdom to speak Your truth in love. May we be faithful ambassadors of Your kingdom, bringing glory to Your name. In Jesus' name, we pray. Amen.

DAY 325

The Armor of God

"Put on the full armor of God, so that you can take your stand against the devil's schemes." - Ephesians 6:11 (NIV)

Ephesians 6:11 calls us to equip ourselves with the full armor of God, a divine provision designed to protect and empower us as we navigate the spiritual battles of life. In a world where we face temptations, trials, and the subtle attacks of the enemy, God's armor is our defense and strength. Each piece of this armor symbolizes a crucial aspect of our faith and our relationship with Christ.

The belt of truth grounds us in the reality of God's word, while the breastplate of righteousness guards our hearts from the lies and accusations of the enemy. The shoes of the gospel of peace equip us to walk confidently in the path of Jesus, spreading His message of hope. The shield of faith extinguishes the fiery darts of doubt and fear, and the helmet of salvation protects our minds, reminding us of our eternal security in Christ. Finally, the sword of the Spirit, which is the word of God, arms us with divine wisdom and power to counter the enemy's schemes.

Putting on the full armor of God is not a one-time act but a daily discipline. It requires intentionality and reliance on the Holy Spirit to strengthen us. As we don each piece of this armor, we are reminded of God's unwavering presence and His promise to fight for us. No matter what battles we face, we can stand firm, knowing that we are equipped and protected by our Heavenly Father.

Heavenly Father, thank You for providing us with Your full armor to protect and empower us. Help us to remember to put on each piece daily, standing firm against the schemes of the enemy. Strengthen our faith, guard our hearts and minds, and fill us with Your truth and peace. Equip us to walk boldly in Your salvation and to wield the sword of Your Spirit with wisdom and power. We trust in Your protection and guidance. In Jesus' name, we pray. Amen.

DAY 326

God's Infinite Mercy

"But you, Lord, are a compassionate and gracious God, slow to anger, abounding in love and faithfulness." - Psalm 86:15 (NIV)

His mercy knows no bounds; it is vast, unending, and overflowing with compassion. In our brokenness and sinfulness, we find solace in knowing that God's mercy extends beyond our comprehension. His love reaches down to lift us up, His grace covers our shortcomings, and His forgiveness restores our souls.

God's mercy is not a distant concept but a tangible reality that we can experience in our lives every day. It is a beacon of hope in our darkest moments, a reminder that no matter how far we may stray, God's arms are always open wide to welcome us back into His embrace. His mercy offers us a fresh start, a second chance, and the promise of redemption.

As recipients of God's infinite mercy, we are called to extend that same mercy to others. Just as God has forgiven us, so too are we called to forgive those who have wronged us. Letting go of bitterness and resentment allows God's love to flow freely through us, transforming our hearts and relationships.

Gracious God, we thank You for Your infinite mercy that knows no bounds. Help us to fully grasp the depth of Your love and forgiveness toward us. Empower us to extend that same mercy to others, showing compassion and forgiveness as You have shown us. May Your mercy transform our hearts and our relationships, bringing healing and reconciliation. In Jesus' name, we pray.
Amen.

DAY 327

The Value of Obedience

"If you love me, keep my commands." - John 14:15 (NIV)

Obedience is not merely a duty or a set of rules to follow; it is a tangible expression of our love for God. When we obey God's commands, we demonstrate our trust in His wisdom, our reverence for His authority, and our desire to align our lives with His will.

The value of obedience lies not only in its outward expression but also in its transformative power within us. As we surrender our will to God's and submit to His guidance, He shapes us into the likeness of Christ, molding our character and molding our hearts to reflect His love and grace. Obedience leads us into deeper intimacy with God, drawing us closer to Him and allowing us to experience the fullness of His presence in our lives.

However, obedience does not always come easy. We may face challenges, temptations, and distractions that pull us away from God's path. Yet, in those moments, we can draw strength from the knowledge that obedience brings blessings and fulfillment beyond measure. God promises to reward those who faithfully obey Him, and He equips us with His Spirit to empower us to walk in obedience each day.

Heavenly Father, we thank You for the gift of Your commands and for the privilege of obeying You out of love. Give us the strength and wisdom to walk in obedience each day, trusting in Your guidance and surrendering our will to Yours. May our lives be a reflection of Your love and grace as we seek to honor You in all that we do. In Jesus' name, we pray. Amen.

DAY 328

Spiritual Mindfulness

"Finally, brothers and sisters, whatever is true, whatever is noble, whatever is right, whatever is pure, whatever is lovely, whatever is admirable—if anything is excellent or praiseworthy—think about such things." - Philippians 4:8 (NIV)

Spiritual mindfulness is about cultivating a deeper awareness of God's presence in our everyday lives, intentionally seeking His guidance and wisdom in our thoughts, words, and actions.

In a world filled with distractions and noise, it's easy to lose sight of God's presence and purposes. But through spiritual mindfulness, we can train our minds to be attuned to the voice of God, to recognize His handiwork in the world around us, and to discern His will for our lives.

Practicing spiritual mindfulness involves being fully present in the moment, opening our hearts to God's leading, and allowing His peace to reign within us. It's about quieting the clamor of our minds and listening for the gentle whispers of the Holy Spirit. As we cultivate a habit of mindfulness, we become more attuned to God's presence in the ordinary moments of life, finding joy and fulfillment in His presence.

Heavenly Father, we thank You for the gift of spiritual mindfulness, which allows us to experience Your presence in our lives in a deeper way. Help us to cultivate a habit of mindfulness, turning our hearts and minds toward You in all that we do. May Your peace reign in our hearts as we seek to live in alignment with Your will. In Jesus' name, we pray. Amen.

DAY 329

The Joy of the Lord

"The joy of the Lord is your strength." - Nehemiah 8:10b (NIV)

Nehemiah 8:10b reminds us that the joy of the Lord is not just a fleeting emotion but a source of strength that sustains us through life's challenges and trials. This joy is not dependent on our circumstances but is rooted in our relationship with God. It is a deep and abiding gladness that comes from knowing and experiencing His presence, His love, and His faithfulness in our lives.

The joy of the Lord is a powerful force that transcends our circumstances. It is not the absence of pain or suffering but the presence of God's peace and comfort even in the midst of our trials. When we fix our eyes on Jesus and trust in His promises, His joy fills our hearts and overflows into every aspect of our lives.

Living in the joy of the Lord is a choice we make daily. It requires us to cultivate a heart of gratitude, to rejoice always, and to find contentment in God alone. As we align our will with His and surrender our worries and fears to Him, His joy becomes our strength, enabling us to face whatever comes our way with courage and resilience.

Heavenly Father, we thank You for the joy that comes from knowing You. Help us to experience the fullness of Your joy in our lives, even in the midst of trials and difficulties. Fill us with Your peace and strength, that we may face each day with courage and resilience. May Your joy overflow from our hearts and be a light to those around us. In Jesus' name, we pray. Amen.

DAY 330

Jesus, Our High Priest

"Therefore, since we have a great high priest who has ascended into heaven, Jesus the Son of God, let us hold firmly to the faith we profess." - Hebrews 4:14 (NIV)

In the Old Testament, the high priest served as the intermediary between God and the people, offering sacrifices for sin and interceding on behalf of the people before God. However, Jesus, as our eternal High Priest, fulfills and surpasses all the roles and responsibilities of the high priests of old.

Jesus understands our weaknesses and struggles because He experienced them firsthand during His time on earth. He faced temptations, endured suffering, and ultimately sacrificed His life to atone for our sins. Through His death and resurrection, Jesus tore the veil that separated us from God, granting us direct access to the Father. He now stands before God as our advocate, interceding on our behalf and offering forgiveness and grace to all who come to Him in faith.

Knowing that Jesus is our High Priest should fill us with confidence and assurance. We can approach God's throne with boldness, knowing that Jesus empathizes with our humanity and advocates for us with compassion and love.

Lord Jesus, thank You for being our High Priest, who understands our weaknesses and intercedes for us before the Father. Empower us to share the hope we have in You with others, that they too may experience the joy of knowing You as their High Priest. In Your holy name, we pray. Amen.

DAY 331

God's Promises Fulfilled

"For no matter how many promises God has made, they are 'Yes' in Christ. And so through him the 'Amen' is spoken by us to the glory of God." - 2 Corinthians 1:20 (NIV)

From the beginning of time, God has been faithful to His word, fulfilling every promise He has made to His people. His promises are not empty words but declarations of His unwavering love, unfailing grace, and boundless power.

Throughout the Bible, we see countless examples of God's promises being fulfilled, often in ways that surpass human understanding. From the birth of a promised Savior to the restoration of broken nations, God's faithfulness shines brightly through every chapter of history. And in Christ, we see the ultimate fulfillment of God's promises—the promise of salvation, redemption, and eternal life.

As believers, we are called to anchor our hope in the promises of God. Even in the face of uncertainty and adversity, we can trust that God's promises remain true. His faithfulness is our steadfast anchor in the stormy seas of life, guiding us through every trial and leading us to victory.

Heavenly Father, we thank You for Your faithfulness to fulfill every promise You have made. Help us to trust in Your word and to anchor our hope in Your unfailing love. Give us the strength to hold fast to Your promises, even in the midst of life's challenges. May Your promises be a source of comfort, strength, and assurance in our lives, leading us ever closer to You. In Jesus' name, we pray. Amen.

DAY 332

The Importance of Scripture

"All Scripture is God-breathed and is useful for teaching, rebuking, correcting and training in righteousness." - 2 Timothy 3:16 (NIV)

The Bible is not merely a collection of words; it is the living, inspired word of God, filled with wisdom, truth, and guidance for every aspect of our lives. As Christians, we are called to immerse ourselves in Scripture, allowing its timeless truths to shape our thoughts, actions, and character.

The importance of Scripture lies in its transformative power. Through the pages of the Bible, we encounter the living God and His unfailing love for us. We find comfort in times of trouble, strength in times of weakness, and hope in times of despair. Scripture illuminates the path of righteousness, guiding us toward a life that honors and glorifies God.

Moreover, Scripture equips us for every good work. It teaches us, convicts us, corrects us, and trains us in righteousness. As we meditate on God's word and apply its principles to our lives, we are transformed from the inside out, becoming more like Christ in thought, word, and deed.

Heavenly Father, we thank You for the gift of Your word, which is a lamp unto our feet and a light unto our path. Help us to treasure Scripture and to prioritize its study in our lives. Open our hearts and minds to receive Your truth and to be transformed by it. May Your word dwell richly in us, guiding us in all that we do and bringing glory to Your name. In Jesus' name, we pray. Amen.

DAY 333

Living in God's Love

"See what great love the Father has lavished on us, that we should be called children of God! And that is what we are!" - 1 John 3:1 (NIV)

It is a love beyond measure, beyond comparison—a love that knows no bounds and surpasses all understanding. To be called children of God is a privilege beyond imagination, a testament to the overwhelming grace and compassion of our Heavenly Father.

Living in God's love means embracing our identity as His beloved children. It means finding our worth and significance not in the fleeting affirmations of this world but in the eternal truth of God's love for us. His love is a constant, unwavering presence in our lives, a source of comfort in times of trial and a cause for celebration in times of joy.

As we abide in God's love, we are transformed from the inside out. His love softens our hearts, strengthens our faith, and empowers us to love others with the same selfless love that He has shown us.

Heavenly Father, thank You for Your unfailing love that surrounds us each day. Help us to fully grasp the depth of Your love for us and to live as Your beloved children. Fill us with Your love so that we may overflow with love for others, reflecting Your grace and compassion to a world in need. May Your love be our guiding light in all that we do. In Jesus' name, we pray. Amen.

DAY 334

The Call to Repentance

"Repent, then, and turn to God, so that your sins may be wiped out, that times of refreshing may come from the Lord." - Acts 3:19
(NIV)

Repentance is not merely a one-time event but a continuous journey of turning away from sin and turning toward God. It is a humble acknowledgment of our need for His forgiveness and a sincere desire to live in accordance with His will.

The call to repentance is both a message of conviction and of hope. It reminds us of the seriousness of sin and its consequences, but it also points us to the boundless mercy and grace of God. Through repentance, we experience the freedom and joy of being reconciled to God, our hearts cleansed and our spirits renewed.

Repentance is not always easy. It requires humility to admit our faults and weaknesses, and it often involves making difficult choices to change our thoughts, words, and actions. Yet, the promise of Scripture is clear: when we repent, God is faithful to forgive us and to bring about times of refreshing and renewal in our lives.

Heavenly Father, we humbly come before You, acknowledging our need for Your forgiveness and grace. Grant us the strength to repent of our sins and to turn wholeheartedly toward You. Fill us with Your Holy Spirit, that we may walk in obedience and experience the times of refreshing that come from Your presence. May our lives be a testimony to Your mercy and love. In Jesus' name, we pray. Amen.

DAY 335

Overcoming Sin

"No temptation has overtaken you except what is common to mankind. And God is faithful; he will not let you be tempted beyond what you can bear. But when you are tempted, he will also provide a way out so that you can endure it." - 1 Corinthians 10:13 (NIV)

As followers of Christ, we are not immune to temptation or sin, but we are not left to battle them alone. God's faithfulness and grace provide us with the strength and guidance we need to overcome sin and live in victory.

Overcoming sin is a journey that requires vigilance, perseverance, and reliance on God's power. It begins with acknowledging our weaknesses and vulnerabilities, recognizing that we cannot overcome sin in our own strength. Instead, we must continually surrender our lives to God, allowing His Spirit to work in us and through us to resist temptation and walk in obedience.

Central to overcoming sin is the practice of repentance and confession. When we stumble and fall, we must humble ourselves before God, confessing our sins and seeking His forgiveness. Through His mercy and grace, God offers us a fresh start, empowering us to turn away from sin and pursue righteousness.

Heavenly Father, we thank You for Your faithfulness and grace in helping us overcome sin. Give us the strength and wisdom to resist temptation and walk in obedience to Your will. May Your Spirit empower us to live lives that honor and glorify You. In Jesus' name, we pray. Amen.

DAY 336

The Role of Deacons

"For those who serve well as deacons gain a good standing for themselves and also great confidence in the faith that is in Christ Jesus." - 1 Timothy 3:13 (ESV)

Deacons are servants, called to minister to the needs of others with humility, integrity, and faithfulness. They play a vital role in the body of Christ, supporting the work of the church and helping to meet both spiritual and practical needs within the congregation and community.

The role of deacons is rooted in the example set by Jesus Himself, who came not to be served, but to serve (Matthew 20:28). Just as Jesus washed the feet of His disciples, deacons are called to follow His example by serving others with love and compassion. Whether it's visiting the sick, caring for the poor, or assisting in the administration of the church, deacons embody the servant-hearted ministry that Jesus modeled for us.

Being a deacon is not just about performing tasks; it's about embodying the love of Christ in all that they do. It's about being a source of encouragement, support, and strength to those in need. By faithfully fulfilling their role, deacons not only serve the church but also grow in their own faith and confidence in Christ.

Lord, we thank You for the example of servant leadership that You demonstrated during Your time on earth. Help us to follow Your example by serving others with humility and love. Give them wisdom, strength, and compassion as they seek to meet the needs of others. In Jesus' name, we pray. Amen.

DAY 337

God's Generosity

"Every good and perfect gift is from above, coming down from the Father of the heavenly lights, who does not change like shifting shadows." - James 1:17 (NIV)

God's generosity knows no bounds; it is limitless, extravagant, and overflowing with love. Every blessing we receive, whether big or small, is a precious gift from Him. From the air we breathe to the relationships we cherish, every good thing in our lives is a reflection of His generous heart.

God's generosity is not confined to material blessings; it extends to every aspect of our lives. He generously offers us His grace, forgiveness, and salvation, freely given to us through the sacrifice of His Son, Jesus Christ. God's generosity is a constant reminder of His unchanging nature and His steadfast love for us.

As recipients of God's generosity, we are called to imitate His example in our own lives. We are called to be generous with our time, talents, and resources, using them to bless others and to further God's kingdom on earth. When we live with an attitude of generosity, we reflect the character of our Heavenly Father and become channels of His love and grace to those around us.

Heavenly Father, we thank You for Your boundless generosity toward us. Help us to recognize and appreciate the many blessings You have bestowed upon us. Teach us to be generous in all areas of our lives, freely sharing Your love and grace with those around us. May our lives be a reflection of Your generous heart, bringing glory to Your name. In Jesus' name, we pray. Amen.

DAY 338

Walking in the Spirit

"So I say, walk by the Spirit, and you will not gratify the desires of the flesh." - Galatians 5:16 (NIV)

Walking in the Spirit is about living in constant communion with God, allowing His Holy Spirit to guide our thoughts, words, and actions. It is a deliberate choice to align our lives with God's will, moment by moment, day by day.

Walking in the Spirit requires us to surrender our own desires and agendas to God's leading. It means yielding to His wisdom and direction, even when it goes against our natural inclinations. As we walk in step with the Spirit, we experience the freedom that comes from living in obedience to God's Word. The Spirit empowers us to overcome the temptations of the flesh and to live lives marked by love, joy, peace, patience, kindness, goodness, faithfulness, gentleness, and self-control (Galatians 5:22-23).

However, walking in the Spirit is not always easy. We may face challenges, distractions, and obstacles along the way. Yet, we can take comfort in the promise that God's Spirit is with us, guiding, comforting, and empowering us every step of the journey.

Heavenly Father, thank You for the gift of Your Holy Spirit who empowers us to walk in Your ways. Help us to live each day in step with the Spirit, surrendering our will to Yours. May our every step be guided by Your Spirit, leading us closer to You and to the abundant life You have promised. In Jesus' name, we pray. Amen.

DAY 339

God's Wisdom in Creation

*"Oh, the depth of the riches of the wisdom and knowledge of God!
How unsearchable his judgments, and his paths beyond tracing
out!" - Romans 11:33 (NIV)*

From the vastness of the cosmos to the intricate details of a single cell, every aspect of the universe reflects the brilliance of His design. God's wisdom in creation is not limited to the physical world but extends to the intricate tapestry of human life and relationships.

Consider the complexity of nature—the delicate balance of ecosystems, the diversity of species, and the intricate interdependence of all living things. It is a testament to God's wisdom that He has crafted such a harmonious and interconnected world. From the tiniest microorganism to the grandeur of mountains and oceans, every aspect of creation points to the genius of its Creator.

Yet, God's wisdom is not only seen in the beauty and order of creation but also in His plan for redemption. Through the sacrifice of His Son, Jesus Christ, God has provided a way for humanity to be reconciled to Him and restored to our original purpose.

Heavenly Father, we stand in awe of Your infinite wisdom displayed in the wonders of creation. Help us to recognize Your handiwork in the world around us and to steward Your creation with reverence and care. May we continually seek Your wisdom in all aspects of our lives, trusting in Your perfect knowledge and understanding. In Jesus' name, we pray. Amen.

DAY 340

The Hope of Glory

"For the creation waits in eager expectation for the children of God to be revealed." - Romans 8:19 (NIV)

The world around us bears witness to the glory of God, eagerly anticipating the day when His children will be fully revealed in all their splendor. From the majestic mountains to the tiniest flower, every aspect of creation reflects the beauty and creativity of our Creator.

As we marvel at the wonders of nature, we are reminded that we are not alone in our journey of faith. Creation itself joins us in longing for the day when all things will be made new. The hope of glory in creation points us toward the ultimate fulfillment of God's redemptive plan, when He will restore all things and reign in glory forever.

In the midst of a broken and hurting world, the hope of glory in creation offers us comfort and assurance. It reminds us that God is at work, weaving His purposes through the fabric of creation, bringing beauty out of ashes and light out of darkness. Even in the midst of trials and tribulations, we can cling to the hope that one day, all creation will be set free from bondage and brought into the glorious freedom of the children of God.

Heavenly Father, we thank You for the beauty and majesty of Your creation, which points us toward the hope of glory in Christ. Help us to be good stewards of the earth and to share Your love and hope with those around us. In Jesus' name, we pray. Amen.

DAY 341

Living with Eternal Perspective

"For our light and momentary troubles are achieving for us an eternal glory that far outweighs them all." - 2 Corinthians 4:17 (NIV)

In the grand tapestry of creation, our lives are but a fleeting moment, yet they are infused with eternal significance. When we view our trials, challenges, and triumphs through the lens of eternity, we gain a deeper understanding of God's purpose and plan for our lives.

Living with an eternal perspective means recognizing that this world is not our final destination. It is a temporary dwelling place on our journey toward our ultimate home with God in eternity. With this mindset, we can face the ups and downs of life with courage, knowing that our present sufferings are but a small part of a greater, eternal glory that awaits us.

This perspective shifts our focus from the temporal to the eternal, from the material to the spiritual. It compels us to invest our time, talents, and resources in things of lasting value, such as loving God and loving others. It prompts us to seek first the kingdom of God, knowing that everything else will fall into place according to His divine plan.

Heavenly Father, thank You for the promise of eternity with You. Help us to live each day with an eternal perspective, knowing that our trials and triumphs here on earth are preparing us for the eternal glory that awaits us. May our lives be a reflection of Your love and grace, pointing others toward the hope of eternity. In Jesus' name, we pray. Amen.

DAY 342

The Power of God's Word

"In the beginning was the Word, and the Word was with God, and the Word was God." - John 1:1 (NIV)

Before the universe came into existence, before time itself began, there was the Word—God's spoken utterance that brought all things into being. The Word was not just a sound or a concept; it was a manifestation of God's divine authority and creative power.

God's Word is not merely a collection of letters and sentences on a page; it is a living, breathing force that sustains all of creation. It is through His Word that galaxies were formed, mountains were sculpted, and life itself was breathed into existence. Every aspect of the natural world bears the imprint of God's spoken Word, testifying to His majesty and sovereignty.

But the power of God's Word extends far beyond the act of creation. It is a source of life and transformation for all who believe. Just as God spoke light into the darkness at the beginning of time, His Word continues to illuminate the darkness in our lives, bringing clarity, hope, and renewal.

Heavenly Father, we thank You for the power of Your Word in creation and in our lives. Help us to approach Your Word with reverence and humility, knowing that it has the power to transform us from the inside out. May Your Word be a lamp to our feet and a light to our path, guiding us closer to You each day. In Jesus' name, we pray. Amen.

DAY 343

Jesus, the Bread of Life

"Jesus said to them, 'I am the bread of life. Whoever comes to me will never be hungry, and whoever believes in me will never be thirsty.'" - John 6:35 (NIV)

Jesus declares Himself as the Bread of Life, a profound statement that speaks to His role not only in our spiritual sustenance but also in the very fabric of creation. From the beginning of time, Jesus has been present, sustaining and nourishing all life. He is the source of our physical sustenance, providing the bread that nourishes our bodies, and He is also the source of our spiritual sustenance, providing the eternal nourishment that satisfies our souls.

Just as bread is a staple of life, so too is Jesus foundational to all of creation. In Him, all things hold together (Colossians 1:17), and by His word, all things were created (John 1:3). Every sunrise, every raindrop, every blade of grass is a testimony to His creative power and sustaining love. He is the bread that satisfies our deepest hunger, the living water that quenches our thirst for meaning and purpose.

As we meditate on Jesus as the Bread of Life in creation, let us marvel at His greatness and goodness. Let us recognize His presence in the world around us, in the beauty of nature and the wonders of the universe.

Heavenly Father, we thank You for the gift of Your Son, Jesus Christ, who is the Bread of Life and the source of all creation. May we be filled with gratitude and awe at Your sustaining love, and may we share that love with others. In Jesus' name, we pray. Amen.

DAY 344

The Fellowship of Believers

"They devoted themselves to the apostles' teaching and to fellowship, to the breaking of bread and to prayer." - Acts 2:42 (NIV)

The fellowship of believers is a cornerstone of the Christian faith, a bond that unites us as brothers and sisters in Christ. It is a sacred space where we can find support, encouragement, and accountability as we journey together in faith.

Fellowship among believers is not merely a social gathering but a spiritual communion rooted in our shared identity in Christ. It is a place where we can share our joys and sorrows, our triumphs and struggles, knowing that we are surrounded by a community of believers who love and care for us. In fellowship, we find strength to persevere through life's challenges and inspiration to grow deeper in our relationship with God.

As followers of Christ, we are called to actively participate in the fellowship of believers. This means prioritizing gathering with other believers, whether it be in worship services, small groups, or community events.

Heavenly Father, we thank You for the gift of fellowship among believers. Help us to cherish and nurture the relationships we have with our brothers and sisters in Christ. May our bonds of fellowship reflect Your love and draw others closer to You. In Jesus' name, we pray. Amen.

DAY 345

Trusting God's Plan

"For I know the plans I have for you," declares the Lord, "plans to prosper you and not to harm you, plans to give you hope and a future." - Jeremiah 29:11 (NIV)

However, trusting in God's plan isn't always easy, especially when circumstances seem uncertain or challenging. Yet, as believers, we are called to place our trust in the One who holds our past, present, and future in His hands.

Trusting God's plan means surrendering our own desires, fears, and doubts to Him, and allowing His wisdom and sovereignty to guide our steps. It requires us to let go of our need for control and to embrace His timing, even when it doesn't align with our own. It's about having faith that God's plan is always better than anything we could imagine, even when we can't see the bigger picture.

In moments of uncertainty or adversity, we can find comfort and strength in knowing that God is with us every step of the way. He is our rock, our refuge, and our ever-present help in times of trouble. When we trust in Him wholeheartedly, we can rest assured that His plan for us is one of hope, abundance, and eternal significance.

Heavenly Father, thank You for the assurance that Your plans for us are good and filled with hope. Help us to trust in Your wisdom and sovereignty, even when we don't understand Your ways. May we find peace and confidence in knowing that You are always with us, guiding us toward Your best for our lives. In Jesus' name, we pray. Amen.

DAY 346

The Power of Prayer

"Devote yourselves to prayer, being watchful and thankful." -
Colossians 4:2 (NIV)

Colossians 4:2 urges us to devote ourselves to prayer, emphasizing the importance of this powerful spiritual discipline in our lives. Prayer is not just a ritual or religious obligation; it is a dynamic and intimate conversation with our Heavenly Father, who eagerly listens to our every word and knows the desires of our hearts.

Through prayer, we have access to the very throne room of God, where we can boldly approach Him with confidence, knowing that He hears us and cares for us deeply. Prayer is our lifeline, our source of strength, and our greatest weapon against the challenges and struggles of life. It is through prayer that we experience the transforming power of God at work in our lives and in the world around us.

When we pray, we invite God to intervene in our circumstances, to bring healing to the brokenhearted, comfort to the grieving, and hope to the hopeless. Prayer has the power to move mountains, to change hearts, and to bring about miraculous breakthroughs.

Heavenly Father, we thank You for the incredible privilege of prayer, for the opportunity to come before Your throne with confidence, knowing that You hear us and care for us deeply. May our prayers be a sweet fragrance to You, bringing glory to Your name and ushering in Your kingdom on earth. In Jesus' name, we pray. Amen.

DAY 347

Overcoming Fear

"For God has not given us a spirit of fear, but of power and of love and of a sound mind." - 2 Timothy 1:7 (NKJV)

Instead, He equips us with a spirit of power, love, and soundness of mind to overcome it. Fear is a natural human emotion, but when it consumes us, it can paralyze us, hindering our faith and preventing us from stepping into the plans and purposes God has for our lives.

Fear often manifests in various forms—fear of the unknown, fear of failure, fear of rejection, or even fear of success. But as followers of Christ, we are called to rise above fear and walk in faith. We are reminded countless times throughout Scripture to "fear not" and to trust in the Lord's provision and protection.

Overcoming fear begins with acknowledging it and bringing it before God in prayer. When we surrender our fears to Him, He replaces them with His peace that surpasses all understanding. We can also find strength in the promises of God's Word, meditating on passages that remind us of His faithfulness and presence with us.

Heavenly Father, we thank You for the promise of Your presence and the power You have given us to overcome fear. Help us to trust in Your provision and to walk in faith, knowing that You are with us always. Replace our fears with Your peace and courage, Lord, and empower us to live boldly for Your glory. In Jesus' name, we pray. Amen.

DAY 348

Faith in Difficult Times

"Now faith is confidence in what we hope for and assurance about what we do not see." - Hebrews 11:1 (NIV)

Faith is not merely believing when everything is going smoothly; it is trusting in God's promises even when circumstances seem bleak and uncertain. It is the unwavering conviction that God is faithful, regardless of the storms that may rage around us.

Difficult times are an inevitable part of life. Whether we're facing illness, loss, financial struggles, or relational challenges, it's easy to feel overwhelmed and discouraged. Yet, it is precisely in these moments that our faith is tested and strengthened. Like a tree with deep roots that withstands the fiercest winds, our faith can anchor us in the midst of life's storms.

In difficult times, we have a choice: to succumb to fear and despair or to cling to our faith with unwavering trust in God's goodness and sovereignty. Even when we cannot see the way forward, we can rest assured that God is with us, guiding us, and carrying us through every trial and tribulation.

Heavenly Father, in the midst of difficult times, we cling to You as our rock and refuge. Give us the strength to trust in Your unfailing love and faithfulness, even when circumstances seem overwhelming. Increase our faith, Lord, and help us to keep our eyes fixed on You, knowing that You are with us always. May Your presence bring peace and comfort to our hearts as we journey through life's storms. In Jesus' name, we pray. Amen.

DAY 349

God's Love for Us

"But God demonstrates his own love for us in this: While we were still sinners, Christ died for us." - Romans 5:8 (NIV)

It's a love that transcends human understanding, a love that is sacrificial, unconditional, and unwavering. Before we even knew Him, God loved us with a love so deep that He sent His Son, Jesus Christ, to die for our sins. This act of love on the cross demonstrates the extent to which God is willing to go to reconcile us to Himself.

God's love is not dependent on our performance or worthiness. It is not earned through good deeds or religious rituals. Rather, it is freely given to us as a gift of grace. No matter how far we may have strayed or how many times we may have failed, God's love remains constant and steadfast. It is a love that pursues us relentlessly, drawing us closer to Him and transforming our lives from the inside out.

Understanding and experiencing God's love for us is essential to our spiritual journey. It fills the deepest longings of our hearts, heals our wounds, and gives us purpose and meaning. When we grasp the depth of God's love, we are compelled to respond with love and devotion, living our lives in gratitude and obedience to Him.

Heavenly Father, thank You for the incomprehensible gift of Your love. Help us to fully grasp the depth and magnitude of Your love for us. May it permeate every aspect of our lives, transforming us from the inside out. Empower us to love others as You have loved us, showing grace, mercy, and compassion to all. In Jesus' name, we pray. Amen.

DAY 350

Seeking Wisdom

"If any of you lacks wisdom, you should ask God, who gives generously to all without finding fault, and it will be given to you."
- James 1:5 (NIV)

In a world filled with uncertainty and complexity, the pursuit of wisdom is essential for navigating life's challenges and making decisions that honor God.

Seeking wisdom is more than just acquiring knowledge or intellect; it is a heart posture of humility and dependence on God. It involves acknowledging our limitations and recognizing that true wisdom comes from above. When we come to God in prayer, asking for wisdom, He promises to generously give it to us, without finding fault or reproach.

Wisdom is not merely about making wise choices in our own lives but also about living in a way that reflects the character of God. It is about seeking His will and aligning our hearts with His purposes. As we grow in wisdom, we become more attuned to His voice and His guidance, allowing His wisdom to permeate every aspect of our lives.

Heavenly Father, we come before You with humble hearts, recognizing our need for Your wisdom in our lives. Grant us the wisdom to discern Your will and to make choices that honor You. Help us to seek Your guidance in all that we do, trusting in Your infinite wisdom and love. May Your wisdom guide our steps and bring glory to Your name. In Jesus' name, we pray. Amen.

DAY 351

The Holy Spirit's Guidance

"But when he, the Spirit of truth, comes, he will guide you into all the truth. He will not speak on his own; he will speak only what he hears, and he will tell you what is yet to come." - John 16:13 (NIV)

The Holy Spirit is not just a vague presence but a personal and active member of the Trinity who walks alongside us, illuminating the path of truth and leading us into God's perfect will.

The Holy Spirit's guidance is essential for navigating the complexities of life. In a world filled with noise and distractions, His gentle voice speaks wisdom and clarity into our hearts, helping us discern right from wrong, truth from deception. He leads us in the paths of righteousness, guiding our steps and directing our decisions according to God's perfect plan.

To receive the Holy Spirit's guidance, we must cultivate a sensitive and obedient spirit. This requires us to quiet our hearts and minds, to listen attentively to His voice, and to yield to His leading. As we surrender our will to His, He empowers us to live victoriously, overcoming obstacles and walking in the abundant life that Christ has promised.

Holy Spirit, Guide and Counselor, we thank You for Your constant presence in our lives. Open our ears to hear Your voice and our hearts to receive Your guidance. Lead us in the paths of righteousness, and empower us to walk in obedience to Your will. May Your guidance bring clarity, wisdom, and peace to every area of our lives. In Jesus' name, we pray. Amen.

DAY 352

Strength in Weakness

"But he said to me, 'My grace is sufficient for you, for my power is made perfect in weakness.' Therefore I will boast all the more gladly about my weaknesses, so that Christ's power may rest on me." - 2 Corinthians 12:9 (NIV)

As humans, we often strive to present an image of strength and self-sufficiency to the world. Yet, it is in our moments of vulnerability and inadequacy that we truly experience the transforming power of God's grace.

Strength in weakness is not about denying our limitations or pretending to be something we're not. Rather, it's about acknowledging our dependence on God and trusting in His ability to work through our weaknesses for His glory. When we surrender our weaknesses to God, He can use them as opportunities to display His strength and power in our lives.

God's strength is not limited by our shortcomings; in fact, it is precisely in our weaknesses that His power is most evident. When we come to the end of our own strength, we discover the limitless reservoir of grace available to us through Christ.

Heavenly Father, we thank You for Your promise that Your grace is sufficient for us, and Your power is made perfect in our weakness. May we boast gladly in our weaknesses, knowing that Your power rests on us. Guide us to rely fully on Your grace, trusting in Your strength to carry us through every trial. In Jesus' name, we pray. Amen.

DAY 353

Living by Faith

"Now faith is confidence in what we hope for and assurance about what we do not see." - Hebrews 11:1 (NIV)

Faith is not merely a belief in something unseen; it is a deep-rooted confidence in the promises of God, a steadfast assurance that He is faithful to fulfill His word. Living by faith means surrendering our doubts and fears to God, trusting in His goodness and sovereignty even when circumstances seem uncertain or daunting.

Living by faith is not always easy. It requires us to step out of our comfort zones, to relinquish control, and to rely wholly on God's provision and guidance. Yet, it is in these moments of vulnerability that our faith is strengthened and our relationship with God deepened. When we choose to walk by faith, we invite God to work miracles in our lives and to lead us on paths of purpose and fulfillment.

Faith is not passive; it is active and dynamic. It compels us to take bold steps of obedience, even when we cannot see the outcome. It empowers us to persevere through trials and to cling to hope in the midst of adversity.

Heavenly Father, thank You for the gift of faith that sustains us and empowers us to live victoriously in You. Help us to trust You more deeply, to surrender our doubts and fears, and to walk boldly in obedience to Your will. Strengthen our faith, O Lord, that we may live lives that bring glory to Your name. In Jesus' name, we pray. Amen.

DAY 354

God's Promises

"For no matter how many promises God has made, they are 'Yes' in Christ. And so through him the 'Amen' is spoken by us to the glory of God." - 2 Corinthians 1:20 (NIV)

Every word spoken by God carries the weight of His faithfulness and power. His promises are not empty words but declarations of His love, grace, and provision for His children. As followers of Christ, we can find hope and strength in the certainty of God's promises, knowing that He is faithful to fulfill every word spoken over our lives.

God's promises are like anchors in the storms of life, grounding us in His truth and guiding us through uncertainty. They are a source of comfort in times of trial, a beacon of light in the darkness, and a testament to His unwavering commitment to His people. Even when circumstances seem bleak, we can hold fast to the promises of God, confident that He will never fail us.

As believers, we are called to not only receive God's promises but also to declare them boldly in faith. Our "Amen" is a proclamation of trust and confidence in God's faithfulness, regardless of what we see or feel.

Heavenly Father, we thank You for Your unchanging and faithful promises. Help us to trust in Your word and to hold fast to Your truth, even in the midst of uncertainty. Strengthen our faith, Lord, as we declare Your promises over our lives and stand firm in Your love. May Your promises be a source of hope and encouragement to us and to all who hear them. In Jesus' name, we pray. Amen.

DAY 355

The Joy of Salvation

"Restore to me the joy of your salvation and grant me a willing spirit, to sustain me." - Psalm 51:12 (NIV)

Salvation is not merely a one-time event but an ongoing journey of restoration and renewal in God's love. It is a gift of immeasurable value, bestowed upon us by God's grace through faith in Jesus Christ. The joy of salvation is not dependent on our circumstances but rooted in the unchanging truth of God's love and forgiveness.

When we experience the joy of salvation, it transforms our lives from the inside out. It fills us with an unshakable peace that surpasses all understanding and a sense of purpose that gives meaning to every moment. The joy of salvation empowers us to face life's challenges with courage and hope, knowing that we are beloved children of God, redeemed and set free from the bondage of sin and death.

As followers of Christ, our joy in salvation is not meant to be kept to ourselves but shared with others. We are called to be ambassadors of God's love and grace, shining His light into the darkness and inviting others to experience the same joy that we have found in Jesus.

Heavenly Father, we thank You for the indescribable gift of salvation that You have given us through Your Son, Jesus Christ. Restore to us the joy of Your salvation, Lord, and fill us with Your Holy Spirit, that we may live each day with hearts overflowing with gratitude and praise. In His name, we pray. Amen.

DAY 356

Forgiveness and Grace

"Be kind to one another, tenderhearted, forgiving one another, as God in Christ forgave you." - Ephesians 4:32 (ESV)

As recipients of God's mercy, we are called to emulate His example by extending forgiveness and grace to others. Forgiveness is a transformative act of love that releases us from the burden of resentment and restores broken relationships. It is a reflection of God's unconditional love and His desire for reconciliation with His children.

Forgiveness does not erase the pain or justify the wrongdoing, but it acknowledges the humanity in both the offender and the offended. It is a choice to let go of bitterness and anger, to surrender our hurt to God, and to trust in His ability to heal and redeem. Through forgiveness, we experience the freedom to move forward in love and grace, unencumbered by the weight of unforgiveness.

Grace accompanies forgiveness, offering unmerited favor and acceptance to those who have wronged us. Just as God's grace knows no bounds, so too are we called to extend grace generously, recognizing that we ourselves are in constant need of God's grace.

Heavenly Father, we thank You for Your boundless mercy and grace toward us. Help us to forgive others as You have forgiven us, releasing the weight of bitterness and resentment from our hearts. May Your forgiveness and grace bring healing and reconciliation to our relationships, to the glory of Your name. In Jesus' name, we pray. Amen.

DAY 357

Serving Others

"For even the Son of Man did not come to be served, but to serve, and to give his life as a ransom for many." - Mark 10:45 (NIV)

Jesus, the Son of God, humbled Himself and took on the role of a servant, demonstrating the depth of His love and the magnitude of His sacrifice. His entire life was a testimony to the transformative power of serving others with selflessness and compassion.

Serving others is not just an optional act of kindness; it is a fundamental aspect of the Christian life. It is an expression of our love for God and our commitment to follow in the footsteps of Jesus. When we serve others, we mirror the character of Christ and participate in His mission to bring healing, hope, and restoration to a broken world.

Serving others also has a profound impact on our own hearts and souls. It teaches us humility, empathy, and gratitude. It reminds us of the interconnectedness of humanity and the importance of community. As we pour ourselves out in service to others, we find fulfillment and purpose beyond measure, knowing that we are making a tangible difference in the lives of those around us.

Gracious God, thank You for the example of Jesus, who came not to be served but to serve. Help us to embody His selfless love as we seek to serve others in our daily lives. May our acts of service bring glory to Your name and be a reflection of Your kingdom here on earth. In Jesus' name, we pray. Amen.

DAY 358

Spiritual Discernment

"But solid food is for the mature, who by constant use have trained themselves to distinguish good from evil." - Hebrews 5:14 (NIV)

Spiritual discernment is the ability to perceive and understand God's will, to distinguish between truth and falsehood, and to make wise choices that align with His purposes. It is a skill that is developed through a deepening relationship with God and a commitment to His Word.

In a world filled with competing voices and conflicting messages, spiritual discernment is crucial for navigating the complexities of life. It enables us to recognize the promptings of the Holy Spirit, to discern the motives behind actions and teachings, and to guard against deception and error. Spiritual discernment empowers us to live with wisdom and integrity, honoring God in all that we do.

Developing spiritual discernment requires intentionality and diligence. It involves immersing ourselves in Scripture, prayerfully seeking God's guidance, and cultivating sensitivity to the leading of the Holy Spirit. As we grow in our understanding of God's character and His ways, our discernment becomes sharpened, enabling us to make choices that honor Him and bring glory to His name.

Heavenly Father, we thank You for the gift of spiritual discernment. Help us to cultivate this precious skill in our lives, that we may walk in wisdom and obedience to Your will. May our discernment be a reflection of Your glory and a testimony to Your faithfulness. In Jesus' name, we pray. Amen.

DAY 359

Devotion

"But seek first his kingdom and his righteousness, and all these things will be given to you as well." - Matthew 6:33 (NIV)

Devotion is not merely a routine or a duty; it is a posture of the heart that seeks after God with fervent love and dedication. It is about centering our lives around Him, aligning our desires with His will, and surrendering ourselves wholeheartedly to His purposes.

True devotion involves a deepening relationship with God, nurtured through prayer, worship, and the study of His Word. It is a commitment to walk in obedience and intimacy with Him, allowing His presence to permeate every aspect of our lives. Devotion is the fuel that ignites our faith, sustains us in times of trial, and empowers us to live out our calling as followers of Christ.

In a world filled with distractions and competing priorities, maintaining a posture of devotion can be challenging. Yet, when we make seeking God's kingdom our primary focus, everything else falls into place. God promises to provide for our needs when we prioritize Him above all else.

Heavenly Father, we thank You for the privilege of knowing You and being known by You. Help us to cultivate a heart of devotion that seeks after You above all else. Strengthen us to prioritize Your kingdom and righteousness in every area of our lives. May our devotion to You be evident in our thoughts, words, and actions, bringing glory to Your name. In Jesus' name, we pray. Amen.

DAY 360

The Fruit of the Spirit

"But the fruit of the Spirit is love, joy, peace, forbearance, kindness, goodness, faithfulness, gentleness and self-control. Against such things there is no law." - Galatians 5:22-23 (NIV)

These qualities, collectively known as the fruit of the Spirit, are not merely character traits to be cultivated through human effort but divine gifts bestowed upon us by the Holy Spirit. As we surrender our lives to God and allow His Spirit to work within us, we begin to bear fruit that reflects the very nature of God Himself.

Love, joy, peace, patience, kindness, goodness, faithfulness, gentleness, and self-control—these are the fruit that testify to the transformative power of God's presence in our lives. They are not only a reflection of our relationship with God but also a testimony to the world of His love and grace.

Living a life marked by the fruit of the Spirit is a journey of growth and surrender. It requires us to continually yield to the leading of the Holy Spirit, allowing Him to prune away the branches of selfishness, pride, and sin, and to cultivate within us the qualities that mirror the heart of Christ.

Heavenly Father, we thank You for the gift of Your Holy Spirit, who works within us to produce fruit that reflects Your character. Help us to surrender to Your leading and to bear fruit that glorifies Your name. Strengthen us, Lord, in love, joy, peace, patience, kindness, goodness, faithfulness, gentleness, and self-control. May our lives be a testimony to Your transformative power at work within us. In Jesus' name, we pray. Amen.

DAY 361

Trust in God's Provision

"And my God will meet all your needs according to the riches of his glory in Christ Jesus." - Philippians 4:19 (NIV)

Trusting in God's provision means placing our faith in His promise to meet all our needs. It's about surrendering our worries and anxieties, knowing that our Heavenly Father cares for us deeply and has abundant resources at His disposal.

God's provision extends far beyond mere material blessings. While He does provide for our physical needs, He also meets us in our emotional, spiritual, and relational needs. His provision is holistic, encompassing every aspect of our lives. In times of scarcity or uncertainty, we can rest assured that God is our faithful provider, and He will never leave us lacking.

Trusting in God's provision requires us to let go of our need for control and to place our complete dependence on Him. It's about shifting our focus from our own abilities or resources to God's infinite power and abundance. As we surrender to His will and trust in His timing, we experience a deep sense of peace and contentment, knowing that we are held in the palm of His hand.

Heavenly Father, thank You for Your promise to meet all our needs according to Your glorious riches in Christ Jesus. Help us to trust in Your provision, even when circumstances may seem uncertain. May we live each day with hearts full of gratitude, knowing that You are our faithful provider. In Jesus' name, we pray. Amen.

DAY 362

Living a Life of Worship

"Therefore, I urge you, brothers and sisters, in view of God's mercy, to offer your bodies as a living sacrifice, holy and pleasing to God—this is your true and proper worship." - Romans 12:1 (NIV)

True worship is not just about singing songs or attending religious ceremonies; it is about offering our entire lives as a living sacrifice to God. It's a lifestyle of surrender, obedience, and devotion that honors Him in everything we do.

Living a life of worship means recognizing God's sovereignty and goodness in every aspect of our lives. It's about acknowledging His presence in our daily routines, our work, our relationships, and even our struggles. When we view our lives through the lens of worship, every moment becomes an opportunity to glorify God and draw closer to Him.

Worship is not just something we do; it's who we are. It's a posture of the heart that acknowledges God's worthiness and responds with love, adoration, and gratitude. Whether we're singing praises, serving others, or simply living out our faith in the mundane tasks of life, our ultimate goal is to bring honor and glory to God.

Heavenly Father, we thank You for the privilege of worshiping You with our lives. Help us to live each day with hearts surrendered to You, offering ourselves as living sacrifices of worship. Fill us with Your Spirit, Lord, and empower us to live as true worshipers in all that we do. In Jesus' name, we pray. Amen.

DAY 363

God's Unchanging Nature

"Jesus Christ is the same yesterday and today and forever." -
Hebrews 13:8 (NIV)

In a world where everything seems to be constantly shifting and evolving, God remains steadfast and eternal. His character, His love, and His promises endure through every season of life, providing us with a solid foundation on which to build our faith and trust.

God's unchanging nature is a source of great comfort and security for His children. It means that we can rely on Him completely, knowing that He will never fail us or forsake us. His love for us remains constant, unwavering, and unconditional, regardless of our circumstances or shortcomings. In a world filled with uncertainty, God's unchanging nature is an anchor for our souls, grounding us in His truth and peace.

As we reflect on God's unchanging nature, let us also consider how we can emulate His constancy in our own lives. We are called to be imitators of Christ, to reflect His love and character to the world around us. This means living lives of integrity, consistency, and faithfulness, even when faced with challenges or temptations.

Dear God, we thank You for Your unchanging nature and Your steadfast love for us. Help us to trust in Your faithfulness and to find security in Your eternal promises. Guide us, Lord, to live lives that reflect Your constancy and faithfulness to the world around us. May Your unchanging nature be a source of strength and hope for us each day. In Jesus' name, we pray. Amen.

DAY 364

Peace in Christ

"Peace I leave with you; my peace I give you. I do not give to you as the world gives. Do not let your hearts be troubled and do not be afraid." - John 14:27 (NIV)

This peace is not merely the absence of conflict but a deep, abiding sense of calm and assurance that can only be found in Christ. It is a peace that surpasses understanding, a peace that soothes our troubled hearts and quiets our anxious minds.

As followers of Christ, we are called to immerse ourselves in the peace of His nature. Just as a calm lake reflects the beauty of the surrounding landscape, so too can our hearts reflect the peace of Christ amidst the storms of life. When we abide in Him, allowing His presence to dwell richly within us, His peace becomes our constant companion, guiding us through every trial and tribulation.

Finding peace in Christ's nature involves surrendering our worries, fears, and uncertainties to Him, trusting in His sovereign control over all things. It means fixing our eyes on Him, rather than on the storms raging around us, and allowing His peace to permeate every aspect of our lives. In the midst of chaos, His peace becomes our anchor, grounding us firmly in His love and grace.

Heavenly Father, we thank You for the peace that surpasses understanding, a peace that can only be found in Your Son, Jesus Christ. Help us to abide in Him, drawing strength and comfort from His presence. May Your peace shine brightly through us, reflecting Your love and grace to a world in need. In Jesus' name, we pray. Amen.

DAY 365

Bearing Good Fruit

"By their fruit you will recognize them. Do people pick grapes from thornbushes, or figs from thistles? Likewise, every good tree bears good fruit, but a bad tree bears bad fruit." - Matthew 7:16-17 (NIV)

Just as a healthy tree naturally produces good fruit, so too should our lives be characterized by the evidence of God's transforming work within us. Bearing good fruit is not simply about outward actions or appearances; it is about the overflow of a heart that is rooted in Christ and surrendered to His will.

When we abide in Christ, allowing His Spirit to dwell richly within us, we become conduits of His love, grace, and truth to the world around us. Our words, actions, and attitudes begin to reflect the character of Christ, bearing fruit such as love, joy, peace, patience, kindness, goodness, faithfulness, gentleness, and self-control (Galatians 5:22-23).

Bearing good fruit is a natural outpouring of our relationship with Jesus. As we draw near to Him in prayer, worship, and study of His Word, we are nourished and empowered to live lives that glorify Him.

Heavenly Father, we thank You for the privilege of bearing fruit for Your kingdom. Help us to abide in You, Lord, so that our lives may be marked by the fruit of Your Spirit. Show us areas where we need to grow and empower us to live lives that honor and glorify You. In Jesus' name, we pray. Amen.

FINAL WORDS

In the pages of this daily devotional for 2025, we've embarked on a profound journey—a journey of faith, reflection, and transformation. Each day, we've explored themes that resonate with the essence of what it means to be a child of God in the year 2025. We've delved into the depths of our hearts, seeking wisdom, courage, and purpose in a world filled with challenges and opportunities.

As we conclude this devotional, let's take a moment to reflect on the lessons we've learned, the moments of inspiration, and the growth we've experienced along the way. We've explored topics like facing fear, pursuing God's calling, enduring through trials, and giving with an open heart. Through these daily reflections, we've sought to strengthen our faith, deepen our relationship with God, and become better stewards of the gifts He's entrusted to us.

Heavenly Father,

As we conclude this devotional journey, we come before you with hearts filled with gratitude and renewed purpose. You have been our constant companion, guiding us through the trials and triumphs of life. We thank you for the inspiration and insights we've gained along the way.

Lord, continue to mold us into men of courage, purpose, and unwavering faith. May the lessons we've learned and the truths we've embraced continue to resonate in our hearts and shape our daily lives.

Help us carry the light of your love, grace, and truth into the world, touching the lives of those around us. May our journey of faith be a testament to your goodness and faithfulness.

As we move forward, Lord, we ask for your continued guidance and strength. Lead us in the paths of righteousness, and may your presence be our constant source of inspiration and hope.

In Jesus' name, we pray.

Amen.

LEAVE US A REVIEW

At Mount Hermon Publications, your feedback matters. We believe that the best way to improve our devotionals and resources is by hearing from you, our valued readers. We invite you to share your thoughts, insights, and experiences by leaving a review.

Your reviews are more than just words on a screen; they are the compass that guides us toward creating better, more impactful devotionals for men like you.

So, if you've found inspiration, wisdom, or transformation within the pages of our devotionals, we encourage you to take a moment to drop a review. Let us know what you loved, what spoke to your heart, and even areas where you think we can improve.

Your voice matters, and we look forward to hearing from you.

Don't forget to follow our Author page on Amazon [Mount Hermon Publication], to get updated information concerning our devotionals, Prayer books, and also when we launch a discount. We would appreciate that.

ABOUT MOUNT HERMON PUBLICATION

Mount Hermon Publications is dedicated to the creation and dissemination of inspirational devotionals and spiritual resources designed to empower and uplift every Christian in their faith journeys. Our mission is to provide Christians with practical, faith-based guidance for navigating the complexities of life while nurturing their spiritual growth.

We understand that being a believer of Christ in today's world comes with unique challenges and opportunities. That's why we are committed to producing thoughtfully crafted devotionals, books, and resources that resonate with the hearts of Christians, offering guidance, inspiration, and practical wisdom to help them live out their faith in meaningful ways.

Our devotionals are designed to be more than just daily readings; they are companions for the journey—faithful allies that walk alongside Men, Women, Boys, Girls, Families, Couples as they seek deeper connections with God and endeavor to live purposeful and impactful lives. We believe in the power of reflection, action, and community to foster spiritual growth, and our devotionals reflect these principles.

Mount Hermon Publications is dedicated to nurturing a community of Christians who strive to be courageous, purpose-driven, and deeply connected to their Creator. We are committed to supporting every Believer as they face life's challenges with faith, embrace their unique callings, and leave a positive impact on the world around them.

With each publication, we aim to inspire Christians to live out their faith with intention, to become better husbands, fathers, mothers, wife, kids, teens, friends, and leaders, and to leave a legacy of love, grace, and truth. We invite you to explore our devotionals and resources, and we look forward to being a part of your spiritual journey.

Together, let us seek to grow in faith, reflection, and action, living as Christians who are anchored in the love of God and empowered to make a difference in the world.

Thank you for joining us in this journey of spiritual building.
May God continue to build and uphold you.
God bless you.

Made in the USA
Coppell, TX
04 February 2025

45411469R10243